Les pénibles adieux.

1. The art of creating elaborate yet edible decorations may have reached its pinnacle in the late 19th century and is shown in these French engravings. These large structures were molded from sugar, marzipan, hardened jellies, nuts, and chocolate to be centerpieces. These specific designs were for military dinners — the cannons.

2. The troops of Spanish Emperor Charles V entered Bologna in northern Italy in 1527. Charles was engaged in a major battle against Pope Clement VII (of the Medici family) and ultimately won that war in the infamous sack of Rome on May 6, 1527. The Spanish troops had interesting tastes in food, such as this ox over a grill; note that the ox is stuffed with smaller animals such as chickens and pigeons. This used to be a typical field meal.

3. This early 19th-century French engraving shows active-duty French soldiers and one invalid veteran who had clearly enjoyed substantial quantities of wine.

MILITARY HIGH LIFE
ELEGANT FOOD HISTORIES AND RECIPES

UNIVERSITY PRESS ✤ OF THE SOUTH, Inc.

This full dress uniform of a 19th century British officer has a tiny pocket, just perfect for holding a small flask such as this one (probably once filled with superb French brandy) inscribed with "68th Field Battery, Peshawar, 1896." On this outpost of British India (now Pakistan), fighting was frequent and heavy and to have served in one of the many battles there was a sign of distinction. (From the collection of Christopher & Karin Ross, New York City)

68th FIELD BATTERY
PESHAWAR
1896

MILITARY HIGH LIFE
ELEGANT FOOD HISTORIES AND RECIPES

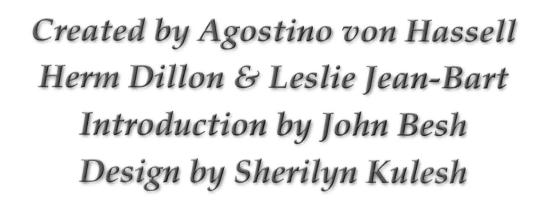

Created by Agostino von Hassell
Herm Dillon & Leslie Jean-Bart
Introduction by John Besh
Design by Sherilyn Kulesh

Published in the United States by:
University Press of the South, Inc.
5500 Prytania Street, PMB 421
New Orleans, LA 70115 USA

E-mail: unprsouth@aol.com
Fax: (504) 866-2750
Phone: (504) 866-2791

Visit our web page:
http://www.unprsouth.com
Visit our partner's web page:
http://www.punmonde.com
Acid-free paper.

Excerpt from ONCE A MARINE, ALWAYS A MARINE by Ben Finney, copyright © 1977 by Ben Finney. Used by permission of Crown Publishers, a division of Random House, Inc.

Excerpt from Armed Forces Journal, February 1993 used with permission of Army Times Publishing Group.

Adapted from Cups of Valor by N.E. Beveridge, copyright © 1968 by Stackpole Books.

Library of Congress Cataloging-in-Publication Data.

Agostino von Hassell.
With Contributors: Herm Dillon, and Leslie Jean-Bart.
Military High Life. Elegant Food Histories and Recipes.
Cooking Cultures Studies Series, 2.
167 pages.
Includes Introduction by Restaurant August, New Orleans, Louisiana, Chef John Besh, Recipient of the 2006 James Beard Foundation Best Chef: Southeast Award.

1. Cooking Cultures Studies. 2. Military History. 3. Military Food. 4. Ancient Egypt. 5. Greece and Rome. 6. The Ottoman Empire. 7. Japan. 8. China. 9. Emperor Napoleon I. 10. United States.

ISBN: 1-931948-60-7.
Printed in China.
2006.

This book is dedicated to the memory
of the brave men and women
who have fought our nation's battles.

To honor them, part of the proceeds of this book
will be used to feed veterans,
so often hungry and homeless.

These funds will be administered by the
Samaritan Village Veterans Program
327 West 43rd Street
New York, NY 10036

U.S. Marines, Beirut, October 1983

This is one dish from the last major dinner of the 17th Bengal Lancer Regiment, held at the Cavalry and Guards Club, Friday, June 6, 1997, London: Salad of Smoked Duck Breast with Asparagus and Walnut Dressing. The dish is presented on a campaign table used in India by the Bengal Lancers. The room is decorated with artifacts of the Bengal Lancers and in particular the famous 17th Lancers. (From the collection of Christopher & Karin Ross, New York City)

CREATED BY AGOSTINO VON HASSELL
INTRODUCTION BY JOHN BESH

Text by Herm Dillon and Agostino von Hassell | Food Photography by Leslie Jean-Bart
Food Styling by Harry McMann | European Research by Teresa Caiado Ramirez
Art Direction by Keith Crossley | Editing by Lisa M. Pellegrino | Design by Sherilyn Kulesh
Photographic Assistance by Kristin Leigh Hoelen | Proofreading by Deborah Fisher

CONTENTS

(Above & Opposite) Former Marine John Besh uses the dramatic stage of his August Restaurant in New Orleans to startle diners with innovate dishes such as "Low Country Shrimp and Grits with Local Andouille," "Huitlacoche Agnoletti with Royal Trumpets, Baby Corn, and Black Mole," or "Parmesan Crusted Hake with Lobster Whipped Potatoes and 'Bouillabaisse' Jus." Besh, drawing on a creativity shaped in the Louisiana countryside and the tough Corps of Marines, has evolved a complex cuisine that celebrates sustainable food sources and the complex, multi-layered history of Louisiana cuisine.

INTRODUCTION

Celebrity chef John Besh's signature dishes attest to the wonderful combination of his classical training and flair for adding local flavor. Techniques he honed at the Culinary Institute of America and stints in some of Europe's finest kitchens, infused with the best of his native Louisiana bayou have won Besh accolades from *Condé Nast Traveler*, *Travel & Leisure*, *Gourmet* and the *New York Times*. Besh won the 2006 James Beard Foundation Award for Best Chef: Southeast.

Few know that prior to being named one of *Food & Wine's* "Top 10 Best New Chefs in America," Besh served with the United States Marine Corps in Operation Desert Storm. Besh had commercial kitchen experience prior to entering the service, so he fully appreciated the differences in cuisine served to soldiers from different coalition countries.

The acclaimed chef operates two fine restaurants, Besh Steakhouse in New Orleans, and Restaurant August in New Orleans. Besh also devotes time to conducting cooking classes at Restaurant August. He has appeared as Featured Chef at New York's famed James Beard House, as a guest on the *Today Show*, and has been the subject of several print media features.

As a former United States Marine grunt, who has spent many nights under stars and storms dreaming of a time and place of dry warmth with great food and wine, it is my honor and pleasure to write such an introduction.

I'm in awe of the work of Agostino von Hassell—gathering and composing this information is no small feat. Agostino has opened my eyes to the elegant history of *Military High Life* and those who preceded me in my chosen profession as an executive chef. As a food history buff, I'm excited to see a book that connects our fine dining of today with that of the cuisine of the leaders of the Roman Legions.

There were times, while in combat, that just the thought of real food was a dream. During Operation Desert Storm, we'd swap whatever we could for food from the British Desert Rats and, at times, the French Legionaries. Their food was so superior to our MREs! One Marine I knew was caught trading his flak jacket for a case of British rations, which included tea, biscuits, and jam.

Most of us ate very little of our American dehydrated food. Instead, we'd receive a three-day supply of MREs and tear them apart just to auction certain prized possessions, like a chocolate bar (which wasn't chocolate) or a mini-sized bottle of Tabasco® hot sauce. These auctions had a similar appearance to the floor of the New York Stock Exchange.It is hard to imagine, as a chef in America, just how special food becomes in times of hardship or war.

Amazingly, that tiny bottle of hot sauce became one of the only comforts one had in a fighting hole. You'd console yourself by thinking of food and how much better it would be when and if you made it home. It was food that brought us together. When even the talk about home grew old, my "hooch mate" and I would always have food to talk about. We all understood good food.

Now I'm no longer that same Corporal Besh, instead, I am operating three restaurants with 173 employees that need paying. I have a book in progress, one tremendously beautiful and patient wife, four of the finest lads you've ever seen and a dog that needs to quail hunt. I am, however, the same corporal while reading *Military High Life* and envisioning the foods of yesterday's battlefields.

In many ways I'm following the footsteps of many of the great chefs before me. Just last year, I had the honor of meeting a table of impeccable looking gentlemen who had enjoyed their meal at Restaurant August and, in turn, handed me a gold Marine Corps emblem. As it turned out it, they were a group of retired USMC generals, one of which was the commanding General in Desert Storm.

Military High Life was an interesting read for me as a former squad leader, mortar man, and forward observer, who now cooks elegant dishes steeped in military tradition. Enjoy this great work!

John Besh
Executive Chef / Partner

Restaurant August – New Orleans
Besh Steak House – New Orleans

THE LORE OF MILITARY FOOD

hen we think of military food today, the first things that come to most American minds are C–Rations, or K–Rations, or even hardtack. Others with more recent experience might consider MREs (Meals, Ready–to–Eat), the fuel that powers our modern military in the field today.

Rest assured, modern field rations are not what this book is about, although there is mention of them. What evades many of us, even professional chefs, is that there is a great deal of fancy food that has emerged from military leaders and organizations, sometimes by necessity, other times by accident, but most often in a concerted and purposeful desire to develop tastes that please the palate.

In many regions of the world, wars have been fought to gain land on which to grow food to feed communities of people. All wars, however, have taught us that the people of one land, one culture, with their traditional tastes for food, sauces, beverages, and even utensils, can learn to savor another's. Sidney Mintz said it best when he wrote, "War is probably the single most powerful instrument of dietary change in human experience." In the end, far more than just arrows or bullets are exchanged. New flavors, cooking styles, and often a melding of cultural cookery lead to new cookery that over time grows in sophistication and dietary nutrition.

Wars and battles are led by generals, emperors, aristocrats, and people of high rank, who throughout history have influenced, and often controlled, what their culture ate. These ranking citizens and warriors used fine dining and drinking to influence, entertain, and occasionally coerce their own staff, diplomatic friends and rivals, and even their enemies to a point of respect, admiration, agreement, and compromise. This is a tradition, renowned in virtually every culture, that has existed from the beginning of time to today.

Without a doubt, more strategic military decisions have been made around a table of fine food and wine than in any office or conference room.

It is with these historical facts in mind that we have written this book, reporting on wars, battles, skirmishes, and people that in some way influenced the palate of a culture. There are many heroes, certainly. Some of them are unsung, and yet vital to the cuisine of a country or culture today.

William Shakespeare may have said it first and best in Henry V in which he writes of the English soldiers, "Give them great meals of beef and iron and steel, they will eat like wolves and fight like devils." Shortly afterward, English soldiers were fed red meat regularly in their mess halls.

Understanding Military Food

In March of 1981, Agostino von Hassell, one of the authors of this book, landed with a United States Marine Corps amphibious force in Northern Norway. The landing site was some 200 miles north of the Arctic Circle, and it was appropriately cold. Actually, as author Hassell describes it, it was quite miserable.

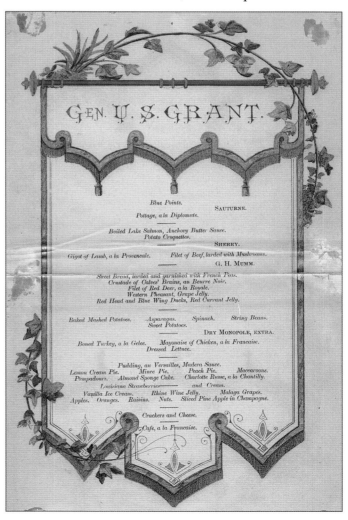

(Opposite) U.S. field rations are what most people associate with military food. While the reality is different, it is worth noting that the U.S. military has been supplied with the most to eat, and most difficult to trade (with Allies), food for over 120 years. Yet one item is a constant: the superb hot sauce made by the McIlhenny Company of Louisiana that helps improve the most basic field rations. Tabasco® sauce is essential to "food" survival in the U.S. military, and their supplier — with a family history chock full of U.S Marines — has done an outstanding job in promoting this critical seasoning.

(Right) This is a menu for a dinner given to General Grant in 1879. This is a wonderful example of the bounty of America, including western pheasant, lake salmon, and red deer complimented by the elegance of fine European wines.

He tells what can only be described as a most "unsavory" story of the events of that landing. It concerned food.

"Issued to us, destroying the many years of developing an expertise with C-Rations and how to make them palatable, were mysterious, heavy-gauge brown plastic bags, labeled 'ASSAULT MENU — PROTOTYPE.' We were, figuratively, guinea pigs. This was the first test for the now commonly used Meals, Ready-to-Eat, or MRE. They were awful."

The importance of good food for the soldier in the field cannot be understated. This assault menu was not good. Marines and other armed forces typically trade food on joint operations, sampling each others' field rations. In this case, the proof was in the proverbial pudding when U.S. Marines learned that no one was interested in trading rations with them. Royal Marine Commandos, on the same operation, flat out refused to trade, preferring to stick to their own rations, which were really quite delicious, in fact, filled with brand-name items such as Cadbury chocolates and nicely done curry dishes. Most of America's allies have rations far superior to what the Pentagon will issue to its armed forces.

On August 19, 2002, *The Marine Corps Times* reported under the headline "Crikey, That's Awful" the following:

"Australian soldiers serving in Afghanistan can handle most privations and dangers in the line of duty — but they're turning noses up at American rations. The leader of an Australian parliamentary delegation who visited Australian Troops in Afghanistan said Aussie soldiers served up only one gripe — U.S. military cooking."

On September 22, 2002, Michael Cooper writing for *The New York Times* described a visit by New York City Mayor Michael R. Bloomberg to Afghanistan, where he shared a meal with the troops: "As the mayor put it delicately after he was asked what he had for dinner: 'I don't want to be ungracious, because they tried very hard. But I cannot identify what the food was, and it is not for security reasons." The Associated Press reported from Kabul that he ate an American-style dinner of pork strips, ham, cornbread, and salad.

The almost paramount disdain for good field rations in the U.S. military is hard to explain. Maybe the desire for elegant food is "not manly" as one Marine

(Below) Few people – inside or outside of the military – will ever realize just how very long it takes to melt snow to make coffee or tea. These United States Marines speculated that it would take just five minutes to melt enough snow for a cup of coffee (Type II). It took almost 20 minutes.

Corps general told Hassell. Or, as is the case with the overall culinary culture of the United States, good, elegant food came very late to the tables and is often still absent from servings in the heartland. The puritanical traditions and the dominant pioneer spirit form most of America's food traditions — meals should be plentiful and solid. Elegance in preparation and delicate selection of ingredients is a frivolous act.

This practice differs markedly from Europe, Japan, China, India, and, of course, ancient Rome and Greece, old Egypt, and much of the Arab world.

For instance, the "Felddienst-Ordung" or "Standing Orders for Units in the Field" of the Royal Prussian Army of 1908 states that war rations should consist of:

750 grams of bread or 400 grams of egg bread and 500 grams of field biscuit
375 grams fresh, salted, or frozen meat
125 grams of rice, gruel, beans or 1,500 grams of potatoes
25 grams of coffee or 3 grams of tea
25 grams of salt

The "Felddienst-Ordnung" also advises troops to be kind to the local population, yet take cows, sheep, and other domestic animals for slaughter by the troops. It contains strict rules against looting.

The experience of World War I changed little in German military manuals. They are consistent in statements of treating the enemy population well and not to loot. A 1924 instruction manual for German artillery recruits emphasizes the need for good, solid food, especially after fighting a battle. "Cooking," the manual states, "almost always takes place in a field kitchen so that troops, after an engagement are quickly served a well cooked meal."

For thousands of years service in the military — particularly in the officer corps — was the duty as well as the privilege of the upper classes, the rulers, the kings, and the princes. Thus it can be of no surprise that elegant food made it to the field of battle and, in turn, influenced the home. Military service was truly the task of the elite — good performance in battle was essential to advance in society.

The common Roman Legionnaire was considered elite. Service under arms to the Roman Empire was viewed as a special privilege, as a way to advance in Roman society. Food is critical in war. Recall Napoleon's adage, "An army marches on its stomach." Good food has a tangible impact on morale.

Military food has had an enormous impact on global culinary culture. Since earliest recorded history, food has been one of the driving forces of military campaigns. Many wars — small and large — were fought over resources, food in particular. Invading armies would also return with new food traditions, new spices, and new ingredients.

Europe's field armies to this day retain much of the traditions and glory of fancy food, albeit in somewhat diminished levels, a reflection of the global transition to a mass society that seemingly seeks to suppress individualism. Recalls Hassell:

"Unforgettable to me were numerous lunches and dinners with the San Marco Battalion in Civil War Beirut in 1982 and 1983. The Italian Marines occupied the sector just north of the U.S. Marine positions. Superb food was the rule of the day for the Italians while most U.S. Marines were limited to the contents of olive-drab cans and early versions of "Meals, Ready-to-Eat."

"Along with decent-quality table wine, the Italians would serve up freshly cooked meals consisting of pasta dishes that varied every day — fresh fish, grilled meats, and a host of well-prepared vegetables. The Italians had transported the very best of Italy's cuisine to the field and pulled it off with appropriate style under combat conditions. Each meal was concluded with espresso served with just the right amount of 'crema.'

"Similar experiences could be had in the headquarters of the French Foreign Legion, occupying the sector adjoining the Italians. Their headquarters was the old 19th-century clubhouse of the Beirut race course, then located just next to the famous 'Green Line,' the center of daily shootings and skirmishes.

"I recall one day when lunch was served by Legionnaires, dressed in white, well-starched jackets and camouflage trousers with submachine guns over their shoulders. The multi-course lunch consisted of a delicate Vichyssoise, followed by herbed grilled chicken, a cheese course, and chocolate mousse. Wine from the Legion's vineyards was served in real glass, and elegant solid sterling covered the white tablecloths. My host, however, profusely apologized about the quality of the table service, saying that the good crystal and better silver had been put away. Why had it been put away? The Syrians — we guess — were happily shelling the top floors of the clubhouse, creating both noise and dust. But lunch had to go on.

"They carry their legends to war with them, along with their insignia-etched glassware, their silver cutlery and the ingredients of a very fine vinaigrette,' wrote Geraldine Brooks for *The Wall Street Journal* on November 13, 1990, from Hafar Al Batin, Saudi Arabia.

"She dined with the Foreign Legion in the weeks before the first ground assault on Iraq and described how the Legionnaires started cultivating fresh tomatoes to improve their diet.

"The food is superb. While U.S. troops sit on the sand, scooping unidentifiable substances from plastic plates, the legionnaires sit at long trestle tables, draped with linen cloths, and pass tureens of fragrant ragout, loaves of crusty baguettes and crisp salads. There is a cheese course, of course, and fruit.'"

This book will take you on a culinary journey through the fancy military cuisines of the world. It is far from complete, as we had to rely on our own combat experience and exposure to foreign military forces and the availability of limited historical research. But the essence of this book remains – it is the first-ever look at just what the military forces since ancient times have contributed to the dining tables of the world. ✄

ANCIENT EGYPT AND GREECE:
CULINARY ARTS AND MILITARY SURPRISES

They eat loaves of bread of coarse grain, which they call cyllestis. They make their beverage from barley, for they have no vines in their country. They eat fish raw, sun-dried or preserved in salt brine.

— Herodotus, *Histories II,* 77

Ancient Egypt

Ancient Egypt's society — fully civilized and organized long before the Greeks started to learn how to write and before the Romans invented the toga — had a highly advanced military force. Food was essential and outstanding logistics mattered, not just for the armed forces but for the country as a whole.

The temperamental Nile River forced Egypt's rulers to develop complex administrative structures. This administrative apparatus controlled irrigation, harvests, and storage and disbursement of food. Without this, Egypt — a society that grew in the middle of a desert, yet made the most of the fertile Nile valley — would have never reached the levels of culture that continue to amaze even the most casual observer to this day.

The riches of Egypt forced Pharaohs to build up strong military forces that could repel invaders eager to seize the apparently plentiful loot. Well-organized forces were needed to secure trade relations and expand the empire.

While Egypt's military logistics pale in comparison to Rome, a culture of superb food evolved. Egypt's soldiers and sailors ate well, and their commanders ate even better.

(Opposite) This Stela of Mentuwoser (ca. 1955 B.C.; Dynasty 12, reign of Senwosret I, year 17; Middle Kingdom, painted limestone) is a prime example of detailed record keeping and instructions. It was created to honor the Egyptian court official Mentuwoser and shows him holding a folded piece of linen in his left hand. He presides over his own funeral banquet asking that he will always receive food offerings. According to the interpretation by the Metropolitan Museum of Art in New York, his daughter is shown holding a lotus "and his father offers a covered dish of food and a jug that, given its shape, contained beer. In order to show clearly each kind of food being offered, the carver arranged the images on top of the table vertically. The feast consists of round and conical loaves of bread, ribs and a hindquarter of beef, a squash, onions in a basket, a lotus blossom, and leeks." This stela and others record in detail food served in ancient Egypt.

Complaints about food are probably the one element common to any military force since the earliest days of humanity. Yet these very complaints show just how well ancient Egyptian soldiers lived.

The administrators of old Egypt, generally known as "scribes," shared the disdain of the profession of arms that seems to infect bureaucrats to this day.

Come, [let me tell] you the woes of the soldier, and how many are his superiors: the general, the troop-commander, the officer who leads, the standard-bearer, the lieutenant, the scribe, the commander of fifty, and the garrison-captain. They go in and out in the halls of the palace, saying: "Get laborers!" He is awakened at any hour. One is after him as [after] a donkey. He toils until the Aten sets in his darkness of night. He is hungry, his belly hurts; he is dead while yet alive. When he receives the grain-ration, having been released from duty, it is not good for grinding.

He is called up for Syria. He may not rest. There are no clothes, no sandals. The weapons of war are assembled at the fortress of Sile. His march is uphill through mountains. He drinks water every third day; it is smelly and tastes of salt. His body is ravaged by illness. The enemy comes, surrounds him with missiles, and life recedes from him. He is told: "Quick, forward, valiant soldier! Win for yourself a good name!" He does not know what he is about. His body is weak, his legs fail him. When victory is won, the captives are handed over to his majesty, to be taken to Egypt. The foreign woman faints on the march; she hangs herself [on] the soldier's neck. His knapsack drops, another grabs it while he is burdened with the woman. His wife and children are in their village; he dies and does not reach it. If he comes out alive, he is worn out from marching. Be he at large, be he detained, the soldier suffers. If he leaps and joins the deserters, all his people are imprisoned. He dies on the edge of the desert, and there is none to perpetuate his name. He suffers in death as in life. A big sack is brought for him; he does not know his resting place.

From the instructions of scribe Wenemdiamun

Yet ancient Egypt's soldiers were — as would be the case later in Macedon, Sparta, Athens, and Rome — known to be members of the very elite:

The warriors were the only Egyptians, except the priests, who had special privileges: for each of them an untaxed plot of twelve acres was set apart…A thousand Calasirians and as many Hermotybians were the king's annual bodyguard. These men, besides their lands, each received a daily provision of five minae's weight of roast grain, two minae of beef, and four cups of wine. These were the gifts received by each bodyguard.

Herodotus, Histories II, 168

Historical records on the diet of Egypt's military forces verify that soldiers and their officers did indeed eat well. The daily issue was a diet of bread, beer, and meat. And for special occasions, such as victory dinners,

commanders would feast on game such as wild geese or Oryx antelopes.

When Pharaoh Seti I (ca. 1318-1304 B.C.) sent a thousand troops to the Silsileh quarry, he "increased that which was furnished to the army in ointment, ox-flesh, fish and plentiful vegetables without limit. Every man among them had 20 deben [about two pounds] of bread daily, two bundles of vegetables, a roast of flesh and two linen garments monthly." *Translated from the Silsileh quarry stela.*

Meats were typically grilled on spits or roasted in simple ovens. According to Herodotus, quail, ducks, and smaller birds were salted and eaten uncooked; all other kinds of birds, as well as fish, excepting those sacred to the Egyptians, were eaten roasted or boiled. Herodotus, in his *Histories*, discussed in some detail forms of food preservation, a natural concern for a society that forever had to worry about failing harvests, lack of water, and the many months of dry weather. His report shows that whatever couldn't

16

(Above) This vase for cooling wine dates to ca. 520-510 B.C. and comes from Attica in Greece. Technically, it is known as a Psykter. According to the New York City Metropolitan Museum of Art, "Around the body, hoplites (foot soldiers) are mounted on dolphins. This procession of identically dressed foot soldiers seems to advance with military precision. A number of other dolphin-riding hoplites appear on vases of this period. All are accompanied by a flute player, suggesting that this scene illustrates a dramatic chorus, probably from a contemporary play. The six dolphins would have seemed to leap and dive as the psykter, filled with wine, bobbed in ice water inside a large krater. Oltos was an early red-figure painter who specialized in decorating cups and other shapes used in symposia (drinking parties)."

(Opposite) Dated to the third quarter of the sixth century B.C., this plate is described by the New York City Metropolitan Museum of Art: "This cup is a paradigm of Laconian vase painting. (The artist is named after two depictions of a boar hunt.) The potting here is fine and sharp. The interior shows, at left, a fully armed foot soldier, his spear on the far side and his shield behind him. His companion bends to put on greaves (shin guards). A shield leans on the 'wall' behind him, and a cuirass occupies the center of the tondo. A bird and a bag for gear complete the picture. In the exergue, two foxes frolic. The fame of Archaic Sparta lay in its military organization, which did not, however, preclude artistic creativity."

be eaten fresh had to be preserved quickly, either by salting and brining, drying, or smoking. A kind of pemmican (pounded dry meat mixed with melted fat) was sometimes made; fish roe, beer, and honey were also used as preservatives.

Greece

Greek cuisine resembles that of the Romans. Both Greece and Italy share similar climates on the Mediterranean, so similar foods were grown and both shared a close relationship with the sea, which highly influenced their diets.

In Greece, however, there was not a permanent military, and generals would call up citizens and build an army for specific threats or wars. Here, quartermaster skills were not nearly as well developed as those in Rome. Greek soldiers may have marched as far as Roman Legionnaires on some campaigns, but they certainly didn't eat as well. The staple of the Greek soldier was grain, primarily wheat, and whatever else could be gained from the poor peasants in their path.

The Greek gourmet Athenaeus in 200 B.C. cited Archilochus of Paros, who wrote that the food of Greek soldiers was essentially barley cakes, but Diodorus of Agyrium wrote that the primary diet of troops commanded by Alexander of Macedon consisted of grain, specifically barley, millet, and wheat, often made into bread.

Perhaps an appreciation for what it took to feed a mammoth army can be gained by estimating the food requirements of Roman or Greek soldiers under different field conditions. In detailed accounts left by Athens General Xenophon, leader of the March of the Ten Thousand from Greece to Persia and back, and from accounts of the march of Alexander's troops from Pella in Northern Greece to India and back, as well as from accounts of various wars fought by the Romans, the energy needs of a typical soldier were estimated at about 1,000 calories per mile. Each soldier required a minimum of 3,600 calories per day. Moving 10,000 soldiers would thus require about four loaves of bread per day per man, or 40,000 loaves of bread per day. Baking, transporting, and distributing 40,000 loaves per day required an entire separate army of support staff.

That would compare to today's American soldiers who are issued MREs (Meals, Ready-to-Eat) in the field, each weighing eight ounces and containing about 3,000 calories. Thus, the food for a 10,000-man force achieving the same caloric intake would weigh 6,000 pounds and could be transported on one truck. Moreover, the MREs provide a more balanced diet of vitamins, minerals, carbohydrates for energy, and protein.

In other accounts of his march from Greece to southern Mesopotamia and back, General Xenophon included numerous food-related notes of how his soldiers plundered the landscape for food, and when they couldn't find any, stole other valuables that could be traded for food. He acknowledged that, at times, supportive civilians fed his army, while at other times his troops were forced to gather and hunt for wild foods.

Consider the logistical problems faced by Alexander of Macedon who campaigned with 65,000 soldiers. The rations required to sustain the Macedonian army were gathered or confiscated from agricultural stores of villages in the army's path. Most soldiers ate three loaves of bread per day and supplemented their diet with cheese, fish, fruits, vegetables, olive oil, and wine. Nevertheless, at the very least, the Macedonian army required nearly 200,000 loaves of bread per day in order to keep it moving. All of this — provisions for soldiers, fodder for animals, and water — on a daily basis would have weighed an estimated 237,500 pounds.

Generally, Greek culinary skills remained quite primitive, based largely on barley that was used to make unleavened bread or a porridge called alphita, which consisted of ground barley boiled into a thick paste. In his play *Lysistrata*, the Greek comic Aristophanes describes soldiers in Athens harassing merchants in the markets and eating alphita from their bronze helmets.

Another staple was salt fish, most of which came from the Black Sea. Called tarichos and consisting mostly of tunny, or tuna as we know it today, these fish were caught in great quantities and salted for preservation. Unlike other civilizations that traded salted fish, the Greeks made it an important staple for feeding the masses and sold it cheaply in markets. It was a foundation of the military diet. The neck, belly, and throat of the tuna were even considered delicacies. Soldiers rarely enjoyed the throats though — they caused severe flatulence, a tricky problem for fighting men who might have to sneak up on an enemy. Tarichos can last up to a year while maintaining 85 percent of the protein value and half of the vitamin B. It was a practical ration for long campaigns — plentiful, cheap, light, and nutritious.

A daily diet of grain and fish was somewhat boring, so chefs used their imaginations and created sauces featuring ingredients such as oregano, thyme, onions, raisins, vinegar, and olive oil. While the sauces added a bit of variety, Greek soldiers did not merely subsist on grains and salted fish. Like soldiers of most other civilizations, the basics were supplemented with seasonal fruits and vegetables as they became available. They also hunted game along the way, cooking it with a little salt and spices on spits over the campfire.

One particular food for which Greeks have been assigned credit is that of baklava, and while the Greeks do deserve credit in developing the thin, flaky dough — phyllo — credit for baklava as we know it today must go to the Turks and the military, and their invasion of Constantinople to the west and eastern regions of Assyria and the entire Armenian Kingdom. ✂

SAUTÉED TUNA FISH

This recipe is adapted from Apicius. It is also a dish a Greek Hoplites — elite Greek soldiers from the various city states — probably would have been able to create. Apicius called this dish "Sauce for Baked Young Tuna-Fish."

Ingredients
¼ cup olive oil
2 pounds tuna filet in thick slices
1 teaspoon pepper
1 teaspoon chopped lovage
1 tablespoon chopped oregano
1 tablespoon green coriander
1 medium-sized yellow onion, minced
¼ cup pitted chopped raisins
1 cup red wine
1 cup fish sauce (can substitute Thai or Vietnamese fish sauce)
¼ cup red wine vinegar

Instructions
Note that Apicius just said, "Instructions: Cook. If you wish, add some honey. This sauce can also be served with poached [tuna fish]."

1. Heat the olive oil in a heavy-duty saucepan.
2. Quickly sauté the tuna filets until brown on both sides (about 2 minutes).
3. Add all other ingredients.
4. Cover and simmer for about 20 minutes on medium heat.

Place in a dish and serve hot.

FAKI SOUP FROM THE BATTLE OF PLATAEA (479 B.C.)

Sixty-thousand Hoplites under the command of the Spartan King Pausanius defeated the Persians in the famous battle of Plataea in 479 B.C. It is likely that some of the Hoplites dined on this substantial lentil soup. Some may even have used their helmets as cooking pots, and shared their meals with each other. Suitable ingredients would have been found among the rations Hoplites carried into battle. It is likely that the soup was accompanied by flat bread baked in embers. Salt-fish, known as tarichos and imported from the Black Sea, would have been another likely accompaniment.

Ingredients
5 tablespoons olive oil
2 yellow onions, finely chopped
6 cloves garlic, chopped
3 turnips, peeled and chopped
2 cups brown lentils, washed
1 stalk celery, chopped
½ cup Italian parsley (flat leaf), chopped
2 quarts water
2 bay leaves
½ teaspoon fresh thyme, chopped
coarse sea salt to taste
pepper to taste
3 tablespoons high quality red wine vinegar
4 scallions, chopped, green part discarded
4 tablespoons olive oil

Instructions
1. Heat 5 tablespoons olive oil over medium heat in a large, heavy saucepan.
2. Add onions, garlic, chopped celery, and turnips, and sauté until the onions are translucent.
3. Add the lentils and sauté for several more minutes, stirring occasionally.
4. Add the parsley.
5. Add water, bay leaves, and thyme.
6. Add salt and pepper to taste (keep in mind the Hoplites would have had very little pepper — then an ultra-expensive spice).
7. Bring to a boil, then reduce heat to a simmer, cover, and cook for an hour and a half.
8. Add the vinegar, stir and cook for one minute.
9. Remove the bay leaves.
10. Ladle into in large soup bowls, add the scallions, and drizzle some additional olive oil.
11. Serve with flat bread or crusty bread.

ROME:
EXCELLENT LOGISTICS, ELEGANT FOOD

I t's no surprise that the essence of military food and truly sophisticated field dining began with the Roman Empire. The first professionally trained, full–time, dedicated military began in Rome. Until the formation of the Roman Empire, armies were part–time military forces organized to do battle in a specific campaign and then discharged back into civilian life. Rome changed all this: it had standing armies supported by a sophisticated supply system that would not be seen again until the Napoleonic wars. The system supported soldiers, horses, and pack animals with both food and water. The logistical complexity of organizing all of this even today would be a challenge, but to have done it successfully for military campaigns that often went for months and sometimes years in the fourth century is a feat beyond comprehension.

Rome began to introduce eastern indulgence in the second century B.C.E., as troops returned from the war with Syria's Antiochus III. Titus Livy, the famous Augustan historian wrote, "the Army of Asia introduced foreign luxury to Rome. It was then that meals began to demand more preparation and expense. The cook, considered and employed until then as a slave at the lowest cost, became extremely expensive. What had been only a job became an art."

The Roman Legions were formed as a standing army when citizens volunteered to give a lifetime of service to the Republic. The Romans were the first to introduce formal military training, rank structure, common uniforms, manuals, pay books, even "paperwork" performed on stones, wax tablets, or papyrus. With this came an orderly and finely tuned logistics system. It used a network of roads that still mark much of Europe and the Middle East.

The movement of men and materiel was key to Rome's success in managing its expansive empire. An important aspect of the logistics system was to ensure that Roman Legions, no matter how distant from Rome, were well fed. Evidence of that comes from notes and letters written by Roman Legionnaires and found in excavations at Hadrian's Wall in Scotland. In the letters, the Legionnaires complained about the delay in the delivery of good olive oil and special types of wine.

(Opposite) Roman Temple in Évora, Alentejo, in Portugal The Roman Temple, commonly believed to have been dedicated to Diana (although it is not known to which god it was really dedicated) is unique and one of the best preserved examples on the Iberian Peninsula. Dating from the end of the second century, it combines both sturdiness and grace. It was built in the Acropolis of the old Roman city then known as Liberalitas Julia, which is now a prosperous town known as Évora. The existing columns are made of granite, while their bases and heads are made of regional marble. The picture depicts some elements of the typical Roman soldier's meal: almonds, olives, and a dish prepared with farro, olive oil, cubes of bacon, onion, and fresh thyme, some red wine in a Roman clay tumbler, and an amphora.

(Left) Trajan Decius, born in 201, ruled as Roman Emperor from 249 until 251, when he was killed in a battle with the Goths. His history is the story of an energetic general who fought all over the Roman Empire. He personally led his Legions, often fighting in the frontlines, and shared increasingly sophisticated meals with his soldiers.

Contemporary reports show that Roman Legions — regardless of where they were stationed in the vast Empire — had easy access to olive oil and wine from Italy and Gaul (modern France). Legionnaires would often feast on fresh seafood and the plentiful wild game of Rome's frontier provinces. A sophisticated supply system cut the time of delivery of amphorae filled with wine and olive oil, as well as various hard cheeses from the south of Provence, to battlefields in the Balkans from several months to just fifteen days.

This silver coin shows the Emperor with the inscription "IMP C M Q TRAIANYS DECIVS AVG." and on the reverse "VBERTITAS AUG." — Uberitas (a symbol of fertility, mostly in agriculture) is standing, holding a purse and the cornucopia, the traditional symbol of plentiful food.

(Above) Rome's Cheeses and Foods: Cielo Peralta of Murray's Cheese on New York City's Bleeker Street is one of the true masters of the fine art of selecting perfectly ripe cheese. Mr. Peralta carries cheeses and food products, such as those shown here, that trace their roots to the elaborate supply systems of Rome's Legion.

The expanding Roman Empire forced the military to hone their skills in preserving fresh products, such as milk or meats, for long journeys. Shown here are Caciocavallo, Parmegiano-Reggiano, Pecorino di Pienza, Mountain Gorgonzola, Formassio di Fossa from The Marches, Provolone Mandorone, Provolone Auricchio (both made in Lombardy now and the Mandorone is aged for three years), Taleggio, Piave, and Serra Da Estrella (from Lusitana or Portugal). The meats shown include aged prosciutto, mortadella, and hard sausages (all ideal food for the Legionnaires' packs).

(Above) Beirut, Lebanon, 1983: These modern Roman Legionnaires are part of the famous San Marco Battalion of today's Italian Navy. Italian Marines served alongside United States Marines during peacekeeping missions in that troubled city. A standard evening dinner concluded with hot, foamy, and excellent espresso.

Some authors have noted that the Roman soldier lived on a diet of plain foods that was extremely limited. In fact, the Roman diet, while not limited in types of food available to the wealthy, was generally plain and remains so to this day. Diodorus Siculus left records on Roman military foods that cautioned against the use of red meat in a military diet, noting a regular diet of meat caused illness among the soldiers. Records left by Julius Caesar and Tacitus reveal that the preferred diet for Roman soldiers was grains, but if grain was unavailable, soldiers should eat meat.

In permanent camps the Roman soldier supplemented his diet with a variety of foods, including bacon, porridge, and even hardtack. Sour wine, called posca, was vinegar diluted with water and could be quite refreshing. Meat, of course, was a staple, and analysis of bones from Roman forts shows that beef, veal, mutton, pork, and even goat were eaten on a regular basis. Many soldiers became hunters and killed red and roe deer, boar, hare, elk, and ox, all of which supplemented their diet.

Roman soldiers in the field kept a watchful eye out for chickens when they passed through villages. They also considered duck, goose, pheasant, swan, woodcock, heron, guinea fowl, bantam, and petrel, a seabird that is now nearly extinct but recovering slowly in the Caribbean, fine supplements to their diet.

Beans and lentils were popular among Roman citizens, and they were readily available to the soldiers, often forming the basis for stews. Less popular were vegetables like peas, carrots, cabbage, asparagus, rice garlic, and chickpeas.

Cheese was another popular food for Roman soldiers because it was easy to carry and store, and it had valuable protein. Hard cheeses such as Parmesan and Pecorino were favorites, especially when flavored with pepper. The demand for cheese was so high that under the rule of Augustus, the Roman Legion supply corps was required to promote the development of cheeses indigenous to the area where the soldiers were serving.

The supply corps popularized English Cheshire cheese, Cantal from the Auvergne, and Beaufort from the Alps. Another popular cheese was called Sbrinz, a very hard cheese still made in Switzerland. Cheeses — mostly hard cheeses — continued to be a staple of military rations for centuries. Even recent C-Rations in the United States military often contained a cheese component, although it was soft.

Whenever possible, Roman soldiers ate fruits such as apples, pears, plums, pomegranates, cherries, strawberries, grapes, blackberries, elderberries, and sloe, or blackthorn as it is more popularly known today. Blackthorn was popular for its medicinal value as a mouthwash for gum sores, a gentle laxative, and a cure for colic. Perhaps the most highly regarded fruit of the Romans was the fig, which is actually an inverted flower. The seeds are drupes, or the real fruit. Romans believed that figs were introduced by the god Bacchus and made the trees sacred. Baccus was often depicted crowned in fig leaves, and the first figs of the season were offered to him.

Nuts, especially walnuts and hazelnuts, were commonly eaten by Legionnaires. They were tasty and packed plenty of fat and calories needed on long campaigns. Their shells made them easy to transport without any fuss.

There is also evidence Roman soldiers ate a variety of freshwater and saltwater fish, including cod, tuna, and sturgeon, as well as whale, porpoise, and even cuttlefish, a cephalopod that was a delicacy and probably led to Italy's current-day taste for calamari. Tuna is quite interesting because in Roman society, as well as among the Legions, tuna had a class status. The neck

(Above) An Italian Marine stir-fries green peppers in Beirut, 1983.

and belly of the tuna were considered delicacies and were eaten only by Romans of status or soldiers with rank. The rest of the tuna was cut up and usually salted and sold at the fishmonger or fed to soldiers of lesser rank.

Roman soldiers also favored fish sauces, especially Garum. Garum, however, was expensive and took a long time to make. Roman soldiers, who were pressed for time, preferred a cheaper and easier-to-make sauce called Muria, which was more like a pickled fish prepared in brine.

What is Garum? Garum is a fermented fish sauce, which was made by layering small fish, the intestines of some larger fish, a few oysters, salt, pepper, and other spices in a barrel. The barrel was then sealed and left in the sun until the contents liquefied. While it is rare to find Garum today, most are familiar with its cousin, Worcestershire sauce, which is based on salted anchovies.

Asia has created a close alternative to Garum suitable for recreating ancient Roman meals. Asian cultures are fond of fermented fish sauce, and have been since ancient times, using them like Westerners use salt. Vietnam has its *nuoc man*. Laos calls it *nam pa*. Thailand calls it *nam bla*. In Burma it is *ngan pya ye*. Although all have their own signature, all are alike in that fish, both saltwater and fresh, are salted, mixed with water, then allowed to ferment in wooden casks. The end product is a clear liquid that is some shade of brown, salty to the taste, and fishy to the smell. Reputedly the best fish sauce is made on Phu Quoc, an island in the Gulf of Thailand, where exquisite and delicate anchovies, called *ca com*, are layered, salted, and left to ferment for months in their wooden casks.

The only ancient cookbook to have survived into modern times is *The Art of Cooking (De Re Coquinaria)* by Apicius, who lived during the reign of Tiberius. The work, which has survived under the name of Apicius, is not in its original form, but is preserved in a later edition prepared in the fourth or early fifth century A.D.

Apicius, according to contemporary records, would send fresh oysters to the field headquarters of Emperor Trajan during his wars against Parthia. The oysters, the reports stated, were chilled with crushed ice (a major accomplishment) and reportedly arrived as fresh as the day they were harvested. By 100 B.C. the Romans had already perfected the art of cultivating oysters.

Each group of Roman Legionnaires assigned soldiers to make bread. They would first have to grind rations of grain into flour, make it into a loaf, bake it in the ashes of a campfire, then distribute it to their troops for eating. Bakers carried sickles with them to harvest local grains along the way. Other troops would be responsible for roasting or boiling the meat. A scene on Trajan's Column depicts a Legionary carrying his kit on a stake; this consisted in part of a string-bag for forage, a metal cooking pot and a messtin, examples of which have been discovered in most parts of the Empire.

Calculations show that each Roman soldier would eat approximately one–third of a ton of grain each year, and that this amount of grain would occupy half a cubic yard of space in the granary. Farro was an important grain to the Roman soldier. Believed to have been popularized in Egypt where Pharaohs were buried with it, every Roman soldier received a bag of it. Often called emmer, farro in Italian (*farina*, Italian for flour), the miraculous little grain with a bold earthy taste, dates back to the Neolithic era in central Italy. It is an early form of wheat and is boiled or milled to make flour. Farro fueled the Roman Legions, and its use spread throughout the Roman Empire. Roman soldiers used their bag of farro to make thick soups, often flavored with salt pork and thickened with beans or other vegetables.

Few foods are as fortifying as farro, which is high in fiber, magnesium, and vitamins A, B, C, and E. It is easily digested and provides lots of carbohydrates for energy and strength. Its flavor is somewhere between that of barley and wheat. Some would describe it as tasting nutty. It was often combined with beans in a "minestra de farro" or milled into flour for pasta and cookies. In Italy, the minestra di farro of Lazio is made with guanciale (pork jowl), parsley, and basil and is served with a fragrant Pecorino Romano. Recently farro has become quite popular in kitchens around the world and is used by the finest chefs, although much of what is believed to be farro today is really spelt or wheat. Farro is still grown in Umbria, Lazio, and Tuscany, growing best in barren, high–altitude terrain, but it is in such high demand that often the other two grains are substituted.

One of the most surprising dishes to come from Roman Legionnaires serving in Great Britain was Yorkshire Pudding. Perhaps one of the most characteristic dishes of Britain today, there is evidence that it was first made by the Romans using farro.

As it was in most other civilizations, salt was of paramount importance to Romans, although it took on different meanings in Rome. A Roman soldier's pay was called *a salarium argentum*, the phrase from which "salary" is derived. The saying, "he's not worth his salt" was coined by Romans referring to slaves purchased with salt. The word "sale" also comes from salt being used as currency. During the Middle Ages, however, salt became linked with superstition. Spilling salt was believed to attract evil spirits. After spilling salt, one was required to throw a portion over the left shoulder, because that was where the evil spirits were believed to congregate. In Leonardo da Vinci's painting of "The Last Supper," Judas is shown with an overturned salt cellar on the table in front of him.

As simple as a Roman soldier's food was, the meals partaken by senior military officials and politicians were of a very different nature. Wealthy Romans loved feasts and imperial banquets. These banquets are reported to have known no bounds. Author Roy Strong, in his book *Feast,* tells a chilling story of Tigellinus, commander of the Praetorian Guard, who was ordered to prepare an imperial dinner for Nero around the summer of A.D. 64. Nero and attendees to the imperial feast reclined on rugs and cushions on a large raft that was towed by barges adorned with gold and ivory. The barges were crewed by "exoleti," or "joy–boys," purposely chosen for their lascivious habits. The lake was surrounded by a park which had been stocked with exotic birds and animals and pavilions of brothels, employing the most beautiful women in the city.

It was at one of these imperial dinners that Nero, hoping to embarrass Britannicus, son of Emperor Tiberius, on the eve of his seventeenth birthday, demanded that Britannicus sing to the assembled group. Britannicus sang, like a bird it is said, but he sang about the cruelty of his father and his expulsion from his father's house and throne.

Nero said nothing of the poor choice of subject Britannicus chose to croon about. But at the next banquet, Britannicus fell dead at the table, poisoned at the hand of Nero.

One of the greatest contributions the Romans have provided to Lucullian fare came from the Roman General Lucius Licinius Lucullus. In history he is rewarded with credit as the conqueror in the Third Mithradatic War when Mithradates resolved to prevent Rome from annexing Bithynia, which had been left to Rome by a deed. Lucullus annihilated Mithradates' army and eventually forced him into Armenia, which gained him great favor. He was made a Praetor in 78 B.C. and a Consul in 74 B.C. Lucullus, however, was never able to end the war, as his troops mutinied and he was recalled and replaced, being forced into retirement. Wealthy and living amidst parks that he designed and built in Rome and villas he constructed at Tusculum near Naples, Lucullus became known for his extravagant banquets and self–indulgence and gained the nickname the "Roman Xerxes." The term "Lucullian" derives from his extravagant standard of living.

The importance of military food is no more steeped in culinary tradition than with the Romans. Few would ever associate lasagna with Prince Alfred zu Windischgrätz, commander of the Austrian forces occupying Ancona in 1799. But it was Prince Windischgrätz that created a type of lasagna called "Vincisgrassi" that has become one of the Marche region's signature dishes. Note here that the Romans had invented modern lasagna, known as *lagana* in Latin. Vincisgrassi, sometimes known as "princisgras," was first written down by Antonio Nebbia in *Il Cuoco Maceratese*. The initial recipe was written before the widespread acceptance of tomatoes, and does omit them, although more modern derivations include tomato sauce, along with chicken giblets, which are credited for giving the dish its characteristic flavor. ✄

RICETTE DI OSTERIE E DI PORTI MARCHIGIANI

The following recipe is published by Slowfood Editore. They note that despite the use of traditional ingredients of the Marche region, the preparation, in particular the baking, has a certain amount of French influence. The dish remains an important one for special occasions.

Ingredients – Meat Sauce

12 ounces chopped chicken giblets
½ cup unsalted butter
1 ⅓ pounds lean ground beef
2–3 whole cloves
1 tablespoon marjoram
2 onions
2 carrots
2 ribs celery
2 pounds beef bones
12 ounces pork bones
8 ounces lamb bones
8 ounces lard (not rendered lard — the cured type found in a deli)
6 ½ pounds blanched, peeled, seeded tomatoes (or use canned tomatoes)
salt and pepper to taste

Instructions – Meat Sauce

1. Finely slice giblets and sauté them in butter with the ground beef, cloves, marjoram, one onion, one carrot, and one stick of celery, leaving the vegetables whole so you can remove them when the sauce is done.
2. In a separate pan, sauté the bones in the lard with the other onion, stick of celery, and carrot, again whole.
3. When the meats have browned, add half the tomatoes to each pan.
4. Simmer both sauces gently, stirring every now and then; the sauce with the ground beef will take about one hour to cook, while the sauce with the bones will take two hours. While the sauces are cooking, begin making pasta.
5. When both sauces are done, remove and discard the vegetables and the bones, then combine the two.
6. Season to taste.

Ingredients – Vincisgrassi (pasta)

5 cups flour
6 eggs
pinch of salt
water

Instructions – Vincisgrassi (pasta)

1. On a smooth work surface, mound the flour and make a well in the center.
2. Put the eggs and salt into the well. Work eggs and flour together until smooth. You may add water, one drop at a time, if needed.
3. Knead for ten to fifteen minutes.
4. Separate dough into two pieces.
5. Flour your work surface and roll out the dough, rolling from the middle and flouring it as necessary to keep it from sticking.
6. Roll dough out dime–thin, and cut it into 4-by-6-inch strips.
7. Cook the strips of pasta a few at a time in lightly salted water until they're just shy of being al dente, 2–4 minutes.
8. Remove pasta from pot with a slotted strainer, run under cold water, and pat dry.

Ingredients – White Sauce

⅓ cup unsalted butter
1 cup flour
3 cups whole milk

Instructions – White Sauce

1. Melt butter over medium heat.
2. Slowly add flour, stirring constantly with a wire whisk.
3. As flour begins to brown, very slowly add milk, continuing to whisk vigorously to avoid lumps.
4. Once all the milk is added, stir sauce slowly until it thickens.

Assembly for the dish

pasta (see left)
meat sauce (see left)
3 balls of fresh mozzarella, diced (about ¾ lb.)
5 cups grated Parmigiano (this should weigh about 10 ozs.)
2 tablespoons nutmeg, freshly grated
white sauce (see above)

Instructions for the dish

1. In an oven–proof dish large enough to hold everything and elegant enough to serve in, lay down a first layer of pasta, followed by meat sauce, diced mozzarella, grated cheese, and a sprinkle of nutmeg.
2. Put down another layer of pasta, making waves in the pieces to absorb sauce.
3. Add a layer of meat sauce and a final layer of pasta.
4. Cover the top layer of pasta with the white sauce and bake at 400° F for 1 hour, checking every 10 minutes. When the dish looks like it is browning, cover the pan with aluminum foil.
5. Remove foil and serve hot.

Makes 4–6 servings.

Fish with Sweet and Sour Onions "Lucretius"

Adapted from Apicius. Since the identity of Lucretius is unknown, the recipe may be much older than the actual writings of Apicius.

Ingredients
6 shallots (or sweet onions)
1 cup fish stock (or a fish bullion cube dissolved in 1 cup of water)
1 tablespoon olive oil
1 pound salt–fish in pieces (If available, use sole, cod, or salmon fillets. If using dried cod, soak for 24 hours, changing the water frequently)
1 tablespoon honey
1 tablespoon white wine or cider vinegar
1 tablespoon boiled wine
fish sauce (you can use Thai or Vietnamese Fish Sauce in the place of Roman Garum)
parsley

Instructions
1. Take shallots, discard the tops, and chop.
2. Place shallots, fish stock, and olive oil in a heavy-duty saucepan. Moisten this bed of onions with a little water.
3. Place salt–fish in the middle, bring to a boil, and then cook gently for about 25 minutes over low heat, basting the fish occasionally.
4. When nearly done, season with honey, vinegar, and boiled wine. Taste and correct for blandness with additional fish sauce and for saltiness with extra honey.

Decorate the dish with parsley and serve.

Farro Soup with Beans

The prosciutto rind, typically discarded when the ham is sliced, is incorporated into this traditional recipe for an earthy, salty flavor.

Ingredients
7 ounces farro
1 ½ pounds shelled borlotti beans (or 4 cans cranberry beans, 8 ounces each)
2 ounces prosciutto rind (or fatty pieces of prosciutto)
¼ cup extra–virgin olive oil
½ onion, minced
1 stalk celery, minced
2 cloves garlic
6 sage leaves
6 sprigs marjoram
1 cup chopped canned plum tomatoes
salt
pinch of each: freshly grated nutmeg, cinnamon, and cloves
freshly ground pepper to taste

Instructions
1. Rinse the farro and soak it overnight in enough cold water to cover all. Drain.
2. If you are using fresh beans, place them in a pot of cold water, bring to a boil, and simmer until tender, about 1 hour; process the beans to a smooth puree in a food processor, and reserve the cooking liquid. If you are using canned beans, process them with 1 cup of the juice from the cans (reserve the rest) in a food processor until smooth.
3. Soak the prosciutto rind in cold water for 10 minutes; scrape the surface with a paring knife and cut it lengthwise into thin strips.
4. Heat all but 1 tablespoon of the olive oil in a deep pot. Add the onion, celery, garlic, sage, marjoram, and prosciutto rind, and sauté until aromatic and lightly browned. Stir in the tomatoes, salt, nutmeg, cinnamon, and cloves, and cook over moderate heat for 20 minutes.
5. Pass contents of pot though a food mill and return to the pot. Add the pureed beans and the farro. Dilute with a little of the bean liquid you have reserved.
6. Bring to a boil, and simmer for 40 minutes, or until the farro is cooked through. Add a little more of the bean liquid if the soup becomes too thick.
7. Add salt to taste if necessary and serve hot, drizzled with the remaining olive oil and dusted with pepper.

(Above) Beirut, Lebanon, 1983: Italian Commander Pier Luigi Sambo cuts into the dessert pie skillfully produced by his Marines, under cooking conditions not all that different from what the Roman's had while marching through Lebanon. The inside and outside of San Marco Battalion's field headquarters in Beirut were riddled with bullet holes and shell damage. The commander amused and chilled his U.S. Marine Corps guests when he toasted them. He pointed out that the last time U.S. Marines served side by side with Italy's Marines, they ended up sharing duty for over 40 years, first in Beijing and then in Shanghai, right after the Boxer Rebellion.

BAKED CONGER EEL FROM APICIUS

Ingredients
eel
pepper
lovage
oregano
onion
pitted raisins
wine
honey
vinegar
fish sauce (Garum)
olive oil

Instructions
1. Combine all ingredients.
2. Cook.

Comments: To recreate this dish, use any oily fish such as tuna, eel, or swordfish. This dish was recreated by using moderate quantities of the spices and quickly sautéing them in olive oil, adding the fish and the fish sauce (use Asian fish sauce here), covering the dish, and cooking it for about 25 minutes. Serve with fresh bread to absorb the juices.

LINGUINE WITH COLATURA OR GARUM

Ingredients
1 pound linguine
sea salt to taste
1 clove of garlic, chopped
coarsely ground black pepper or red chili pepper
    flakes to taste
6 ounces of Asian fish sauce (a substitute for Colatura
    or Garum)
juice of two lemons
1 sprig of fresh oregano (or two tablespoons of dried
oregano)
olive oil
pepper and salt to taste

Instructions
1. Cook linguine in salted boiling water until al dente.
2. Drain.
3. Combine other ingredients in a bowl.
4. Add drained linguine.
5. Mix vigorously.
6. Add olive oil, pepper, and salt.

COOKED FLAMINGO

The conquests of Alexander opened up Asia and Africa to the Greek world, and vastly increased the range of foodstuffs available for luxurious consumption. Apicius collected and designed new recipes for the tables of the fabulously wealthy Roman elite during the period of Rome's greatest wealth and power. He made a fortune from his skills. According to legend, Apicius died in the following way: one day he was counting his fortune and he worked out that he had so far spent a hundred million sesterces, mainly on food, and only had ten million sesterces left. So he poisoned himself rather than renounce his gourmet lifestyle. Following is his recipe for flamingo. Gourmands such as Apicius especially prized the flamingo tongues.

Ingredients
flamingo
water
salt
aniseed
vinegar
chives
coriander
boiled wine
pepper
cumin
laser root
mint
rue
vinegar
dates
starch

Instructions
1. Free the flamingo of its feathers.
2. Wash, dress, and put it in a pan.
3. Add water, salt, aniseed, and a little vinegar.
4. When the bird is half cooked, bind a bouquet of chives and coriander and cook (with the flamingo).
5. Before the bird is fully cooked, pour boiled wine over it for coloring.
6. Put pepper, cumin, coriander, laser root, mint and rue into a mortar. Bruise these seasonings together.
7. Pour vinegar over them, and add some dates and drippings from the pan.
8. Empty the contents of the mortar into the same pan (with the flamingo).
9. Thicken the sauce with starch and pour it over the bird. Serve.

The same method can be used for cooking parrot.

THE OTTOMAN EMPIRE: FUSING TASTES FROM AROUND THE GLOBE

The Ottoman Empire is a fine example of a civilization developing sophisticated cuisine through the melding of local and exotic foods. Its military built some of the finest cooking in the Mediterranean region. As warriors and invaders, the Turks exchanged many customs from Armenia, Bulgaria, Greece, Persia, Egypt, North Africa, Assyria, Mesopotamia, Yugoslavia, and even France and Hungary. Of particular interest to the Turks was food, and they captured and imported the finest chefs from these regions, bringing them to Constantinople where they were placed in the employ of the wealthy, most of them military leaders.

Turkey did, however, through its once formidable military, almost inadvertently create major culinary victories. The croissant, shaped like the half-moon of the Turkish national flag, was reportedly first baked in Vienna to celebrate the successful defeat of the Ottoman siege in 1683. Is this legend true? No concrete proof exists, yet the complex layering that makes up a flaky croissant does suggest a Middle Eastern influence. Vienna coffeehouses, renowned as places of celebration and excellent brews, are said to be another result of combat with the Turks.

Turkey's military also refined the art of spit roasting meats on skewers over an open fire. Roasting on swords, sticks, lances, and other pointy instruments has been the most traditional way of cooking meats, and soldiers thrive on it. Images on the Bayeux Tapestry record in great detail the Norman invasion of Britain in 1066 in which William the Conqueror's troops are shown spit roasting meats. What the Turkish troops did was truly refine the art, combining vegetables such as succulent peppers and eggplants, spices, and marinades based on yogurt, creating the shish kebab.

Ottoman Empire chefs became some of the most renowned of their time, combining foods and recipes from many different regions. One recipe that gained early fame was that for baklava, not the same baklava brought from Greece, but the light phyllo dough with two new ingredients, honey and walnuts. Both of these new ingredients were believed to be aphrodisiacs, and they gained great favor with Turkish sultans.

Later, even more ingredients were added to baklava to improve its aphrodisiac qualities. In fact, the pastry

took on a separate recipe for each gender with cinnamon being added for females and cardamom for males. Sometimes cloves were added for an extra romantic boost.

Greeks may take offense with this, but it was Ottoman chefs who in the 18th century gave baklava the form that has endured to this day. Until the 18th century, the phyllo dough was traditionally layered and cut into squares or triangles. The shape of baklava changed when the general manager of the Imperial Kitchen in Istanbul's Topkapi Palace (the home of the sultans) hired Monsieur Guillaume, a former pastry chef of Marie Antoinette who had been exiled in the Ottoman Empire.

According to "The Kitchen Project," an article by Stephen Block and Stephen Holloway, Chef Guillaume

(Opposite) Ottoman Empire ca. 1905 – Shish-Kebab served on a brass plate, okra salad served in a Syrian copper bowel inlaid with silver, fruit juices, spiced yogurt sauce, and Turkish eggplant make a tasty and elegant meal.

(Right) Shish-kebab is a common military dish. This image comes from the Bayeux Tapestry, in Bayeux, in Normandy, France. It is probable that Bishop Odo of Bayeux, half-brother of William the Conqueror, commissioned this 70-meter-long tapestry in the 1070s. It tells the story of the 1066 Norman invasion of Britain and the bloody war between William the Conqueror and Harold, Earl of Wessex. It also gives us an idea of food in war. This panel shows the Norman soldiers arriving in the South of England near Pevensey. Soldiers are gathering food. Subsequent panels show chicken — shish kebab style — cooked on skewers over and open fire and how the soldiers load the food on their shields to serve at a feast attended by William, his military leaders, and Bishop Odo.

created the "dome" technique of cutting and folding the baklava squares and named it "Baklava Franscaise" after his native country.

Under the Turks, palace kitchens took on a new role being designed and built with four main areas based on the social rank of the diners. The most important was the *Kushane,* named after a cooking pot and most likely derived from the Latin word for kitchen, *cucinare.* This kitchen was for preparing foods for the sultan. The second kitchen area was named *Has Mutfak* and was where food for the sultan's immediate family and select members of his harem was prepared. Other kitchens prepared meals for the remaining members of the harem, the chief eunuch, the state chancery, and members of the palace guard according to their rank.

Probably the strongest connection between decent food and the military was the Ottoman's own foreign legion of sorts. This was the elite guard known as the Janissary Corps, whose members were mostly slaves obtained in previous conquests.

This Corps — for a while the single most influential power in the Ottoman Empire, revolting against ministers and even sultans — was organized like a kitchen.

Various scholarly reports claim that this may have been based on religious reasons as well as the responsibility to feed the poor, one of the duties of the sultan (a duty inherited from the Romans. It was common that emperors would care for the populace of Rome and Byzanz, by opening grain storages on feast days).

According to cook and author Clifford A. White, the Turkish name of the complete corps was *ocak* (hearth) and was commanded by an *aga* (master). The *qazan-I sarif* (sacred cauldron) of *sorba* (soup) — a gigantic kettledrum — was the emblem of the whole Janissary Corps. These cauldrons were also used for cooking. When the Corps was upset, they would turn these cauldrons or drums upside down as a sign of their displeasure.

But there was more. Their headgear was decorated with a spoon and senior officers were called *sorbadji* (soup men). Many other lower ranks had designations such as *asçıbası* (head cook), *karakullukcu* (scullion), *corekci* (baker of round bread), and the *gozlemici* (pancake maker).

The food prepared in these kitchens was of the finest caliber. There were strict guidelines on the quality and freshness of food that entered the palace, all of this enforced by the head butler, who had charge over the staff of bakers, desert cooks, helva makers, pickling chefs, and the chief yogurt maker. The staff constantly experimented with new dishes

(Opposite) This sixteenth century Turkish miniature shows food stalls at an Ottoman army encampment. Some of the stalls are distributing rice, wheat, and other loose provisions, while others sell bread, soup, milk, yogurt, and stews cooked in great cauldrons. Source: *Nusretname,* f. 93a. Topkapi Palace Museum H. 1365, Istanbul.

and recipes that were often served in an extravagant manner to nobles and state officials.

Turkish culinary art was expanded further as chefs were encouraged to form guilds where they traded ideas and set standards for food quality, as well as trained new chefs for the palace. The guilds fostered secret recipes, many of which were handed down for generations. They often forbade that the recipes be written down or even shared outside the empire. For this reason, today some of the best Turkish recipes are those that have been passed down through oral traditions.

Ms. Pricilla Mary Isin has developed a fascinating and useful web site devoted to Turkish food and culinary history. The following, found on www.ottoman-cuisine.com, is reprinted here with permission from Ms. Isin:

Mahmud Nedim bin Tosun, a lieutenant in the Ottoman infantry, completed his cookery book in H. 1316 (1898), and it was published in Istanbul in H. 1318 (1900). He presented the finished manuscript to the kaymakam (local government director) of Bulanık in Mus, an eastern province of Turkey, where he himself was posted at the time. Kaymakam Ali Rıza Bey returned the manuscript with an enthusiastic review, praising the "young officer" for providing an alternative to translations of European cuisine to meet the needs of Turkish housewives, who "not only in families of just one or two people, but even in quite large families are both head cook and mistress of the household, while the cook's assistants are the other female members of the family," and have to "personally procure and prepare all the household provisions."

Mahmud Nedim was evidently a man of good education, fascinated by cooking, which he learned from his mother as a child. If his clearly written and detailed recipes are anything to go by, he was an accomplished cook, who specifies whether the spoon used should be a metal or a wooden one, or the exact state of the fire (ashes with sparks, etc). He makes a point of never using either cooking jargon or food terms without exact and careful definitions.

He is writing with the inexperienced cook in mind, not only housewives, as he explains in his introduction, but also unmarried officers, to whom he addresses occasional pieces of advice in the recipes. If they do not know how to roll out the paper thin yufka pastry, for instance, they are recommended to ask private soldiers, some of whom are sure to be able. Not only does he provide detailed technical instructions but takes the trouble to explain why: Add salt to tripe after it is well cooked so that it does not become tough, a state of affairs known as "kirt" in culinary terminology. He tells his readers in a bracketed aside, do not substitute citric acid for lemon wedges when pickling cabbage as it will cause it to go off, and if you add grapes which have not been boiled in syrup for decoration to rezaki grape hosaf they will rise to the surface because their specific gravity is less than the juice. Complicated recipes requiring skill, such as çırçır böreği and stuffed mackerel, are described with clarity.

We learn lots of useful tips: plunge a non-ashy hot coal into muhallebi to see if it is cooked to the correct consistency — if not it will extinguish the coal; add a large chickpea-sized piece of yellow beeswax to your rice pudding to obtain a rich yellow skin on top; if you do not possess a serrated pastry wheel, the rowel of your spur will do the trick. The latter example is further evidence that he was writing partly for his brother officers.

From his wide repertoire of regional recipes we gather that he had served widely across the Ottoman Empire of the time, including the Balkans, Rhodes and Erzurum, and applied his keen observation not only to the cooking techniques, but to the kitchen equipment, local terminology, and ingredients. Erzurum's famous demir tatlısı (literally "iron pudding") required special waffle irons manufactured in "many finely executed shapes," which were copied elsewhere in the region. However, even if these copies "take the first time, at the second they fail," so he advises readers to obtain a couple of authentic Erzurum waffle irons to reproduce the dish.

The many interesting recipes in this book includes stuffed okra, pogaça with kıkırdak (scratchings), aubergine pudding ("This is most delicious and it is impossible to guess that it is made of aubergines."), tel helvası (the Turkish prototype of candy floss, also known as keten helvası, having several regional variations. Mahmud Nedim attributes its origin to Bayburt in the northeastern province of Gümüshane), testi kebabı (jug kebab), green olives preserved with sour orange juice, melon seed sherbet, aside (the favourite dish of black Africans), mock bone marrow (cooked in the knots of reeds), purslane and broad bean shoot pickle (which is "delightful, sir, delightful" to eat), unripe almond pickle, bitter almond cakes made with haricot bean purée, and fried green peppers with sour orange juice and garlic.

My own [Ms. Isin's] favourite recipe is that for gaziler helvası (warriors' helva), which Mahmud Nedim describes first in ordinary quantities for a family, and then as prepared for a company of soldiers in the field: this requires at least 15 kıyye (18 kilos) of clarified butter to be melted in a cauldron (larger quantities to be divided between two cauldrons). Two privates are then detailed to add the flour slowly by rubbing it between their hands while another stirs with the large wooden meblag. Finally the hot syrup simmering in a second cauldron is poured over and stirred in.

More so than in any other culture prior to the Ottoman Empire, the Turkish kitchen from the 11th century to the 20th century underwent a historical revolution that took foods from many regions of the world and combined and blended those foods into cuisine that is uniquely Turkey's. With its sophisticated and orderly methods of preparing food, presenting it, dining and entertaining along with the establishment of high-quality standards for ingredients, Turkey, often viewed as an unlikely place for fine cuisine, has evolved into a most extraordinary culinary experience with a wide range of recipes, most of them originating somewhere else, but all with their own Turkish character, as stated by Ms. Isin. ✂

SHISH KEBAB (SIS KEBABI)

In Turkish, shish kebab literally means "gobbets of meat roasted on a spit or skewers." It is probably the most famous preparation for grilled lamb, and there seems to be countless recipes. It is said that shish kebab was born over the open-field fires of medieval Turkish soldiers, who used their swords to grill meat, yet it is possible it originated even earlier.

Ingredients
1 cup high-quality, full-fat plain yogurt
3 tablespoons extra virgin olive oil
3 tablespoons onion juice (grated from 1 medium-size onion)
Salt and freshly ground black pepper to taste
2 pounds boneless lamb, cut from the leg with its fat into 1/2-inch cubes
8 10-inch metal or wooden skewers
4 pieces of pita bread (optional)
1 cup cacik (optional)

Instructions
1. Stir together the yogurt, olive oil, and onion juice in a glass or ceramic pan or in a bowl and season with salt and pepper. Add the lamb cubes, coat with the marinade, and refrigerate, covered, for 4 hours.
2. Prepare a charcoal fire and let it die down a bit, or preheat a gas grill for 15 minutes on low. Set the skewers in a skewer holder over the fire and grill until golden brown and succulent, turning often, for about 20 minutes. Or, lacking a skewer holder, place them on the grill and grill to perfection, turning frequently.

Serve with or on a piece of warmed pita bread with cacik on the side.

Minced Meat with Mastic (Kiyma Püryâni), 18th-century cooking manual

This recipe is reprinted from www.ottoman-cuisine.com with the permission of Ms. Pricilla Mary Isin.

Ingredients
mutton
parsley
salt
pepper
mastic
water
cinnamon
lemon juice

Instructions
1. Take the best mutton of a curly-fleeced sheep, and place in a fairly deep pan.
2. If parsley roots are available, chop a few into it, and add salt, pepper and two lumps of mastic.
3. Add plenty of water and cook over hot coals until the meat is tender.
4. Remove from the heat and add cinnamon, pepper and, if desired, lemon juice.

Kebab in Paper (Kagit Kebabi)

This recipe is reprinted from www.ottoman-cuisine.com with the permission of Ms. Pricilla Mary Isin.

Ingredients
lamb ribs, may substitute breast or leg meat
2 onions, finely chopped
salt
pepper
allspice
basil

Instructions
Although ribs are properly used for this dish you may take about 300 dirhem (900 g) of meat from the breast or leg. If using ribs, cut the meat carefully into portions without separating them completely. Finely chop two onions, and add salt, pepper, allspice and dried basil leaves to taste. Mix and rub mixture onto meat. Leave for half an hour. Place the meat in the center of a sheet of paper known as battal kagit (a kind of thick paper polished on one side only used by Ottoman government offices for making drafts), then take the four corners and bring them together in the center and squeeze together tightly. Use a length of string to tie first the opening and then the four sides tightly. It should remain for exactly two hours in a slow oven, and then be eaten immediately while hot.

Sometimes the meat is wrapped in the gut and then in paper, but when cooked that way it is impossible to avoid its having a powerful odor. Sometimes baked kebab is made in a tin or çukali (earthenware casserole). In this case the bakers sample it to check its flavor and to determine whether it is cooked.

Eggplant Dish (Saksuka)

This dish was served to Agostino von Hassell aboard the Turkish frigate *Gaziantep*. It has been adapted for civilian use.

Ingredients
1 large, plump eggplant
2 potatoes
4 green peppers
2 cups olive oil
sea salt to taste
5 garlic cloves, finely chopped
6 tomatoes, peeled, seeded, and chopped

Instructions
1. Slice the eggplant into slices ¾ of an inch thick.
2. Peel the potatoes and slice.
3. Cut peppers into ¼-inch cubes.
4. Combine these three vegetables and fry at high heat in olive oil until tender. Set aside.
5. In a second saucepan combine additional olive oil, two teaspoons of sea salt and the chopped garlic. Fry, while stirring constantly, until the garlic is soft and golden.
6. Add the chopped tomatoes to the garlic and salt mixture.
7. Add the eggplant, potatoes, and green peppers to the tomato-garlic mixture. Stir well and serve in a pre-warmed bowl.

Sea Bass in White Wine (Beyaz Sarap Soslu Levrek)

Ingredients
olive oil
red onion, finely chopped
2 cups white wine
1 cup whipped cream
water
8 small filets of sea bass (Chilean sea bass is
  also suitable)

Instructions
1. In a saucepan heat some olive oil and stir in the onion. Cook until translucent.
2. Add the fish filets and brown on both sides.
3. Add the wine and cover the pan. Cook at medium heat for 6-7 minutes.
4. With a spatula, remove the fish from the pan and place on a warmed serving plate.
5. Reduce the remaining fluid in the saucepan.
6. Take the saucepan off the stove, add the whipped cream, stir, and pour over the fish.

Variation: you may add capers to the sauce for flavor.

(Above) Detail of a 16th-century Turkish miniature depicting food stalls at an Ottoman army encampment. The stall shown here is distributing rice. Source: *Nusretname*, f. 93a. Topkapi Palace Museum H 1365, Istanbul.

Noodle Soup (Kesme Hamur Çorbasi), *Asçibasi, 1900*

This recipe is reprinted from www.ottoman-cuisine.com with the permission of Ms. Pricilla Mary Isin.

Ingredients
2 eggs
salt
water
flour
soup stock

Instructions
In almost every house pastry for this soup is prepared in autumn, cut and dried, and stored for the winter. However, since my [Mahmud Nedim's] object in preparing and writing this manual is to usefully serve my unmarried comrades at arms, who cannot carry a supply of strip noodles or dried dough for soup around with them, and since my manual is designed so that a soldier may prepare whatever he wishes, it appears necessary to explain how this dough — which can be prepared in a short time — is made.

Break two eggs into a bowl, add a little salt and beat with water. After adding sufficient flour to this mixture to form a dough, knead well.

As to rolling out the pastry into yufka (very thin circles of dough), many private soldiers know how to do this. On the underside of a cooking tray, roll out tiny lumps of dough, then wrapping them around the rolling pin (use one 80 cm long and 1.75 cm wide at the centre, tapering to 1.5 cm at either end) make a cut lengthwise along the rolling pin with a knife. The rolling pin is thus revealed. Then cut the layers of pastry crosswise again at intervals of approximately one and a half fingers. Take each of these strips and cut them again with a knife into pieces at most the width of a kebab skewer. But you must sprinkle flour amongst them so that they do not stick together. Now you have very narrow rectangular pieces of pastry. When you have finished cutting up the pastry in this way, seive them to remove the excess flour and toss them into a saucepan of boiling stock for soup. Let it come to the boil a couple of times at most, just so that the doughy smell disappears, gently stirring with a ladle at the same time, since the eggs in the dough may cause it to boil over. When it is ready remove the pan from the heat and pour into a bowl. Sprinkle seasoning over and it is ready to eat.

WARRIORS HELVA (GAZILER HELVASI), ASÇIBASI, 1900

This recipe is reprinted from www.ottoman-cuisine.com with the permission of Ms. Pricilla Mary Isin.

The author of this book was an Ottoman infantry officer, and here he first describes making helva for an ordinary household and then in military cauldrons for a detachment of soldiers.

Ingredients
clarified butter
flour
syrup
powdered sugar
cinnamon
almonds, hazelnuts, pine nuts, or pistachio nuts
  (optional)

Instructions
For a family:

Place 100 dirhem (320 g) of clarified butter into a pan and set it over the heat. When it is scorching hot set aside. When cooled slightly sprinkle in fine flour with one hand while with the other stirring to a consistency slightly thicker than yogurt. When this consistency is reached place the pan back on the heat and stir constantly. Meanwhile on another stove let there be some cut syrup boiling, and toss one spoonful of this syrup into the helva pan; if it suddenly swells up and spits then it has reached the correct state. Alternatively take a spoonful of syrup and a spoonful of the mixture and stir them together into helva. If it tastes floury or sticks to the teeth then that means it is not yet ready. If it is ready remove the pan from the heat, pour the hot syrup over and cover. Stir with a ladle for a couple of minutes and if it is not sufficiently sweet add some more syrup and cover. Leave for about half an hour, and then when stirred well it will crumble like bulgur. Then with a metal spoon or ladle press firmly into the helva to make neat shapes and turn these out upside down onto plates. Sprinkle with a little powdered sugar and a little cinnamon before eating. It is most delicious and attractive. If blanched almonds, hazelnuts, pine nuts or pistachio nuts are added while cooking and roasted with the flour they add an extra degree of delicacy to the helva.

Now let us come to helva in army cauldrons:

The number of tabla [8-10 people ate around one tabla or circular tray] should never be considered. If there is more than fifteen kıyye (19.245 kilos) of clarified butter then it should be divided between two cauldrons. If there is fifteen kıyye then cook the helva in one cauldron. If this method is followed exactly the result will be excellent. Put the clarified butter into the cauldron and set it over the fire. When it begins to scorch toss a spoonful of water into the cauldron. When the sizzling stops remove from the heat. Let it cool slightly then two soldiers should rub the flour between their fingers as they pour it into the cauldron, while one person stirs it with a large mablak [a huge wooden implement with a flat circular end]. When it is the consistency of thick yogurt set the cauldron back on the heat. But the heat should be low. As far as possible try not to scorch the base. As before when the right stage is reached pouring some of the boiling syrup from the other cauldron and stir, and then five minutes later pour in some more. In short, if this method is followed the helva will be delicious. But the syrup must be hot or the fat will be exuded, and to avoid that only care is required.

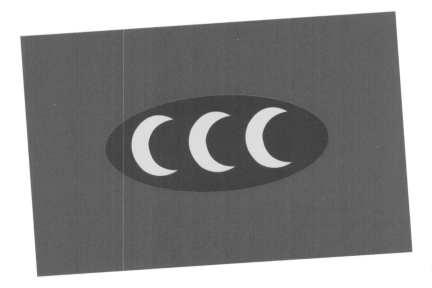

(Left) The Croissant and the Grand Vizier: Shown here is the flag of the Grand Vizier of the Ottoman Empire. He held the highest rank in the military/administrative hierarchy of the Ottoman Empire.

One famous Grand Vizier was Kara Mustafa Pasha (1634-1683) who led the rather unsuccessful Ottoman siege of Vienna in 1683. The Viennese, celebrating that victory, started – or so it is claimed – baking croissants in the half-moon shape seen on this flag. Co-author Agostino von Hassell was offered an unusual cocktail in 1984 during joint training with Turkish naval officers in Izmir. The drink was called the "Grand Vizier." It is made with $1^1/_2$ shots Grand Marnier, $^3/_4$ shot vanilla liqueur, $^1/_2$ shot fresh lime juice, and 1 shot apple juice, stirred and chilled.

JAPAN AND CHINA:
REFINEMENT AND RITUAL IN BATTLE

China

It is difficult to separate Chinese imperial cuisine from the country's fancy military dishes. The reason is simple: China was essentially a feudal society until the revolutions of the twentieth century, and China's military leaders during feudalism were part of a very limited aristocracy. As in ancient Rome, these leaders often served in multiple roles in religious, administrative, or military circles. Julius Caesar, one of Rome's most accomplished military leaders, started his career as Pontiff, a high priest of the Roman Republic. The dividing lines between religion, government, and the military were vague at best.

Chinese imperial food has incredible variety and depth, and is steeped in hundreds of years of tradition. These factors are most likely attributable to the periods when China was primarily a slave society, able to employ enormous amounts of man-hours toward growing and preparing fine foods for the cultural elite. Even early Chinese emperors had a delicate and varied palate, and they expended tremendous effort at employing the finest chefs capable of collecting and developing great delicacies to provide for their tables.

Imperial food was exclusive to the royal families, generals, ministers, and nobles, but the raw materials came from peasants, herders, and fishermen, who also often provided imperial chefs with recipes. While we often think of the ancient Chinese using simple accoutrements such as chopsticks, they reveled in sophisticated cooking instruments that were made by some of the finest craftsmen.

Fancy food preparation is impossible without skilled chefs, so emperors sought out the finest culinary talents

and cherished their gifts. *The Historical Records* by Sima Qian, a famous historian of the Han Dynasty (206-220 B.C.), includes a reference to Yi Yin, who became the first prime minister of China, and played an important role in helping Emperor Tang overthrow Emperor Jie, the last ruler of the Xia Dynasty. Yi Yin was born into a family of slaves and worked as a professional chef before entering politics. In his attempts to prove to Tang that he was worthy of a top position in government, Yi Yin brought his kitchen utensils with him on his first visit to the palace and dazzled the emperor. Tang became convinced that anyone who had such impressive skills in the kitchen also had the skills to govern the country and thus named Yi Yin prime minister.

Food continued to play an important role in shaping China's early history. Zhuan Zhu of the Wu State was an assassin in the late years of the Spring and Autumn Period (770-476 B.C.). He conspired with Prince Guang, who was desperate to ascend to the throne of the Wu State (and ultimately reigned 515-496 B.C.), to eliminate his cousin, Prince Liao. Prince Liao had one weakness; his love of fancy food. Zhu went to great trouble to become a chef, albeit not a well-rounded one. He learned the unique skill of "roasting fish" from a famous chef. His skill got him an invitation to Prince Liao's kitchen where, as he was serving the delicacy to the prince, Zhu promptly assassinated him and made room on the throne for Prince Guang.

It was during this same period that Chinese eating and drinking habits underwent a great deal of change. Intellectuals studied how food and drink related to everyday life, and as medical science developed, the concept of diet therapy evolved. Diet therapy is the use of food, herbs, spices, and condiments to promote good health and longevity. It is often used to develop specific diets that prevent or cure disease. No other civilization focused as strongly on the health aspects of food than the Chinese, and many of these ideas and concepts found their way into recorded history and were shared. Several hundred writings about using food and diet therapy for better health exist, and the topic is still being written about today. Diet therapy remains very popular in China and has been promoted, often under other names, in many other regions of the world.

Diet therapy prompted the use of written recipes that could be sent to others with similar health concerns. In fact, the earliest cookbooks can be traced back to Chinese dynasties as early as 200 A.D. During the Han period in China, food technology and nutritional

(Opposite) "The Sword of Autumn" – Imperial China. Served on a bed of rice are savory grilled fishes, known as "Sword of Autumn." The dish is spiced with wild chives and a dark soy sauce spiced with chopped chives. This is an exceptionally simple yet elegant dish. Simply grilling the fish and serving it with rice is very well within the capabilities of field kitchens along China's long coast line. This particular meal is based on records from the writings of Kao Tzu, a Warring - States-period philosopher. The Warring States period was a time of intense civil war in China and took place from 475 to 221 B.C. The photograph is enhanced with two key military manuals of China: Mao-Tse Tung's military writings and the all-time classic *The Art of War* by Sun-Tzu.

(Above) Circa 1800: Elaborate food presentations such as this phoenix made from quail eggs, cucumbers, daikon roots, salmon roe, and ginger were common elements of Imperial Chinese banquets. China is believed to have first domesticated chickens more than 4,000 years ago, and chicken — represented by the phoenix - holds a key role in Chinese cuisine. The phoenix - symbolizing life rising from ashes — is a key element of banquets and is "a must" presentation during New Year's celebrations. The chicken/phoenix is also the symbol of the empress, while the dragon is the symbol of the emperor and the empire.

The connection among food, politics, and military affairs is critical to our understanding of Chinese cuisine. Many accomplished chefs became political leaders in China.

Just 50 years ago, one title for the chief executive of the Chinese government was still defined as "adjusting the tripod." The tripod is a catchall term for cooking implements. Typically a pot was suspended from a tripod over an open fire, and the cook changed and improved flavors of a dish by adjusting the tripod. It is also of interest that an elaborate phoenix was served to British General Charles "Chinese" Gordon (1833-1885, who lost his head in Khartoum). General Gordon fought while leading the "Ever Victorious Army" in 1862-1863 around Shanghai, helping to suppress a local insurrection. He was honored by the Chinese Imperial Court with fancy banquets as well as the rare privilege to wear bright yellow imperial robes.

science made huge strides, with much of the new information written down in manuals on how to grow, process, store, and prepare food. *The Seven Advices*, one of the first books dedicated to culinary art, was written by Mei Cheng, a politician in the State of Wu. The book provided advice to the crown prince of the State of Chu in the Western Han Dynasty (206 B.C.). Although the book exaggerates the deliciousness of food, it still gives a glimpse of imperial cuisine at that time. This food consisted of tender calves' meat, fresh bamboo shoots and vegetables, thick soup of flattened dog meat, and rice balls covered with fresh rock mushrooms that melt the moment they are placed on the palate.

The Han Dynasty's imperial kitchens grew vegetables in hothouses so their availability was not limited by the seasons. New milling techniques were developed to extract oil from seeds. Sesame and perilla seeds became important sources of cooking oils during this period.

Ancient Chinese literature tells us that during the period of the Three Kingdoms (220-280 A.D.), Cao Zhi, prince of Chenliu and the son of Cao Cao, made a thick soup of camel's hooves that cost 1,000 ounces of gold. Cao Zhi called it Seven Treasure Soup. Cao Cao usurped dynastic power by taking the emperor hostage and acting in his name during the final years of the Han Dynasty, a circumstance that led to major changes in palace customs, including culinary tastes and eating habits. In particular, Cao Cao and his chefs paid great attention to the variety of food, its flavor, and the quality of dinnerware used.

The development of cooking oil quickly led to the use of the wok, a pan with a curved bottom that only required a small amount of oil for cooking. The wok was versatile in that it could be used for stir frying, deep frying, and even steaming vegetables. During this same period, Chinese chefs began to substitute tea for wine at the table.

The Shin Dynasty that followed Han, began to unify China, and with that unification came the spread of Chinese food technology. China's small and independent farmers became more productive and eventually shared their technology with the people of other lands they invaded. The wheelbarrow is a perfect example of a Chinese innovation that spread throughout the world. As Chinese farmers began growing increasingly larger crops, they needed a better way to move the harvest from the field to the market.

During the Chinese-Cham War (431-446 A.D.), the King of Champa invaded Chinese-controlled Nam Viet (what is now North Vietnam) and with his victory gained many of China's agricultural secrets, in particular modern methods of growing rice. The Chinese military eventually crushed the invaders, and forces led by General Liu Fang marched southward, overwhelmed Champa, and looted its capital. After the Chinese withdrew, Champa King Sambhuvarman is reputed to have asked Chinese Emperor Yang Kuang for forgiveness.

By the end of the sixth century in China, Emperor Sui had established a national granary that would help keep prices stable and provide reserves in the event of shortages, as had happened so many times in China's past. During this period, a socialized agricultural society developed in China where a male householder would receive five mu (a *mu* is the equivalent of about one acre) of land to work for his active lifetime or until age sixty. At that time, the land reverted back to the emperor. Military leaders and other noblemen received as much as 10,000 mu of land that could be inherited by their children. The socialized system of agriculture led to very wealthy landowners that became some of the first commercial farmers in history.

Another key change that evolved during this period was the habit of taking meals as a group or a family, instead of eating alone, which was the norm. This practice became particularly prevalent in the military, where some of the first formal messes began to appear with senior leaders taking meals together.

By the early seventh century, Chinese military leaders were importing honey from Tibet and using it as a sweetener on certain foods. This led to the first instance of boiling sugar cane, extracting the sweet juice, and processing it into a granular substance. The Chinese learned sugar manufacturing techniques from a military mission sent to India. The Chinese immediately implemented these practices, most notably at the confluence of the Yangze River and the Grand Canal, which served as a sugar manufacturing center for centuries.

The new taste for sweets did not change the basics of the regional diet. Rice, of course, remained a staple of Chinese meals, but it was supplemented with yams, taro root, and often with domesticated and wild birds such as chicken, duck, goose, and even songbirds. While the Chinese of the time ate wild game such as hare or pork, they rarely ate beef or meat from other large animals.

Chinese living in coastal regions and along rivers added fish as a dietary staple during the seventh century, but their choice in fish was much different than the choices being made in the Mediterranean and Atlantic coastal regions. Carp was a favorite of the Chinese, with eels running a close second. Crabs, oysters, and shrimp were also popular.

Chinese military leaders brought the traditions of imperial cuisine with them to the battlefield. Grand field headquarters with fancy meals were normal. An imperial banquet — and from what records of the nineteenth century tell us, fancy "victory" dinners —would, for mythological reasons, always include a dragon and a phoenix, meticulously created with food.

There are numerous legends surrounding Chinese emperors and military leaders, perhaps the most popular of which is General Tso's Chicken, otherwise known as Chicken Peng Teng.

As the legend goes, General Tso Tsungtang was born on November 10, 1812, near the end of the Qing Dynasty. As a young man he failed to pass his school final exams three times, a fate that disgraced both him and his family. Fed up with school, he returned home, married, and began a career as a farmer growing silkworms and tea leaves. Often compared to U.S. Civil War General William T. Sherman, who after graduating from West Point saw little military action and resigned his commission to teach school only to later become a general during the Civil War, Tso led a gentleman's life and took the nickname "The Husbandman of the River Hsiang."

In 1850, Tso was 38 years old and a successful farmer when the Taiping Rebellion began. The rebellion lasted for twenty years and resulted in millions of deaths. Tso was drafted into the military as an adjutant and named secretary to the governor of the Hunan Province, where the unlikely champion became one of China's best-known war heroes. Tso built an army of 5,000 volunteers and in 1860 drove the Taiping rebels from the province into coastal Zhejiang, where he promptly captured the key cities of Shaozing, then went south to Fujan and Guangdong where he crushed the Taiping rebels in 1864.

There are, however, some doubts regarding the relationship between General Tso and the chicken dish that bears his name. The recipe, according to Chinese cooking experts, is not particularly original and resembles certain other Chinese chicken stir-fry dishes. Moreover, the recipe calls for the use of dark meat instead of the white meat preferred by Chinese nobility. It is, some speculate, a poor man's dish and not the feast of a military hero.

Some Chinese chefs have advanced the theory that rather than naming a dish to honor a military hero, as Arthur Wellesley, the Duke of Wellington, is honored with Beef Wellington, General Tso's Chicken may have been developed and mockingly popularized by his enemy the Taipings. Still another theory is that General Tso's Chicken may have been popularized in a Chinatown restaurant in Manhattan, perhaps in the early 1970s.

Thus, there is a fair chance General Tso never tasted the dish that has been named after him. Nevertheless, General Tso's Chicken remains a favorite among Chinese dishes around the world today.

Mongolia

The Mongolian armies once ruled the majority of Asia. Moving swiftly on horseback and over great distances, the Mongols were truly creative in developing campaign rations the individual solider could carry along. Fancy food as we understand it now was rare.

During a campaign, a typical strategy included sending 200 men two day's ride ahead to act as scouts, 200 more to the rear, and 200 on each flank so the army could not be attacked by surprise.

Each rider carried a pignate, a small earthen pot for cooking meat. If they killed an animal and had no pot, they took out the stomach, emptied it, filled it with water, and cooked it over a fire. When it was done, they ate their meal, pot and all.

Mongols could ride ten days without food or fire, living on blood from their horses. They carried dry milk in two leather flasks, to which they added water before drinking. The reconstituted milk provided a nourishing drink that was centuries ahead of its time. In addition, they also carried qumiz, millet, and dried meat.

Japan

While Europeans were busily fighting wars, an entirely new type of cookery was evolving in Japan, nearly all of it from Japanese samurai traditions. With it came a model of artistic expression, much of it derived from Chinese Buddhist temples and introduced to Japan by monks during the twelfth century. The essence of Japanese cooking, as also expressed by its military, was an almost obsessive attention to ritual and presentation.

Harry Cook, author of *The Story of a Warrior Tradition,* accurately describes the art of *Cha no Yu,* or tea ceremony, as a means to develop a sense of natural simplicity, an experience of reality, uncluttered by intellectual considerations.

Japan's senior military warlord Toyotomi Hideyoshi, who reunified Japan in a pact with Oda Nobunaga, popularized the art and practice of the tea ceremony in the sixteenth century. The son of a foot soldier turned peddler, Hideyoshi rose steadfastly through the ranks to become one of Nobunaga's best generals and continued to fight for Japan's unity after Nobunaga's death in 1591. He also continued to promote the tea ceremony, which rose to great popularity among the samurai.

The utensils for the tea ceremony are often made of plain and natural materials, yet they can hold extraordinary value, both sentimentally and monetarily. Pieces have been used by warriors to show off their artistic acumen, have been raided as spoils of war, and have been offered as symbols of peace.

(Opposite) Macao cuisine is distinct from Chinese cuisine, since it has incorporated many traditional Mediterranean ingredients that are not used in China. For example, olive oil and many spices are popular in Macao dishes, but not in Chinese cooking.

This Macao dish called "Fat Rice" is on a china plate from The East Indies Company — China Trade (King Dynasty, Quianlong reign, ca. 1750), on top of a wooden table with Chinese motifs engraved in mother of pearl. In the background, the red symbolizes joy and happiness, and the yellow, used exclusively for the emperor, indicates imperial power.

Utensils once owned by historic figures are highly sought after by private collectors and museums, and many are considered priceless.

Tea parties have remained an important ritual for Japanese soldiers throughout the centuries and in modern times are used to mark special events ranging from birthdays to holidays. They are typically held among close friends and seldom involve more than six or seven people. Guests are usually seated on cushions around a low table and are served small cakes, rice cakes, or biscuits with, of course, tea. Serene background music is often played to help guests relax.

Japan was perhaps the first culture where cleanliness and food preparation became just as important, in fact more important, than eating it. Around 1192, he Japanese daimyo Yoritomo Minamoto won an imperial appointment as shogun and established his seat of government at Kamakura as he continued to war with the Fujiwara clan in the north. Minamoto's

soldiers ate three times a day rather than the customary two meals, and when the hostilities ended, the Japanese continued to follow this practice. The Kamakura court began to follow traditional, ceremonial dietary codes based on rice, vegetables, and preserved fish, but the samurai class had a freer style of eating habits based more on wild game. *Hochoshi* (cutting specialists) became established in Japanese kitchens during the Kamakura period. Each group had its own stylized secrets of cutting fish, meat, and vegetables, handed down by word of mouth from one generation to the next. Ceremonial cutting became a spectacle for the nobility.

Curry of the Japanese Navy

Indian curry and Japanese curry are as different as pizza and coffee. Indian curry is a catchall for a variety of styles while Japanese curry refers to a specific type of dish that is made the same way throughout Japan. Japanese curry is thickened with flour, to give it a consistency like stew or gravy, and is served with rice. Properly called curry-rice, the dish usually consists of potatoes, onions, carrots, and any type of meat.

According to records from Japan's Maritime Self Defense Force, curry-rice was born of necessity in 1882 when a Japanese naval ship sailing to South America had 160 of its 400-man crew come down with beriberi. Twenty-five men died. The Japanese borrowed a recipe for curry from a British Royal Navy cookbook, this form of curry being largely based on Indian curry. In order to make it more palatable to Japanese sailors and to help ensure that it would fight future outbreaks of beriberi, the Japanese navy modified the recipe, adding potatoes, peas, carrots, and stringed konnyaku, and spicing it with soy sauce and sugar. Typically pork, beef, or chicken was added to the thick sauce and then served over rice.

The dish became an immediate favorite among sailors who, upon returning home, told friends and families about the fine curry they were served aboard ship. Japanese naval ships still serve a special curry dish, typically on Friday, to both sailors and officers. Admiral Richard M. Dunleavy, U.S. Navy, partook of this fine food onboard ships of the modern Japanese navy. Curry is usually served with a glass of milk, a tradition of unknown origin.

There are many curry-rice restaurant chains in Japan, as the dish is a national favorite, highly rated among people of all ages. It is so popular it has inspired good-natured competition among at least four Japanese port cities boasting to be the birthplace of curry-rice. Regardless of its exact origins, this naval food has crossed over to mainstream cuisine and is today considered a home-cooking staple. ✄

(Above) Warriors — shown here on the cover of a menu from 1902 — were, to the surprise of many, often vegetarians. Japanese military food was accompanied by ritual.

CURRY-RICE

NOTE: The quantities below are a mere average. The amount can be increased/decreased, ingredients can be added or subtracted. Meat is totally optional. The navy usually uses chicken, pork, or beef. You can add a half-tablespoon of sugar, bean curd, or spice of your choice to suit your taste.

Ingredients
4 tablespoons vegetable oil
1 onion, sliced
1 carrot, diced
1 pound of meat, cut into bite-sized cubes
1 clove fresh garlic, minced
¼ teaspoon fresh ginger, grated
4 cups chicken broth (may substitute with water)
3 potatoes, diced
8 tablespoons white flour
2 ½ tablespoons curry powder
½ tablespoon salt

Instructions
1. Heat 2 tablespoons of oil in a pan and fry onion, carrots, and meat until tender.
2. Add garlic and ginger.
3. Add broth or water; let it simmer for 15 to 20 minutes.
4. Skim the broth, then add potatoes.
5. In a different pan, heat 2 tablespoons of cooking oil on a low flame and stir-fry the flour until brown. Remove from heat and add the spices.
6. Add a few spoonfuls of the broth into the flour and stir. It should be like a paste.
7. Slowly add the contents of the frying pan, stirring constantly so the mixture remains smooth.
8. Let mixture simmer for 30 minutes or until it thickens.

Serve with plain rice.

CHICKEN CURRY

Ingredients
1 teaspoon salt
½ teaspoon pepper
½ teaspoon curry powder
12 chicken legs
1 teaspoon ginger root, finely chopped
1 clove garlic, minced
1 onion, thinly sliced
3 cups water
¼ pound Japanese curry roux

Instructions
1. Sprinkle salt, pepper, and curry powder on chicken legs.
2. Sauté chopped ginger, garlic, and sliced onion.
3. Add chicken legs in the pan and sauté well.
4. Add water and simmer for 30 minutes.
5. Add curry roux and stir lightly.
6. Simmer for 5 minutes.

Makes 4 servings.

(Below) The wars in China this past century brought enormous deprivations to the Chinese population, illustrated by this sad card, circa 1905, of a young Chinese boy begging a soldier.

No. 44. Poor Chinese Boy Begging Rations.
Copyrighted, 1905, by T. W. Ingersoll.

(Above and Right) The sushi chef who deftly handles his ultra-sharp knife to create paper-thin slices of fatty tuna, toro or many other delicacies is, in some ways, a direct descendent of the sword mastership of the samurai warriors. The knives used by Japanese sushi chefs are created with extreme skill, many of which are based on how the famous swords of the samurai were crafted.

This screen shows the major battle of Heiji in 1159. During the twelfth century, the power of the emperor had faded and been replaced by a new leadership class, the samurai fighters who would dominate Japan's culture, food, politics, trade, and religion for the next centuries. The emperor would not regain full power until the nineteenth century.

The Samurai class created an entire culture, built on ritual and bravery in battle. The skill in sword fighting was a central part of their tradition and now carries forward into the Zen-like concentration displayed by sushi chefs

(Japanese, The Battle of Heiji, Edo period (1615-1868), seventeenth century. Pair of six-panel folding screens; ink, color, and gold on paper; 60 15/16 in. x 11 ft. 8 in.)

General Tso's Chicken Peng Teng

Ingredients

4 chicken legs with thighs
½ cup soy sauce
½ cup distilled white vinegar
½ cup water
1 clove garlic, minced
1 teaspoon ginger root, peeled and minced
1 teaspoon cornstarch
1 large egg, lightly beaten
⅓ cup cornstarch
4 dried hot chilies, seeded

Instructions

1. Remove bone from the chicken legs and thighs by scraping the meat from the bone with a sharp knife, starting at the bottom of the leg and working downward and keeping close to the bone. Pull the meat down over the bone (pulling it inside out like a glove) and cut it free from the bone. Discard the skin and cut the meat from each leg into 6 pieces.
2. In a bowl, combine the soy sauce, vinegar, water, garlic, and ginger root.
3. In another bowl, combine the egg and cornstarch and dip the chicken pieces.
4. Heat oil in a wok or a deep, heavy skillet until very hot. Add the chicken and sauté for 4-6 minutes, or until it is crisp. Transfer the chicken with tongs to paper towels to drain.
5. Pour off all but 1 tablespoon of the oil from the wok. Add the soy sauce mixture, the chili peppers, and the chicken, and cook the mixture over moderately high heat for 2 minutes, or until heated through.

Kung Pao Chi Ting

During the time Lord Li Hung Chang was the minister of Naval, Military, and Diplomatic Affairs of Northern China, he enjoyed this dish very much. Later, it was introduced to the Imperial Court. Lord Li Hung Chang was the first ambassador to the United States from Imperial China.

Ingredients

½ pound boneless chicken, cut into ½-inch cubes
¼ teaspoon black pepper
¼ cup cornstarch
2 teaspoons green onion, finely chopped
1 teaspoon ginger root, finely chopped
4 tablespoons sesame oil
1 red pepper, seeds removed and julienned
3 tablespoons soy sauce
2 teaspoons sugar
1 tablespoon wine (white wine or rice wine, if available)

Instructions

1. Sprinkle chicken cubes with black pepper and dredge with cornstarch.
2. Add 1 teaspoon onion and ½ teaspoon ginger root to the chicken and mix well.
3. Bring 3 tablespoons sesame oil to a boil in a pan over high heat. Sauté chicken cubes, stirring briskly, for 2 minutes and remove from the pan.
4. Heat 1 tablespoon sesame oil in another pan over high heat. Sauté red pepper until slightly burned, and add 1 teaspoon onion, ½ teaspoon ginger, soy sauce, sugar, and wine.
5. Bring to a boil and add the fried chicken cubes. Sauté, stirring constantly, for 1 to 2 minutes.

Serve hot.

(Left) A formal "Chinese Imperial Banquet" — often served to senior military officers such as Britain's General Charles Gordon — included dramatic displays and moments of great ceremony. Incense burners, such as this antique burner from Beijing that was collected during the Boxer Rebellion, were used. This bronze vessel is decorated with the sacred and mythical Foo Dog, a symbol of good fortune, luck, and wisdom — all essential for military leaders. The Foo Dog is second only to the dragon in importance for the Chinese.

THE AGE OF NAPOLEON

apoleon Bonaparte, who ruled as Emperor Napoleon I from 1804 to 1814, correctly stated that "An army marches on its stomach." This adage is just as true today as it was in the nineteenth century. Napoleon was a major military innovator, and maintaining a reliable food supply was essential as his armies roamed and pillaged much of Europe. Napoleon so firmly believed his own adage that he offered the equivalent of a modern $250,000 prize for the discovery of a way to get better food to the French army. Nicholas Appert, a confectioner, won the prize in 1795 by discovering the process of hermetically sealing food. In 1810, a patent was taken out in England for Appert's method, and soon the idea spread to America, where lobster and salmon were the first foods canned. In 1823, an American, Thomas Kensett, invented the tin can.

The Vivandière were critical to Napoleon's military supply system. Dressed in colorful clothes, these women, most married to enlisted men, were the principal guardians of the food supply. Their name may be based on several words — the true etymological origin is unclear. It may be based on old French for "Viande" or "meat," or the Latin "vivenda" or "food."

Vivandière first became part of the French forces as early as the 1650s. They were allowed into active combat, clearly separating them from the other key food suppliers such as the Cantinières (as in "Canteen") who were restricted to camp and rear areas.

By the time Napoleon took charge, Vivandières had begun carrying wooden kegs, often painted red, white, and blue and containing brandy. By 1860, the Vivandière had formal military status and were entitled to remuneration, decorations, and a small, curved sword. Even though their designation was replaced in 1854 with the name of their counterparts, Cantinières, the term would stick around along with specific rules of how many would serve with a specific unit.

Maréchal Jean Jacques Canceres, one of Napoleon I's generals, was not only a great soldier, but also a great gourmet. During a general staff meeting which dragged on in the general's house, he became more and more nervous. Finally, he beckoned a staffer, and dispatched a note. Napoleon, always suspicious, intercepted the messenger, expecting to find espionage, treason, or worse, but roared with laughter when he read the message. All it contained was a short order to Maréchal's cook: "Save the soups and the entremets, the roasts are spoiled now anyway." Entremets are little side dishes, served with or after the roasts.

On June 14, 1800, Marengo, a small town just south of Turin, Italy, became the site of a battle that Napoleon regarded as one of the most brilliant of his career. Napoleon had led his army in a march across the Alps, through the Saint Bernard Pass, into the Po Valley. His army clashed with the Austrians at Marengo, and Napoleon's troops would have been defeated had reinforcements not arrived.

He pursued his enemy with such vigor that he left the commissary behind, but kept his cook, Dunand, close at hand. Napoleon, as was his habit, had not eaten before the battle and was certain to be famished upon its conclusion. When he called for a meal, he demanded immediate service and swiftly ate it once he was served.

Dunand was desperate. Foragers were sent out and turned up only meager booty: a scrawny chicken, four

(Opposite) Chicken Marengo – Battle of Marengo, 1800
This was one of Napoleon's favorite dishes. It was first cooked on the battlefield of Marengo by the emperor's personal chef, Dunand, who used the meager supplies he could find: a small chicken cut up with a sword, some eggs, stale bread, crawfish, garlic, and brandy.

(Above) Vivandière in the colorful uniforms issued in the nineteenth century.

tomatoes, three eggs, a few crayfish, a little garlic. The only cooking utensil Dunand could scavenge was a frying pan, but he could not find any butter, just some olive oil.

He cut up the chicken with a saber and fried it in oil, crushed garlic, and water made more palatable with a little cognac filched from Napoleon's own canteen. He added some emergency–ration bread supplied by one of the soldiers. The eggs, fried in the same liquid, went on the side, and the crayfish was on top. A measure of Dunand's desperation was the unholy combination of chicken and crayfish; he used every morsel of food he could scrape together and there wasn't much.

Napoleon found the dish excellent and ordered that it be served after every battle. On the next occasion, Dunand tried to improve the dish by substituting white wine for water, adding mushrooms, and leaving out the crayfish. Napoleon noted the disappearance of the crustaceans and demanded that they be restored to the dish, but not for gastronomic reasons. Napoleon was highly superstitious and in his mind chicken with crayfish was associated with victory.

The name "Marengo" has since been awarded to numerous other dishes such as Sauce Marengo (fried pulped tomatoes with mushrooms and truffles, onions, and garlic) and Eggs Marengo, a simple dish where eggs are fried in olive oil, served with fried ham and Madeira sauce. Some sources claim "meringue" is a variant of the spelling of Marengo, and during much of the nineteenth and early twentieth

(Below) A French solider fell asleep while waiting for his meat to cook, and his comrades seized the opportunity to steal the succulent beef with their saber.

(Opposite) The Salamanca Battle, or the Arapiles Battle, between the French Napoleonic Army and the Anglo–Spanish–Portuguese Army, started June 13, 1812, and ended on July 22, with a loss by the French army.

The battle served as a turning point in the Peninsular War and marks the beginning of the decline of the French occupation in Spain. Many of the soldiers in this battle were Portuguese and are known to have fought bravely.

The picture shows "The Plan of the Battle of Arapiles near Salamanca — the previous movement of the armies from the Douro to Tormes," published in London in 1814 by T. Cadell & W. Davies Strand.

On top of it lies a book titled *Nourishment for the Army*, printed in Lisbon, Portugal, in 1865. Concern among Portuguese officers for the type of nutrition that their men were getting dates back many years.

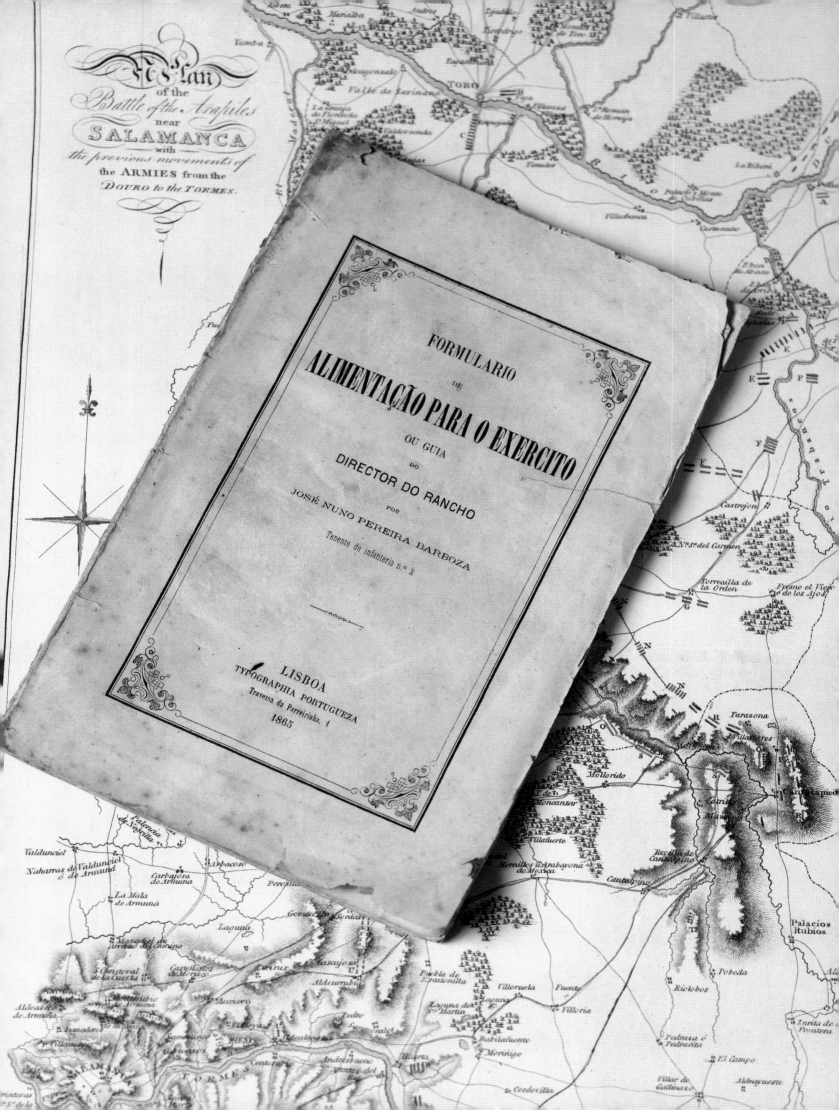

FORMULARIO

DE

ALIMENTAÇÃO PARA O EXERCITO

OU GUIA

DO

DIRECTOR DO RANCHO

POR

JOSÉ NUNO PEREIRA BARBOZA

Tenente de infanteria n.º 2

LISBOA
TYPOGRAPHIA PORTUGUEZA
Travessa da Parreirinha, 1
1865

centuries, meringue dishes were served on June 14, the anniversary of the victory.

Napoleon's opponents also loved great food.

Among those fighting Napoleon was British General George Thomas Keppel, 6th earl of Albemarle (1799–1891). Numerous dishes are attributed to him including Albemarle Sole and Albemarle Pudding.

England's Arthur Wellesley, duke of Wellington, who defeated Napoleon along with Prussian Field Marshal Prince Blücher, became the source for another famous dish: Beef Wellington. Just how he is connected to this dish is very unclear and there is no proven historical record. ✕

(Above) The inside of kitchens of all armed services changed little over the centuries until the advent of refrigeration. Here French army cooks in the late nineteenth century prepare multiple dishes. Note the sausage machine (then an innovation) in the foreground and the open hearth in the back.

(Left) The Peninsular War pitted Napoleon's army against British troops, led by the duke of Wellington, and assisted by the Portuguese regular army and Spanish irregulars. Many towns and cities were destroyed, yet numerous reports of good food survived. Some have been published in diaries of soldiers who fought in this campaign. This nineteenth century color engraving depicts the French 3rd Line Infantry Regiment, commanded by General Jean–Andoche Junot, cooking over an open fire in the ruins of a building after winning the Battle of Saragossa on February 21, 1809.

(Opposite) Onion Soup Savoyarde
Onion soup was one of Napoleon's favorites, but culinary historians have never been able to agree whether he favored onion soup Savoyarde or onion soup gratine. Shown here is the Foreign Legion version served with wines made by Legion veterans. It is worth noting that this superb wine is made in the Rhone Valley — often in the same vineyards first started by veterans of the Roman V Legion who brought viniculture to the province.

ENGLISH MILITARY GAME PIE

Hunting was and is certainly a gentleman's sport. For instance, fox hunting was a much–encouraged sport for members of the British armed forces as it kept horse and rider in training during the peacetime lull.

This recipe was supplied to one of the authors by an officer of the Coldstream Guards. That officer and this writer were together during jungle training in Borneo, waiting to complete a fire mission.

Discussion about food in that dreaded hot and humid climate came naturally after both had devoured absolutely horrible rations. Game pie filled with partridge figured prominently in the menus for the Duke of Wellington during the Peninsular War.

Apart from being quite tasty, such pies have the benefit of tasting good when eaten cold, spiced up with some quince jelly or, in a more formal environment, proper game sauces.

Ingredients – Pie

2 pounds of minced pheasant, hare, partridge, venison, grouse, or any other available game
10 ounces lean pork, minced
10 ounces fatty pork, minced
5 cups Port
1 batch basic pie pastry (see below)
1 onion, minced finely
1 ounce olive oil
2 bay leaves
salt and pepper to taste
1 cup Madeira
½ cup Brandy
1 egg, lightly beaten

(Opposite) Partridge Pie – Saint George Castle – ca. 1147
In the warm light of a winter evening, the wall of the castle of Saint George had to be the perfect place to depict a "Game Pie," a famous dish served frequently at festive occasions. The setting overlooks Lisbon's old roofs and the Tagus River flowing gently toward the ocean, the city's characteristic vast horizon line basking in the glow of a peculiar light.

The castle was built over the previous hilltop citadel that had existed there since the Roman times. King D. Afonso Henriques, the first Portuguese king, commissioned it as the Portuguese kings, official residence after conquering Lisbon from the Moors in 1147.

A game pie is composed of dough and stuffing. The better the meats one uses to prepare the stuffing, the richer the taste of the pie.

Instructions – Pie

1. Take all the meats, cut into bite–sized chunks, and marinate in Port for 24 hours.
2. Grease a 9-inch deep-dish pie pan. Divide dough in half. Roll out the dough on a floured surface until it is large enough to line the baking pan and have a quarter–inch overhang. Line the pan.
3. Remove meat from marinade. Discard marinade. Take marinated meats and onion and quickly brown on all sides in a pan with olive oil. Add bay leaves, salt, and pepper.
4. Remove onion and meat from pan. Discard bay leaves.
5. Place onion and meat into a food processor, add Madeira, Brandy, and Port, and process until it has the texture of well–cooked grits.
6. Place mixture into pie pan.
7. Cover mixture with the rest of the pastry. Pinch edges together and trim excess pastry into strips or leaf shapes for decorations. Do not overfill the pie as the meat mixture will expand during baking.
8. Make a hole in the center of the pie to let the steam escape.
9. Brush the pie with egg wash.
10. Bake the pie at 375° F for 2 ½ hours.
11. Remove from oven.
12. Fill the "steam hole" with quince jelly or game sauce.
13. Allow to cool and once cooled, store in refrigerator until the next day.
14. Demold and slice.

Ingredients – Basic Pie Pastry

2 cups flour
1 teaspoon salt
⅔ cup vegetable shortening
¼ cup water

Instructions – Basic Pie Pastry

1. Sift flour and salt together into a bowl.
2. Cut in shortening with a knife until particles are the size of peas.
3. Add water 1 tablespoon at a time; mix lightly with a fork.
4. Gather dough together with your fingers and form into a ball.

Refrigerate at least one hour before rolling out.

ALBEMARLE SOLE

Several sources claim that General George Thomas Keppel, 6th earl of Albemarle, who fought with distinction at Waterloo, inspired this fish dish.

Ingredients
4 fillets of sole
½ pound shad roe
2 tablespoons extra virgin olive oil
1 tablespoon lemon juice
1 ounce butter
1 cup gherkin pickles, julienned
1 cup white mushrooms, julienned
1 cup red pepper, julienned
butter
salt to taste
lemon juice

Instructions
1. Heat olive oil in a frying pan on high heat.
2. Quickly sauté the sole and roe (about five minutes). Be careful while turning the sole so the filet does not break.
3. Transfer the oil, fish, and roe to an ovenproof casserole.
4. Cover with the pickles, mushrooms, and red peppers, some butter, and salt.
5. Cook in a 300° F oven for no more than 20 minutes.
6. Remove from the oven and finish with some lemon juice.

QUENELLES DE BŒUF

Ingredients
1 pound chopped beef
1 egg
1 teaspoon breadcrumbs
1 tablespoon cream
2 teaspoons finely chopped dill pickles
salt, pepper, and thyme to taste
4 round steaks, very thin
½ teaspoon wine vinegar
4 ounces red wine
1 bay leaf, chopped
1 tablespoon butter
flour

Instructions
1. In a large bowl, prepare the stuffing by thoroughly mixing chopped beef, egg, breadcrumbs, cream, pickles, salt, pepper, and thyme.
2. Place round steaks flat on a wooden board. Beat with the flat side of a meat tenderizer or the side of a cleaver until very thin.
3. Lay stuffing lengthwise in the middle of each piece, using just enough to still be able to fold both sides of the meat over the stuffing. Secure with string or toothpicks.
4. Heat butter in a frying pan. Fry the meat quickly, turning it frequently.
5. When the meat is well browned on all sides, add the wine vinegar, red wine, and bay leaf.
6. Cover the pan and let simmer for 30 minutes.
7. Thicken the sauce with flour if necessary.

(Right) The 5th Dragoon Guard celebrated its annual dinner on June 5, 1895, at London's Willis's restaurant with this impressive menu. General Sir Thomas Westropp McMahon, the colonel–in–chief of the regiment at that time, presided over this dinner. Virtually all of the dishes are based on the French culinary arts — typical for that time period when a handful of chefs, such as Auguste Escoffier, dictated the very best cooking all over the world. Among the dishes served was a filet of French Charolais cattle and French roasted capon. Plain Whitebait fish and ham from York (albeit braised in Port wine) are the only significant departures from this otherwise all–French menu.

Properly known as the 5th Princess Charlotte of Wales's Dragoon Guards, this regiment fought all over the globe and in famous battles such as Blenheim, Ramillies, Oudenarde, Malplaquet, Beaumont, Salamanca, Vittoria, Toulouse, The Peninsula War, Balaklava, Sevastopol, Defense of Ladysmith, South Africa 1899–1902, and in major battles in the First World War.

In 1922, this regiment was amalgamated with The Inniskillings (6th Dragoons), to form the 5th/6th Dragoons.

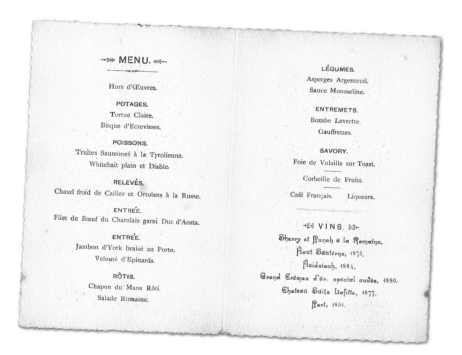

ONION SOUP GRATINE

Onion soup was one of Napoleon's favorites, which he would consume with copious amounts of Chambertin, a superb Burgundy.

Ingredients
4 tablespoons butter
4 large Spanish onions, sliced into rings
paprika, salt, and pepper to taste
32 ounces beef consommé
2 ounces Roquefort cheese
4 slices French bread, toasted
4 tablespoons grated Parmesan cheese

Instructions
1. Melt 2 tablespoons of butter in a saucepan over medium heat, add onion rings, cover the pan, and sauté until the onion is soft.
2. Remove cover, and raise heat to medium–high until the onions take on color.
3. As soon as they begin to brown, add spices and consommé.
4. Let it boil, and then reduce heat and simmer for five minutes.
5. Ladle soup into onion soup crocks, dividing the onions evenly.
6. Combine Roquefort and remaining butter and spread mixture on each slice of toast.
7. Place toast on top of each crock, and sprinkle with Parmesan.
8. Grill crocks under the broiler set on low and watch carefully.
9. Remove as soon as cheese begins to bubble and serve.

Serves 4.

ONION SOUP SAVOYARDE

Ingredients
3 tablespoons butter
6 large Spanish onions, sliced into rings
48 ounces beef consommé
48 ounces water
1 clove garlic, whole
salt and pepper to taste
¼ teaspoon thyme
2 egg whites, beaten
4 cups cream
2 egg yolks, beaten
4 drops wine vinegar
6 slices French bread, toasted

Instructions
1. Melt 2 tablespoons of butter in a saucepan over medium heat, add onion rings, cover the pan, and sauté until the onion is soft.
2. Remove cover, and raise heat to medium–high until the onions take on color.
3. As soon as they begin to brown, add consommé, water, and spices.
4. Let the soup boil in an open pot until it is reduced to half its original volume.
5. Add beaten egg whites.
6. Boil again till the egg white has set, then remove the pot from heat.
7. When the bubbling has ceased, stir in cream, egg yolks, and vinegar.
8. Place toast into individual crocks. Ladle soup over toast. Serve immediately.

Note: this soup cannot successfully be reheated.

(Above) This nineteenth century miniature silver cannon is a faithful copy of a British 12–pound gun. It's actually a cigar lighter, designed to roll along the officers' dinner table so the men could light the "cheroots" after dinner while sipping their Port. Rolling implements on mess tables were quite popular for a time. Contemporary nineteenth century reports tell of elaborate miniature silver wagons, designed to carry Port and Brandy flasks, pulled by little dogs along the long mahogany tables common to a mess. (From the collection of Christopher & Karin Ross, New York City)

BEEF WELLINGTON

Ingredients
2 sheets puff pastry
flour
3 ½ pounds beef tenderloin
1 tablespoon vegetable oil
2 tablespoons butter
8 ounces liver pâté (may substitute foie-gras mousse)
2 eggs, beaten

Instructions
1. Preheat oven to 425° F.
2. Roll out the puff pastry and sprinkle with flour. Set aside.
3. Trim and tie up the beef at 1 ½-inch intervals with fine string so it retains its shape while cooking.
4. Heat oil and butter in a frying pan and brown beef on all sides.
5. Lower the heat, cover pan, and leave the beef in the pan to roast for about 15 minutes.
6. Remove beef and allow to cool.
7. Remove the string.
8. Spoon pate into the center of one sheet of puff pastry. Using the back of the spoon, spread pâté out to match the size of the beef.
9. Place beef on top of the pâté.
10. Brush the edges of the pastry with the beaten egg and fold the pastry edges over to form a tight roll.
11. Turn the roll over so the seam is at the bottom.
12. Lightly oil a baking tray and place the beef roll on it.
13. Brush the beef roll generously with beaten egg.
14. The second pastry sheet is used to create shapes for decorations. Some artistic-minded regiments in the United Kingdom would create elaborate copies of the regimental badges.
15. Place the decorations on the beef roll and brush with beaten egg.
16. Place tray in oven and bake for 50 minutes.
17. Cover the beef with foil and bake for an additional 25 minutes.
18. Allow to rest for 10 minutes before slicing.

QUOORMA CURRY

From *Culinary Jottings: A Treatise in Thirty Chapters on Reformed Cookery for Anglo-Indian Exiles* by "WYVERN" (Colonel Arthur Robert Kenney-Herbert, a British Army officer), published in Madras by Higginbotham and Co., 1885. The colonel wrote about this dish: "The 'Quoorma,' if well made, is undoubtedly an excellent curry. It used, I believe, to be one of the best at the Madras Club, in days when curries commanded closer attention than they do now." Note that the term Quoorma normally applies to spiced Pakistani or Indian stews of mutton and yogurt. His recipe, without yogurt, follows with notes for the modern cook in parenthesis:

Cut up about a pound of very tender mutton (use leg of lamb) without any bone, and stir the pieces about in a big bowl with a dessertspoonful of pounded green ginger, and a sprinkling of salt. Melt a quarter of a pound of butter in a stew-pan, and throw into it a couple of white onions cut into rings, and a couple of cloves of garlic finely minced. Fry for about five minutes, and then add a teaspoonful of pounded coriander seed, one teaspoon of pounded black pepper, half a teaspoon of pounded cardomoms, and half a teaspoon of pounded cloves. Cook this for five minutes, then put in the meat, and stir over a moderate fire (medium setting) until the pieces seem tender and have browned nicely (this takes about 10 minutes). Now, take the pan from the fire, and work into it a strong infusion obtained from four ounces of well-pounded almonds and a cup of cream. Mix thoroughly, adding a dessertspoonful of turmeric powder, and a teaspoonful of sugar. Put the pan over a very low fire, and let the curry simmer as gently as possible for a quarter of an hour, finishing off with the juice of a couple of limes. This, it will be perceived, is another curry of rich yet mild description. The total absence of chilli, indeed, constitutes, in the opinion of many, its chief attraction.

(Above) An individual Beef Wellington decorated with a regimental logo made of pastry. This is a standard dish of the British officers corps.

(Opposite) British regiments commissioned a wide variety of elaborate silver items to present to honored and retiring officers. This silver figure of a hussar on a horse was presented to a colonel retiring from a British cavalry regiment. The uniform and accoutrements are typical for regiments that fought during and right after the Napoleonic Wars. These statues were often used as table decorations. Today, the prestigious Cavalry and Guards Club boasts similar silver trophies, some of which are two feet tall. Ornate silver decorates all key parts of this elegant club on London's Piccadilly Circus. (From the collection of Christopher & Karin Ross, New York City)

Napoleon's Rum–Banana Fritters

Napoleon's cook faced quite a challenge on the desolate island of Saint Helena since most of the cooking ingredients were dreadful. The one bright spot was the abundant bananas. Batter boosted by rum transformed them into delectable fritters.

Ingredients

6 firm bananas
1 ¼ cup rum
1 cup orange juice (may substitute pineapple juice)
2 egg whites
2 tablespoons cornstarch
2 tablespoons flour
oil for frying
½ cup sugar
1 tablespoon water
3 tablespoons butter, melted

Instructions

1. Slice bananas in halves, and then into quarters, lengthwise.
2. Marinate them for an hour in 1 cup of rum mixed with all the orange juice.
3. Combine egg whites, cornstarch, and flour to make batter.
4. Coat each piece of banana thoroughly with the batter, and fry in deep fat until light brown.
5. Remove from oil and drain.
6. In a small bowl, add sugar and water to the melted butter and stir until sugar dissolves.
7. Add remaining ¼ cup rum to make syrup.
8. Place the bananas in a buttered, oven–proof serving dish, and generously drizzle with syrup.
9. Heat for a few minutes in a warm (200° F) oven.

Serve as a hot dessert.

Foie Gras

In the 18th century a chef named Clause, who headed the kitchen of the Marechal de Contades, created a dish with foie gras in a pastry crust and called it pâté lá Contades. When King Louis XVI tasted it , he loved the new creation so much he rewarded Clause. Clause used the money to marry a Strasbourg pastry cook, Marie–Anne Maring. The combination of his pâté and her pastry earned the newlyweds a small fortune.

Ingredients

1 goose liver
salt and pepper
quatre epices
thyme
bay leaf
6 ounces Madeira
1 ounce Armagnac
½ pound sliced bacon

Instructions

1. To prepare the liver, separate the two lobes. Split them lengthwise with a long, pointed knife in several places and carefully remove all the blood vessels. Remove the skin covering the liver.
2. Sprinkle both lobes with a mixture of salt, pepper, and quatre epices. Place them in a terrine with a sprig of thyme and half a bay leaf. Lightly mash.
3. Pour the Madeira and Armagnac over the lobes, then cover and marinate in a refrigerator for 24 hours.
4. Remove the liver from the marinade. Reserve marinade in a small bowl.
5. Line the terrine with bacon slices, then replace the liver and press it down.
6. Pour in a little of the marinade, enough to moisten.
7. Fold the tops of the bacon over on top of the liver.
8. Cover with greaseproof paper folded into quarters, then with the lid.
9. Cook the terrine in a steamer in a low oven for 1 ¼ hours.
10. Allow it to cool before turning out.

(Left) This silver hunting horn was crafted for a British Regimental mess. It is actually a lighter and was used by officers to light cigars after an elegant repast. There is a close link between fox hunting and the military. British commanders encouraged their officers to engage in hunting. It was a wonderful way to keep horses and riders fit and agile between campaigns. The elegant food served upon the conclusion of the hunt, known as the formal hunt breakfast, is very similar to dishes served after battle, such as game pies and savory soups.

Today, the 7th Hussars are part of the Queen's Royal Hussars (Queen's Own and Royal Irish), which was formed on September 1, 1993, from the amalgamation of The Queen's Own Hussars and The Queen's Royal Irish Hussars. The Regiment traces its roots back to 1685.

The 7th Queen's Own Hussars — which had previously been amalgamated into The Queen's Own Hussars — originated with Cunningham's Dragoons, which were raised in Scotland in 1689 and won their first battle honor at Dettingen. Later renamed the 7th Hussars, they fought during the Peninsular War and gained the admiration of Wellington for their heroic service at Waterloo. The 7th Hussars were then sent to Canada to help repulse an American invasion.

Field Marshal Douglas Haig may have used this cigar lighter. He joined the 7th Hussars in 1885.

Napoleon's Chicken Marengo

Chicken Marengo is a simple dish, quick and easy to prepare. Basically it is just chicken pieces browned in olive oil and then cooked slowly (not as Dunand did it on the battlefield of Marengo) with peeled tomatoes, crushed garlic, parsley, white wine, and cognac, seasoned with crushed pepper and served with fried eggs.

Ingredients
1 whole chicken, cut into pieces
1 teaspoon salt
1 turn of the pepper mill
2 tablespoons flour
4 tablespoons olive oil
1 yellow onion, chopped
½ clove garlic, minced
½ cup peeled, seeded, and chopped tomato
½ cup of Cognac (may substitute Sherry)
½ cup white truffles, sliced thinly (optional)
6 eggs for garnishing
crayfish (optional)

Instructions
1. Sprinkle chicken with salt, pepper, and flour and brown in oil. Set aside.
2. Mix onions and garlic in same pan. Add chicken and rest of ingredients (except eggs and crayfish), cover, and simmer until tender (30–40 minutes).
3. Fry the eggs and place one on each dish as a garnish.
4. If available, boil crayfish until it turns red and place on top of the dish.

Muscat Wine Sherbet (Spoom au Vin de Muscat Sorbets)

Ingredients
2 ½ cups sugar
¾ cup water
juice of 2 lemons
juice of 1 orange
2 cups Muscat wine
2 egg whites

Instructions
1. Make syrup by dissolving 2 cups plus 3 tablespoons of the sugar into the water. Boil, stirring until the liquid is clear. Let cool.
2. Add the lemon and orange juice to the syrup. Strain and add the wine.
3. Pour syrup into a tray and place in freezer.
4. Put the remaining sugar in a small saucepan and add just enough water to dissolve it. Boil until you have a syrup.
5. In a small bowl, beat the egg whites to a froth and pour the boiling syrup into them, whisking until the bowl and contents are completely cold. The result is what is called Italian Meringue.
6. Gently mix this meringue into the first, frozen mixture.

Serve in chilled glasses.

(Left) Setting an elegant table has long been a must for the better regiments of Europe. These candlesticks were presented to Major William Stephen Raikes Hodson (1821–1858) of the 10th Bengal Lancers. The regiment was properly known as 10th Duke of Cambridge's Own Lancers. Founded in 1857 for duty in India, the regiment was noted for major accomplishments in various campaigns. In 1921, the regiment was amalgamated with 9th Hodson's Horse, to form 4th Duke of Cambridge's Own Hodson's Horse.

General Hugh Gough, Hodson's commander in the Raij, once described Major Hodson by writing, "A finer or more gallant soldier never breathed. He had the true instincts of a leader of men; as a cavalry soldier he was perfection; a strong seat, a perfect swordsman, quick and intelligent."

Between the candlesticks is a British silver presentation menu holder, typical of that used for fancy dinners of the 12th Lancers. It shows the "lances" carried by the cavalry along with the regimental colors. This regiment was founded also in 1857 (a time of crisis in India) and was first known as the 2nd Sikh Irregular Cavalry. In 1861, it became the 12th Regiment of Bengal Cavalry. It was later amalgamated with 11th King Edward's Own Lancers (Probyns's Horse) to form 5th King Edward's Own Probyns's Horse.

The silver items speak of rough life on the Indian campaign fields, chutney, tea, and enormous courage. (From the collection of Christopher & Karin Ross, New York City)

(Above) 1911. This beautiful tenderloin of beef is served with red wine sauce, roasted potatoes, and honey–glazed carrots. This silver presentation platter, with the Star of the Prussian Guards, was a wedding gift to Lieutenant T. von Studnitz from the 4th Guard Artillery Regiment. The heavily decorated cup depicts a monument to the guard artillery. The flatware is decorated with a fiddle–thread pattern and the coat of arms of Lieutenant von Studnitz on the front and the cipher of the guards on the back.

THE MESS:
FINE FOOD IN THE MOST EXCLUSIVE CLUBS OF THE WORLD

The word "mess," most often used to describe where soldiers dine, is a contradictory term. Civilians typically use the word to describe something that is in disarray. In fact, the word comes from the Latin *missum* or *mittere*, which means to send or put in place.

The British military is believed to be the first to begin using the term mess to describe where their officers dined in the 16th century, during Tudor times. In those days, portions for two to four officers were prepared on a platter and then served at a table in the mess. As time went on, however, the officers' mess took on new meaning and became the pride of every British regiment. The mess was the home for officers of a regiment, as well as a place of culinary excellence and innovation.

For example, some of the finest contributions of military food to the general public are a result of the mess. English regiments serving in India often lived a life of luxury and insisted on the very best in terms of food and service. Today, Major Grey's Chutney, first created for British regiments in the 1800s, is sold in supermarkets.

In 1827, Prince Pückler–Muskau wrote, "I was invited to dine in barracks by a Major of the Horse Guards. There is a most advantageous custom prevalent throughout the English army, I mean the so–called 'Mess.' Each regiment has its common table, to which every officer is bound to contribute a certain sum, whether he chooses to avail himself of it or not. By this he is entitled to the privilege of dining at it daily. ...The table was admirably served. There was not wanting either the elegant service of plate, or champagne, claret, or any of the requisites of luxury."

Many foods served in the mess resulted from major battles. An example is "Alma Pudding," named after a river in Russia where British and French troops won a major victory on September 20, 1854, during the Crimean War. The rich, steamed pudding is studded with preserved cherries and served with cherry sauce. One source claims

(Left) This dish is medium-rare lamb served with green beans and mint jelly, and dark brown English beer. Pictured are samples of trench art manufactured by soldiers out of the brass parts of ammunition, including a knife, a fork, a fish knife marked "Marne," a shell casing used as a cigarette holder (oval cigarettes were typical for the period), a flask, a small ashtray with the regimental logo of the Welsh Guards, and a matchbook with a looted belt buckle cover of a Prussian soldier.

(Above) This silver, gold, and enamel helmet is a faithful copy of the helmets worn by Prussian's Garde du Corps. Used in the Corps' "casino," it was a communal drinking vessel — passed from officer to officer — to salute grand days in the history of the guards, the King of Prussia (who was also the emperor of Germany), and visiting dignitaries. The Garde du Corps was heavily armored cavalry and represented the cream of Prussia's aristocracy. Among its officers were many men of royal blood whose names are inscribed on the back of this helmet. (From the collection of Christopher & Karin Ross, New York City)

This "drinking cup" was used by the Prussian Regiment of the Garde du Corps, which was personally commanded by Wilhelm II. The names on the helmet list the then (1888) commander; Lieutenant Colonel Baron von Bissing, Major Henry XIX, Prince of Reus; 1st Lieutenant Georg Prince Radziwill; 1st Lieutenant Albert Christian Adolph Carl Eugen, Prince of Schleswig–Holstein–Sonderburg–Glücksburg; and other famous names from Prussian history, such as Brühl, Arnim, Sydow, Count Finck von Finkenstein, Spee, and Count von Schlieffen, who would rise to the rank of general and formulate the famous "Schlieffen Plan" during World War I.

the cherries convey the image of the scarlet uniforms of the British troops.

Maintaining a good mess was the pride of the regiment. Through this ultimate institution of British military life, regiments competed against each other over who had the best food, wine, silver, and china. Much of the decorations in the mess conveyed the rich history of a regiment. Silver, crystal, and china, along with paintings and "war loot" carefully collected over

hundreds of years, were a permanent museum of a regiment's accomplishments and honors. In Britain, much of the better items were donations from officers serving with a regiment.

Some family pieces were just too valuable or rich in sentiment to risk being lost forever. Imperial Germany's Grand Admiral Alfred von Tirpitz, one author's great–grandfather, is known to have commissioned special china and silver to be used on board his ships. They brought refinement and elegance to the table without putting dear heirlooms in jeopardy should the ship sink.

Possibly the oldest "war loot" displayed by any British regiment is the Abyssinian Coptic Cross (dated to either the sixth or seventh century), believed to come from the Church at Magdala, at the end of the Abyssinian Campaign in 1868.

Champagne is occasionally served for all officers of a cavalry regiment from the silver chamber pot that belonged to Napoleon, and which was "liberated" from his brother, Joseph Bonaparte, by the 14th Light Dragoons during the Peninsular War.

The tradition of giving commanders fanciful dinner services was quite common among the royal houses of Europe and generated a plethora of elegant dinnerware. Frederick the Great commissioned special china to reward his commanders. Prussian King Frederick Wilhelm III presented Britain's Duke of Wellington fine china decorated with scenes from the war against Napoleon. The dinner service was manufactured by the famous Royal Prussian Porcelain Manufactory or Königliche Porzellan Manufaktur (KPM).

Catherine the Great, never to be outdone by her western counterparts, was famous for keeping the Russian Imperial Porcelain Factory busy making elaborate regimental china. She would also provide favorite officers (and lovers at times) with elaborate silver drinking cups.

It was common in most of the better Russian regiments to have a miniature of the regimental helmet (reproduced in silver and gold and gilded inside). Included as part of each place setting, this helmet could be

(Above) In most Prussian regiments, such as the Guard Artillery Regiments, officers had their own set of cutlery, engraved on one side with their personal coat of arms and on the reverse the regimental cipher. Photographed on top of a map from the Seven–Year War.

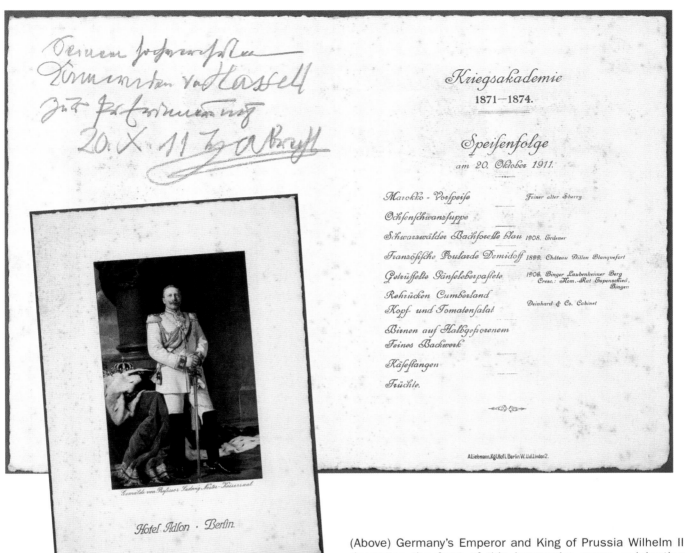

Hotel Adlon · Berlin.

(Opposite) These are the actual items used by the Life Guards, the British Crown's most famous household regiment. The Life Guards are one of the two components of what is now called the Household Cavalry Mounted Regiment. The other is The Blues and Royals (B&R). These are the men who ride horses and wear breastplates and plumed helmets — Life Guards with red tunics and white plumes, B&R with blue tunics and red plumes. They take turns providing what is called the Queen's Life Guard at the Horse Guards arch in Whitehall, London, which is the ceremonial entrance to the former Whitehall Palace (it burned down in the seventeenth century). The two units also provide the mounted escort when a royal family member or a state visitor is in a ceremonial procession.

The meal is an individual Beef Wellington with a reddish, almost translucent sauce; greens for garnish; and tiny, partially peeled red potatoes. The focus is on the Beef Wellington. The crust of the Beef Wellington is decorated with a simplified version of the regimental badge which is quite elaborate. To the left on the table is the mess cap worn while attending the mess. This one belonged to Field Marshal Lord Kitchner of Khartoum.

(Above) Germany's Emperor and King of Prussia Wilhelm II decorates the front of this impressive menu, celebrating alumni of the War Academy in Potsdam. Ulrich von Hassell, who served in the Royal Hanoverian Army prior to Prussia conquering Hanover in 1866, attended this dinner on October 20, 1911. The menu shows some of the elegance of the event. Officers were served fresh trout, truffled goose liver pâté, a rack of venison with Cumberland sauce, and a whole chicken cooked in the French "Demidoff" style.

That last dish was served by the President of France Félix Faure at a state dinner on May 22, 1895. The dish is named after Antole–Nicolaïevitch Demidoff, an Imperial Russian noble who was married to Princess Mathilde, the daughter of King Jerome Bonaparte (1813–1870). The dish was created by chef Louis Bignon, who later became the chef of the Café Riche and Maison Doree and heavily influenced French cuisine in the 19th century. Demidoff also gave his name to the famous accompaniment for caviar: "Blinis Demidoff."

This 1911 menu demonstrates that Prussia's officers' corps dined well, somewhat in contrast to the popular assumption that food in Prussia was uninspired. The wines included French and German vintages, as well as old sherry.

turned upside down to become an instantly available vodka glass.

The Russian tradition of regimental finery continued through World War I when the wives and mothers of officers approached Fabergé with a rather surprising request: would they kindly make some copper pots the men could take with them for cooking at the front? The House of Fabergé graciously complied, and today the creations are valuable to collectors and chefs alike.

Of course, soldiers are natural born competitors, and even gracious dining can be taken to extremes. Thus was the case in 1762 when His Royal Majesty D. José, king of Portugal, felt compelled to issue a formal decree regarding the general's table during campaigns. The Portuguese king was perturbed so many fighting men were being diverted from defending the motherland to lug loads of silver serving pieces hither and yon during wartime. He forbid the use of silver with the exception of eating utensils and coffeepots and declared that fine china (from China) was unnecessary in the field. Reminding his men that dining in the field should not be the same as dining at home, his majesty set a limit of no more than twenty persons at the general's table and no more than twenty dishes being served, excluding fruit and dessert. One can only wonder if the generals on the receiving end of

(Opposite) Bengal Lancers: This is one dish from the last major dinner of the regiment, held at the Cavalry and Guards Club, London, Friday, June 6, 1997: Salad of Smoked Duck–Breast with Asparagus and Walnut Dressing. (From the collection of Christopher & Karin Ross, New York City).

(Below) Prussian Garde du Corps mess plate bearing the Coat of Arms of Count Rittmeister (Captain) Rudolph von Brandenstein–Zepplin. The arms of the Counts von Brandenstein–Zepplin depict a green wolf grasping a dead swan in its jaws on a yellow shield.

It was common for officers serving in the better regiments to have elegant plates commissioned for use in the mess. Count Brandenstein came from a long line of warriors. Some fought against Napoleon and others fought for Finland in the grim Winter War against the Soviets. Two officers of this family earned the Pour le Mérite decoration (equivalent to the Victoria Cross or the U.S. Medal of Honor) in World War I in service to king and emperor. Another Brandenstein was awarded the same decoration in 1815 in the battles against Napoleon.

This mess plate belonged to Baron Rudolf Wilhelm Georg Otto von Brandenstein (1871–1957) who then served as a lieutenant in the 1st Regiment of the Guard, Infantry. The plate carries his coat of arms. (From the collection of Christopher & Karin Ross, New York City).

(Above) Built in 1824, the house of the superintendent of the United States Military Academy at West Point, New York, is one of the oldest structures on that post. Famous American generals have lived, worked, and, of course, entertained there. Among them are such stellar figures as General Robert E. Lee (who donated some of his furniture to the house) and General William C. Westmoreland, U.S. Army, who would go on to command troops in Vietnam.

The cooks at this house describe it as one of the most intensive "entertainment environments" with hundreds of formal dinner receptions for presidents, members of Congress, foreign dignitaries, and other officers, hosted every year.

this decree were disappointed they could no longer put on such an elaborate show for their fellow officers, or were relieved that they could concentrate their energies on the battles at hand.

The British tradition of each officer financially supporting the regimental table remains part of the United States Navy, where upon joining a ship, an officer must be formally admitted to the mess or ward-room and is assessed a daily fee.

Other armies and navies around the world also adopted the British tradition. In Prussia, for instance, instead of the word "mess," officer dining rooms were referred to as the casino.

Like the British officer, the Prussian officer was required to pay a sum of money for the privilege to dine there. A Prussian officer could expect to be served the finest food, and imbibe superior wines and liquors. Rich coffees and cigars, along with premium brandies, were enjoyed in casual conversation following dinner. Casinos were often decorated with original art and paintings, gorgeous tapestries, antique military hard-ware and banners or other souvenirs taken in battle.

Ulrich von Hassell, in his memoirs for the years 1848–1918, wrote enthusiastically about his time in a Hanoverian regimental mess. "That these regiments were molded in the British tradition is not surprising considering the House of Hanover ruled England from 1701 until the ascension of Queen Victoria. Many of the better Hanoverian regiments fought as part of the King's German Legion and were instrumental in the defeat of Napoleon."

Wrote Hassell:

The "mess" was an establishment that Hanoverian officers who had served for long years in the German legion under English leadership in Spain and other places had brought home from England. One gathered in the mess hall for lunch, which was usually eaten in the late afternoon (around five o'clock) during the long time of peace from 1815 until 1866 and often stayed together in these rooms at night too. The mess was run by the officer corps itself through competent people and was sometimes located in the barracks, sometimes in rented houses. The maxim was: off duty the officer is a gentleman, differences in rank are not eliminated but take second place as far as possible. On duty: strictest subordination; off duty: casual exchange, finest manners. As a principle no one talked about work at table. Apart from the president, no one had a designated seat at the lunch table. Everyone sat down as he arrived, which led to frequent interactions between older and younger officers. Unmarried men had to dine in the mess so that officers rarely frequented public houses. The food was good, even very good, but measured by the lower income of the younger officers. Good, cheap table wine was provided for, usually red wine; only later light wines from the Moselle and the Rhine were supplied as a result of improved railway connections. Life in the mess was family like so to speak. On "guest days" strangers were invited, often civilians too, to meet social obligations. Of course the mess was also great fun, but the entertainment never crossed certain lines.

"I have seen the beautiful mess halls in Hanover myself, namely those of the Gardejäger. Without exception they had class and were very tasteful. Every incoming officer donated a set of cutlery so that as time passed by the mess halls amassed considerable treasures of silverware. In other respects too there was no lack of donations and gifts, paintings, tableware etc. — in short, the mess halls made a very comfortable impression. It was a strange custom that the tablecloth was replaced with a fresh one every day and that this cloth that hung down very far was used to wipe one's mouth — there were no napkins. Pretty heavy punches were popular; I got to know the light punches based on Moselle wine only on the Rhine. I suppose it was said later that the Hanoverian officers who transferred to the Prussian and Saxon armies introduced some traditions to the local mess halls there that were a little sumptuous. The truth is that these officers

(Below) At Quarters 1 at West Point, Army cooks can truly shine. On a well–set table covered with elegant silver, fine crystal, and delicate lines, Army cooks present diners with the best of what the lush Hudson Valley has to offer. This particular dinner featured pan–roasted Hudson Valley Foie Gras and local pheasant breasts.

helped to make the mess halls homier than before 1867, for they all had been almost uncomfortable in their simplicity.

Mess halls had rules as well. *The Armed Forces Journal International* in February 1993 reprinted — perhaps as a reminder — the rules of etiquette applicable to junior officers invited to dine with the Archduke of Austria in 1624. Young men were told:

1. They are to come neatly dressed wearing coats and boots and not enter in a drunken condition.
2. At table they are not to tilt up their chairs; or rock themselves therein, nor stretch their legs at full length;
3. Nor drink at each mouthful, for if they do they will get tipsy too soon, and they should wipe the mouth and moustache in a cleanly manner;
4. Neither are they to thrust their hands into the dishes, nor throw the bones under the table;

5. Nor to lick their fingers, nor to expectorate in their plates, nor wipe their noses on the tablecloth;
6. Nor to drink so beastly as to fall from their chairs; and make themselves incapable of walking straight.

If you think fine dining isn't important to the military, then you haven't visited West Point. Most scenes of cadets at the revered U.S. Military Academy show them marching in precision drill, or training with full battle gear wearing camouflage, but there is a much more civilized repertoire for cadets that attend the academy. Washington Hall is the largest building on the West Point campus. It occupies nearly six acres of space, and the precision of its operations is on par with the precision close order drill of senior cadets.

The kitchen of Washington Hall is enormous, designed for maximum efficiency. It has to feed as many as 4,450 hungry cadets three times a day. Imagine preparing 10,000 hot dogs for lunch while 500 pies are prepared for dinner. The kitchen, operated by the largest staff at the academy, works around the clock and serves three meals a day with every cadet served within six minutes from the time the order to serve is given. The cadets are seated at some 450 tables and are served an entrée on a plate with the rest of the meal served family style. A senior cadet is seated at one end of the table and a plebe at the other end. The plebe is responsible for pouring beverages, knowing ahead of time what everyone at the table will drink. The plebe is also responsible for serving dessert, cutting pie in equal portions for those at the table who will have pie for dessert.

Washington Hall is also the most decorated building at West Point. The walls of the six wings of the cadet mess are hung with pre–Revolutionary War flags, portraits of former superintendents, and the flags of the 50 states.

A conspicuous and unusual work of art adorns the entire back wall of the C Wing of Washington Hall. The 2,450–square–foot mural, painted in 1936 by T. Loftin Johnson, captivates onlookers. It took Johnson one year to paint the mural, which consists primarily of battle scenes, some going back thousands of years. Several mysteries surround the mural, among them why King Richard the Lion Hearted was depicted with two right hands, or why a man, seemingly bowing to Queen Elizabeth, has no face. Among the anomalies in the painting are a horn from a 1930s car, a spark plug, a gas mask, and other incongruous objects like the bottle of Coca–Cola ® rumored to be somewhere in the painting along with a pack of cigarettes. Few people, if any, have been able to find them but they are alleged to be there.

Throughout the year, there are many important dinners served at Washington Hall. The Graduation Banquet, 100th Night, 500th Night, the Yearling Banquet, the Plebe/Parent Banquet, along with

MARINS RUSSES A PARIS MANGEANT LE PAIKI NATIONAL

(Above) Russian sailors enjoying fresh soup. Nourishing soup has been a staple for sailors from around the globe since Roman times. Many accounts of life aboard ship mention soup as a key food item where a variety of ingredients were combined and served from a communal pot.

holidays, all represent dinners with special Army pomp and circumstance.

One of the more significant holiday meals is Christmas dinner, held a week or so before the Christmas break since most cadets go home for the holidays. The Corps Christmas Dinner commemorates the end of the first session at West Point, although cadets are in the middle of finals and will go home after exams end the following week. Cadets wear full dress uniforms for this special repast and are served an elaborate turkey dinner.

As cadets arrive at Washington Hall they are treated to live music — Christmas carols played by the cadet jazz band. Every table in Washington Hall is decorated, most of them in a Christmas theme, but often in a rather bizarre manner. Plebes spend the afternoon decorating their respective tables, and it's a high–pressure mission because, before dinner is over, there are awards for the best or most originally decorated tables. There is another curious tradition. Most of the place settings also include a cigar. Smoking, of course, is not permitted at West Point, but on this one evening, eyes look the other way.

Following dinner, cadets honor a tradition by standing, holding hands, and singing *The Twelve Days of Christmas*. When the song is completed, a cadet at each table places a chair on the center of the table and a plebe, sometimes two, mounts the table and stands on the chair. The remaining cadets at the table then lift it into the air. It's a raucous time, especially when one considers the table alone weighs nearly 400 pounds!

When the table dancing is over, the cadets all gather outside and surround General Washington's statue where they light their cigars as they begin to say goodbye to fellow cadets.

There's more to Washington Hall, however, than just eating. The U.S. Army calls it "The Art of Dining In," and it is most certainly an elegant affair. Every cadet is required to host a Dining In before he or she graduates. At West Point, a Dining In begins with chimes, then the boom of a gavel in the Black and Gold Room in Washington Hall. This room, named after the academy's colors, is a formal dining room, equipped with crystal, silver utensils, fine china, and silver serving dishes and is used to train cadets in proper U.S. Army dining traditions.

A senior officer in the corps will give the order to "Post the Colors." A bugle sounds calling the guests to attention. A drum roll follows. There is a brief invocation followed by toasts to visiting dignitaries. While it may be a mock event, the Dining In exercise is done with the same finesse and panache as battlefield training from the protocols followed for sending invitations and planning the meals, to a mock selection of wines and cigars.

(Above) U.S. Army officers tended to dine in style and with elegant food in the late 19th century when this French engraving was produced. It is titled "Missouri German Artillery" and pokes fun at the Americans, perceived then (and maybe even now) by the French as uncultured and boorish. That the unit was also a German–style U.S. Army unit adds to the French eagerness to be full of satire. Note the freshly shot pheasant in the basket at the officer's right foot along with a probably delicious country ham.

At the U.S. Naval Academy at Annapolis, the fare and traditions are a bit different but no less special. *Brigade Seats!* is the name of the Naval Academy Cookbook, written by Karen Jensen Neeb and published in 1984. Like West Point, the Naval Academy is a superb ballet of precision–timed logistics, feeding wholesome fare to some 4,000 midshipmen. Standard seafood dishes that exploit the rich fishing grounds of the Chesapeake Bay highlight the menus. Recipes for Spiced Shrimp or Crab Imperial are common. The Spiced Shrimp dish requires 1,373 pounds of large shrimp for all the midshipmen and 1,320 pounds of crabmeat are needed to feed the mess with Crab Imperial. Ironically, the least favored dish served to cadets at West Point is fish. ✂

Bengal Lancers' Shrimp Curry

This dish was popular with Bengal Lancers serving in India.

Ingredients
1 pound medium shrimp, peeled and deveined,
  tails left on
½ teaspoon salt
¼ teaspoon turmeric
½ teaspoon mustard seeds
1 teaspoon cumin seeds
4 garlic cloves, peeled
1 half-inch piece fresh ginger, peeled
2 dried red chili peppers, stemmed
1 tablespoon lemon juice
2 tablespoons mustard oil or light olive oil
1 cup onion, finely chopped
1 ½ cups chopped tomato
¼ – ½ cup water
freshly cooked basmati or long-grain rice

Instructions
1. Sprinkle shrimp with salt and turmeric. Toss well to coat; cover and set aside for 15 minutes.
2. Combine mustard, cumin, garlic, ginger, chilis, and lemon juice in a blender and puree. Set aside.
3. Heat oil in a large heavy skillet over medium-high heat. Add onions and cook until soft, about 3 minutes.
4. Add pureed spice mixture. Cook, stirring, until fragrant, about 5 minutes.
5. Stir in tomato and cook until soft.
6. Add shrimp and stir gently to coat them evenly.
7. Pour in the water and bring to a boil, stirring constantly.
8. Reduce heat to medium, cover, and cook until shrimp are just opaque, about 5 minutes.
9. Mound rice onto heated serving plates. Spoon curry over and serve.

Bengal Lancers' Beef Curry Cubes

Ingredients
3 ½ pounds beef tips, cubed
3 tablespoons Dijon mustard
5 tablespoons vegetable oil
1 four-inch piece of ginger, peeled and minced
8 cloves garlic, peeled and minced
2 tablespoons garam masala
2 tablespoons curry powder
2 ½ to 3 teaspoons salt, to taste
1 teaspoon black pepper, or more, to taste
1 fresh jalapeño or serrano chili, seeded and minced
1 cup low-salt chicken broth
⅓ cup chopped cilantro for garnish

Instructions
1. Toss beef with mustard until the meat is coated. Cover and refrigerate overnight or at least 2 hours.
2. Heat 3 tablespoons of oil in a large wok on medium. Stir-fry ginger and garlic until soft, about 2 minutes.
3. Stir in garam masala and curry powder and cook, stirring often, for another 2 to 3 minutes. You should end up with a thick paste-like mixture.
4. Remove curry paste mixture from the pan and reserve.
5. Heat remaining 2 tablespoons of oil on high.
6. Stir-fry beef with the reserved curry paste, salt, pepper, and half the jalapeño.
7. Lightly brown the beef cubes, but avoid cooking them all the way through, about 4 to 5 minutes using a large wok on high heat.
8. Turn heat to low. Stir in chicken broth. Simmer 5 minutes for the flavors to blend.
9. Garnish with chopped cilantro.
10. For a spicier dish, add reserved jalapeño.

Serves 8.

Abkochen

(Left) Here senior officers of a Prussian Regiment are dining in the field during a maneuver in the days before World War I. Then, as now, the mess would leave the garrison and travel into the field. Note the almost frantic activity in the background where enlisted soldiers prepare the meal for the officers.

(Above) British 17th Lancers' mess items, including dinner plate, silver napkin ring, and match box. At the top are silver napkin holders engraved with the Lancers' motto, "Death or Glory." (From the collection of Christopher & Karin Ross, New York City)

Russian Borscht

Ingredients

12 ounces fresh beets
1 pound boneless beef or pork, cubed
  flour for dredging
2 tablespoons oil
4 ½ cups beef stock
1 28-ounce can diced tomatoes
2 cups shredded red cabbage
1 medium onion, diced
2 carrots, peeled and sliced
2 celery stalks, sliced
1 3-ounce can tomato paste
2 tablespoons red wine vinegar
2 teaspoons lemon juice
2 cloves garlic, crushed
1 ½ teaspoons sugar (optional)
salt and black pepper to taste
dairy sour cream, for garnish
fresh dill, chopped, for garnish

Instructions

1. Roast beets in a 350° F oven until tender, about one hour. Allow to cool and cut beets into thin strips.
2. Dredge meat in flour and brown in hot oil.
3. Add stock and tomatoes. Bring to a full boil, then reduce heat and simmer until meat is tender, about 30 minutes.
4. Add cabbage, onion, carrots, celery, and tomato paste.
5. Simmer until vegetables are tender, about 30 minutes.
6. Add beets, vinegar, lemon juice, garlic, sugar (optional) and simmer for 15 minutes.
7. Add salt and pepper to taste.
8. Serve in bowls garnished with sour cream and dill.

USMC Capered Shrimp Salad

Ingredients

1 pound shrimp, peeled and deveined
½ cup chopped celery
½ cup mayonnaise
2 tablespoons capers

Instructions

1. Boil shrimp until pink yet still firm.
2. Allow shrimp to cool. Once shrimp is cooled, add remaining ingredients and mix well.
3. Refrigerate at least 2 hours.
4. Serve on bread or crackers.

Makes 4 to 6 servings.

Recipe provided by Gunnery Sergeant D. E. Blakeman

Egg Rolls from the Marine Commandant's House

Ingredients

1 pound lean ground beef
3 celery stalks, finely chopped
6 green onion stalks, finely chopped
1 cup finely chopped cabbage
4 tablespoons butter or margarine
2 to 3 cups grated sharp cheddar cheese
¼ cup soy sauce
½ teaspoon garlic powder
¾ teaspoon fresh ground pepper
1 package of 50 won ton wrappers

Instructions

1. In a frying pan, brown ground beef and drain.
2. In a separate pan, sauté celery, onion, and cabbage in butter.
3. Add vegetable mixture to the meat, along with cheese, soy sauce, and spices.
4. Place 1 teaspoon on each won ton wrapper and wet wedges with water.
5. Fold edges in and over and deep fat fry to a golden brown.
6. Serve with mustard sauce or sweet and sour sauce.

Makes 50 egg rolls.

Recipe provided by Staff Sergeant A. P. Schneider

(Above) This post card, from the days before World War I, pokes fun at the dining habits of French reservists serving in the infantry. They were easily sidetracked by good food and wine and the always-present baguette — a mainstay of French rations in war and peace. Note the colorful uniforms: French infantry went into World War I in red trousers, presenting themselves as perfect targets to the advancing forces of the German Empire. Needless to say, the baguette remained while the uniforms changed rapidly.

(Above) Egg Rolls – U.S. Marine Corps
These are special egg rolls created by the cooks serving at Marine Corps Barracks at 8th and I Streets in Washington, D.C., and are typically served at glamorous receptions for Washington's elite. These receptions are hosted by the Commandant of the Marine Corps.

NAVAL TRADITIONS:
MORE THAN RUM AND COFFEE

"Englishmen, and more especially seamen, love their bellies above anything else, and therefore it must always be remembered in the management of the victualling of the navy that to make any abatement in the quantity or agreeableness of the victuals is to discourage and provoke them in the tenderest point, and will sooner render them disgusted with the King's service than any other hardship that can be put upon them."

— Samuel Pepys, 1686

Samuel Pepys kept a detailed diary and served as First Sea Lord supervising the victualling of a rapidly expanding British Royal Navy in the late 1600s. It is under his administration that the Royal Navy first codified the basic rules for shipboard provisions, including the use of rum, pickled meats, and biscuits.

Pepys certainly took a major interest in the culinary arts. His diary is loaded with detailed references to food and his library contained many recipe books, a true rarity in his time.

He theorized that a well-fed crew is more likely to be a happy crew. In 1686, Samuel Pepys wrote that; "Englishmen, and more especially seamen, love their bellies above everything else." Pepys was writing when food was often in short supply, and in the years that followed the Admiralty developed an elaborate system to ensure that seamen's bellies were filled.

A seaman's staple drink was eight pints of strong beer a day. Requirements for beer were so great that in 1760 the Navy's brewery in Gosport produced 4 million gallons of beer.

The navy ran the first bottle bank. The seaman's food was stored in wooden casks, glass jars, and canvas bags. Empty casks and jars were expensive so great efforts were made to recycle them. When they were empty, casks could be "shaken down" into separate staves and hoops. These were then taken back to port, cleaned, and reassembled.

Critics of the seaman's diet claimed the food was so bad that the hard Suffolk cheese was made into buttons or recycled into cannon balls; raisins were used as wadding in the guns; and butter was used to grease the ship's blocks. These were probably just good stories, but certainly wine, which was too

vinegary to drink, was recycled and used to clean the decks.

Officers, on the other hand, ate very well. It cost more than £500 per year to feed a Commander-in-Chief. In 1806, when Earl St. Vincent took command of the Channel fleet, he spent more than £500 in four months with grocers in Portsmouth. In contrast to the monotonous food eaten on the lower deck, his steward cooked from a great variety of the choicest ingredients. He drank Turkish coffee, milk chocolate, suchong and

La Vie du Marin.
Le Maître-Coq.

(Opposite) These samples of the personal silver of Admiral von Tirpitz are engraved with his coat of arms. They were photographed on top of a painting of SMS *Barbarossa*, a battleship constructed in 1903.

(Above) A French naval cook in the days before World War I poses with his enormous chef's knife in the porthole of a French ship. Cooks aboard ship have always been treated with respect. Their skill in turning out good food under often difficult conditions — such as in heavy storms or with dwindling supplies — is essential for maintaining morale.

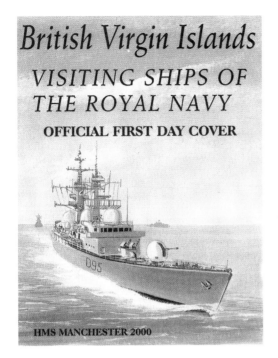

British Virgin Islands

VISITING SHIPS OF THE ROYAL NAVY

OFFICIAL FIRST DAY COVER

HMS MANCHESTER 2000

(Above) The tradition of sending warships on diplomatic missions around the world dates back to the first days of naval power. This set of stamps from the British Virgin Islands celebrates visits by famous British Royal Navy ships including (left to right) HMS *Manchester* 2000, HMS *Wistaria* 1923-30, HMS *Dundee* 1934-5, HMS *Eurydice* 1787, HMS *Pegasus* 1787, HMS *Astrea* 1807, and HM Yacht *Britannia* 1966.

(Opposite) "Captain Rasher demonstrating..." is the caption on this 19th century British illustration. It shows a senior naval officer instructing young midshipmen and other junior naval officers in the fine art of table manners. The Royal Navy expected officers to be accomplished in social circles as well as in the line of battle.

hyson tea, in addition to his stock of wines. He flavored his food with ginger, allspice, cloves, India soy sauce, ketchup, and a great number of pickles and vinegars.

In 1792, Commander Juan de Bodega y Quadra, assigned to North America's west coast, was sent to Nootka Sound to settle matters with the British — represented by Captain George Vancouver — concerning the Spanish "sovereignty" of Nootka. As was common to those times, this naval diplomacy was accompanied by all the needed implements for top class entertainment.

During the negotiations, the tables were set with heavy silver cutlery. "Dishes, knives and forks, and indeed every thing else, were of silver and always replaced with spare ones . . . . On purpose they let us see the quantity of silver," noted one British officer.

Dinner "consisting of a superfluity of the best provisions, was served with great elegance. (We) were gratified with a repast we had lately been little accustomed to, or had the most distant idea of meeting with at this place," Vancouver noted in his journal, *A Voyage of Discovery to the North Pacific*, and *Round the World*. He noted that oysters, salmon, and game were served alongside potatoes, cabbages, lettuce, artichokes, and tomatoes.

To this day, naval ships of all nations make great efforts on foreign port visits to impress and convey not only an image of power, but also an image of elegance. When, on November 19, 2003, the USS *Vandergrift* became the first U.S. war ship to call on Vietnam since the fall of Saigon, plans were in the works to invite local Vietnamese dignitaries aboard for elegant entertainment.

In November 2003, the British Royal Navy's HMS *Manchester* visited Tortola in the British Virgin Islands. The captain hosted an elaborate cocktail party for local politicians and dignitaries. The exquisite food included honey roasted Lincolnshire sausages, pork

satays, quiche, smoked salmon en croute, rough chopped "Marie Rose" scallop tartlets, and wild mushroom and herb tartlets. The wines were reported to have been superb.

The ship's chef, Petty Officer Harris, had a reputation for serving his captain and crew elegant food. Menu items have included such delicacies as sirloin steak parmentiere garnished with sautéed sliced mushrooms and a burnne noisette, gazpacho garnished with a nab tower tian finished off with an herb drizzle, and seared fillet of beef served with fondant potato garnished with julienne of steamed leek and pepper finished off with a wild mushroom and red wine jus lie.

A review of other menus of the HMS *Manchester* finds items such as poached chicken served on a bed of fresh saffron pasta taglitelle accompanied with roasted shallots and sugar snap peas, and capped with a julienne of steamed leek with a honey and tarragon jus lie. Others include pan fried gresingham duck supreme with a honey glaze, a wild boar terrine with juniper berries and gypsy-style pan fried sea bass.

Desserts on board have included a Bavarian Orange Bavious, Iced Grand Marnier Soufflé, White Chocolate Cups Au' Citron, and a Ginger and Peach Panna Cotta. If English seamen truly love their

Captain Rasher demonstrating

MAJOR-GEN. BARON VON STEUBEN
PRESIDENT OF THE GERMAN SOCIETY OF THE CITY OF NEW YORK 1785-1795

1784 · 1902

118th Anniversary Banquet
of the
German Society
OF THE CITY OF NEW YORK
Saturday evening, March eighth
at the Waldorf-Astoria

TIFFANY & CO.

GUESTS

—

HIS ROYAL HIGHNESS PRINCE HENRY OF PRUSSIA
HIS EXCELLENCY THE GERMAN AMBASSADOR, DR. VON HOLLEBEN
STAFF OF HIS ROYAL HIGHNESS PRINCE HENRY OF PRUSSIA

HIS EXCELLENCY VICE-ADMIRAL VON TIRPITZ, Secretary of State for the Navy
HIS EXCELLENCY GENERAL VON PLESSEN, His Imperial Majesty's Adjutant-General
HIS EXCELLENCY VICE-ADMIRAL BARON VON SECKENDORFF, Hofmarschall
HIS EXCELLENCY VICE-ADMIRAL VON EISENDECHER
CAPTAIN VON MULLER
COMMANDER VON GRUMME, His Imperial Majesty's Aide-de-camp
LIEUTENANT-COMMANDER SCHMIDT VON SCHWIND, Aide-de-camp
LIEUTENANT-COMMANDER VON EGIDY, Aide-de-camp
LIEUTENANT-COMMANDER VON TROTHA, Aide-de-camp
STAFF SURGEON DR. REICH

DETAILED BY THE PRESIDENT OF THE UNITED STATES

HON. D. J. HILL, First Assistant Secretary of State
REAR-ADMIRAL ROBLEY D. EVANS, U. S. N.   ADJUTANT-GENERAL HENRY C. CORBIN, U. S. A.
COLONEL T. A. BINGHAM, U. S. A.
COMMANDER WILLIAM S. COWLES, U. S. N.

—

HON. SETH LOW, Mayor of the City of New York
HON. CARL SCHURZ
PROF. NICHOLAS MURRAY BUTLER, President Columbia College
FRED'K W. HOLLS

RUDOLPH KEPPLER
CONSUL-GENERAL K. BUENZ
GRAF QUADT
CONSUL GEISSLER

JOHANNES WILDA

STAFF OF OFFICERS OF HIS IMPERIAL MAJESTY'S YACHT "Hohenzollern"

REAR-ADMIRAL COUNT VON BAUDISSIN
COMMANDER VON HOLLEBEN
COMMANDER HIPPER
LIEUTENANT-COMMANDER KARPF
LIEUTENANT-COMMANDER VON DER OSTEN
LIEUTENANT-COMMANDER VON MANTEY

LIEUTENANT REBENSBURG
LIEUTENANT SEIDENSTICKER
LIEUTENANT VON HAXTHAUSEN
ENGINEER (LIEUTENANT) STEINMEYER
ENGINEER (LIEUTENANT) NICHOLAI
NAVAL SURGEON DR. UTHEMANN

MENU

—

HUÎTRES

—

POTAGE À LA JENNY LIND

—

BOUCHEES À LA COLOMBINE

—

RADIS   OLIVES   CÉLERI   AMANDES SALÉES

AIGUILLETTES DE FILET DE BASS À LA CHEVALIÈRE

TOMATES FARCIES AUX CONCOMBRES

—

COQUILLES DE VOLAILLE À LA VIERCHAUX

—

ESCALOPES DE FILET DE BOEUF, SAUCE AUX CHAMPIGNONS FRAIS

POMMES DE TERRE SAUTÉES EN QUARTIERS   CHOUXFLEURS AU GRATIN

—

ASPERGES, OYSTER BAY, SAUCE HOLLANDAISE

—

SORBET AU MARASQUIN

—

CANARD TÊTE-ROUGE RÔTI

HOMINY FRIT   SALADE À LA WALDORF

GLACES DE FANTAISIE

PETITS FOURS   FRUITS

CAFÉ

Chateau Cérons

Amontillado Pasado

Rudesheimer 1889

St. Emilion

Pommery Sec
Pommery Brut
G. H. Mumm's Extra Dry
Clicquot, Yellow Label
Clicquot Brut
Dry Monopole
Moet & Chandon
Rheingold

Apollinaris
Liqueurs

(Opposite and Above) On March 8, 1902, an amazing dinner was held at New York's Waldorf-Astoria Hotel. It was advertised as the 118th Anniversary Banquet of the German Society of the City of New York, but the event's real purpose was to honor a senior Imperial German Naval delegation. Germany's Navy was, at that time, experiencing a major growth spurt spearheaded by Grand Admiral Alfred von Tirpitz. An inspection visit to the United States was seen as an essential element of developing plans for growth. As the list of honorees shows, key German naval officers were at the Waldorf: H.R.H. Prince Henry of Prussia, Tirpitz and others who would gain fame during World War I naval engagements.

The all-French menu — with 13 different wines, including a choice of eight different Champagnes — combines Escoffier-influenced dishes such as a filet with a sauce composed of fresh mushrooms, along with some unique American contributions such as Oyster Bay oysters, fried hominy grits (something the Waldorf most certainly does not serve anymore) and the famous Waldorf Salad.

bellies, those aboard the HMS *Manchester* must be happy indeed.

Admiral Horatio Nelson was quite fond of excellent cooking as well as wines. Large quantities of Marsala were served to him aboard his ships. Contemporary records strongly suggest that he directly supervised the creation of "Consommé Nelson." Other dishes are also associated with his name such as "Sole Nelson" (folded fillets of sole with white wine sauce, garnished with sautéed roe and potatoes) and various meat dishes such as "Tournedos Nelson." The meat dishes all call for sautéing meat in butter and are served with a simple Madeira sauce.

Naval Coffee

Good Navy coffee can be a superb elixir during long nights on the bridge or put into a thermos before an amphibious landing. So much so that in 1913 the Portuguese government passed a law that allowed the brandy bonus to the sailors "to be replaced by strong warm coffee during the night shifts, when the weather was cold or rainy."

But at times naval coffee has had a bad reputation. One senior U.S. naval officer describes the "genuine Navy coffee" as follows: "Never clean the coffee mug. Never clean the percolator. Brew coffee. Reheat daily for one week until it tastes burned. Then serve it."

The following story was told to Agostino von Hassell, but may apply to some other admirals. Grand Admiral Alfred von Tirpitz, when in command of the German Imperial East Asia Squadron (which scoped out Tsingtao as a decent colony and trading post for Germany in 1896), liked his coffee served in a cup filled to the very top, on a saucer with two dry cubes of sugar on the side. On the battleship SMS *Kaiser,* he was served such coffee almost every night. The coffee was brought up by a steward from the galley all the way up to the bridge … and even in heavy storms, the coffee arrived perfect — cup filled to the top, the sugar perfect and dry. One day, the mess man fell ill and his replacement struggled mightily with the task, carrying the coffee cup up ladder wells … disaster. Half of the coffee spilled, the sugar cubes were soaked. The replacement asked the steward how he did this. "Simple…I put the sugar into my pocket, the spoon and saucer into the other pocket, take a healthy sip of coffee and keep it in my mouth … run up the ladder well and just before entering the bridge spit the coffee back into the cup, get the saucer and the sugar … voila perfection." ✂

(Opposite) Inventory of the Royal Biscuit Plant of Vale de Zebro

"Biscuit Royal Plant of Vale de Zebro" describes how the biscuits used to feed the Portuguese navy were prepared. The page seen on the left lists the number of biscuits prepared during the month of March and the beginning of April in the year 1787.

The elaborately decorated hand-tooled leather binding is "wallet style" with exterior seams. These two books belong to the Portuguese Navy Central Library-Central Archive.

(Above) Chipped Beef on Toast – U.S. Navy

Chipped beef on toast is a standard breakfast in wardrooms of the U.S. Navy and a dish that has crossed over onto the tables of U.S. civilians. Coffee (black, of course) is served in a mug from the USS *Iowa*.

Pan Seared Marinated Buffalo Stuffed with Vidalia Onions, Shitake Mushrooms, and Black Tiger Prawns

The U.S. Navy's fast attack submarine *Buffalo* (SSN 715) is the third U.S. Navy ship to bear the proud name of the *Buffalo*. The USS *Buffalo* is the Navy's 25th Los Angeles Class fast attack submarine. She was commissioned on Nov. 5, 1983 in Norfolk, Virginia and is now home-ported in Pearl Harbor, Hawaii. Upholding a long tradition of superb food aboard submarines, the chefs serving on this boat created this dish with the subtitle *"A Crews Recipe for Success. From the chefs onboard the nuclear powered submarine while deployed to the Western Pacific Ocean 1999."*

Marinade Ingredients
2 cups virgin olive oil
¼ cup white wine vinegar
3 ¼ teaspoon fresh ground black pepper
½ teaspoon fresh ground white pepper
1 teaspoon fresh garlic, grated
½ teaspoon fresh thyme, minced
½ teaspoon fresh oregano, minced
2 ½ teaspoons mesquite BBQ seasoning
¼ teaspoon Tabasco™ sauce
½ teaspoon worcestershire
¼ teaspoon sea salt
pinch of fresh marjoram, minced
½ teaspoon onion powder

Main Ingredients
2 12-ounce buffalo prime rib steaks, trimmed
  (may substitute porterhouse)
2 Yukon Gold potatoes
8 ounces Shitake mushrooms, sliced
1 Vidalia onion, cut into strips
¼ cup 2 percent milk
6 ounces real sour cream
½ pound honey cured bacon
¼ pound sharp cheddar cheese, shredded
1 orange and yellow bell peppers, cubed small
2 green Poblano peppers, cubed small
16 black tiger prawns, peeled and cleaned
1 teaspoon butter

Instructions
1. Trim the fat off of the steaks and butterfly (like cutting a pocket in the side).
2. Mix all marinade ingredients together. Place the steaks in the marinade, cover container, and refrigerate 24 hours.
3. Cook the bacon and drain it well on paper towels. Once cool, crumble into pieces and set aside.
4. Place potatoes in a preheated 350° F oven and cook for about one hour or until soft inside. When the potatoes are done, cut in half lengthwise and scoop out the centers into a bowl. Leave some potato to hold up the skin and structure of the potato. Do not scoop all the way down to the bare skin.
5. Add the milk, sour cream, bacon, and cheddar cheese to the potato scoopings and mix gently. Refill the potato and garnish on top with the small cubed peppers.
6. Sauté the mushrooms and onions in the butter until translucent.
7. Throw in the shrimp and pour on a cup of the marinade.
8. Reduce the liquid while simmering for a few minutes. This allows for the shrimp to get drunk on the marinade as well.
9. Grill the buffalo steaks and stuff them with the mushroom, onion, and shrimp mixture.
10. When steaks are nearly done, heat up the stuffed potatoes in the microwave.
11. Place two stuffed potato halves and a steak on each plate, and garnish with the small cubed peppers.

Note: Serves two. Can easily be scaled up for more people.

(Opposite) Italian Navy – 1989
This is a dish served on the Italian Amphibious Assault Ship *Garibaldi*. An Arugala salad accompanies breaded chicken cutlets topped with prosciuto, melted cheese, and a fried egg. The meal is served with a red wine typical for shipboard duty. The personally signed photograph of Italy's King Vittorio Emanuele was given to Admiral von Tirpitz during the Naval Review in Kiel in 1913. The scarf is from the Battaglione San Marco (Italy's Marine Corps), and the ashtray is decorated with the coat of arms of today's Italian Navy.

Nelson's Soup for the Sick and Hurt

This nourishing soup was likely concocted under the command of Admiral Nelson.

Ingredients
1 meaty beef shinbone cut into 3 large pieces (may substitute ½ pound stew meat)
1 ham or bacon hock
1 ounce anchovies
3 carrots, washed and sliced
1 head of celery
water
cayenne pepper

Instructions
1. Put the shin bones and ham into a large pan. Slowly brown on low heat. You won't need any extra fat if it is heated gently.
2. Add carrots, celery and anchovies plus enough water to cover everything in the pan.
3. Bring to a boil and skim all that rises to the surface.
4. Cover and simmer for four hours.
5. Remove the bones and strain the broth through cheesecloth or muslin into a clean pan.
6. Refrigerate overnight and the next day skim fat from the top of the liquid.
7. Boil liquid until it is reduced by about two-thirds. The color should change to a rich dark brown.
8. Add a small amount of cayenne pepper and pour the mixture into a shallow glass or earthenware bowl.
9. Leave overnight then cut the soup into "coins" about 3-inch diameter.
10. Allow the "coins" to dry out a few days.
11. Once dried, store "coins" in an airtight container with paper between each "coin."

Note: Do not add any salt to this recipe, the anchovies provide it.

To reconstitute — place one "coin" in a bowl, add boiling water and stir well.

Nelson's Consommé

Probably created under direct supervision of Admiral Nelson while cruising in the Mediterranean.

Ingredients
2 pounds of fish bones
water
1 yellow onion, sliced
1 leek, chopped
1 stalk of celery, chopped
½ cup parsley, chopped
1 bay leaf
1 clove
1 pound ground sirloin
2 egg whites
2 cups cooked white rice
salt and pepper to taste

Instructions
1. In a heavy saucepan combine three quarts of water with the fish bones, onion, leek, celery, parsley, bay leaf, and clove.
2. Boil this mixture for at least 30 minutes and set aside.
3. Strain and reserve the broth.
4. In a separate saucepan, mix the ground sirloin and egg whites.
5. Slowly add the fish broth.
6. Simmer mixture for 10 minutes.
7. Strain through cheesecloth.
8. Add boiled white rice.
9. Add salt and pepper to taste, and serve.

Skillgallee

Ingredients

2 cups of flour
¾ to 1 cup of water
1 tablespoon of Crisco or vegetable fat
6 pinches of salt
fried pork

Instructions

1. Mix ingredients together into a stiff batter, knead several times, and spread the dough onto a baking sheet at a thickness of ½ inch.
2. Bake for 30 minutes at 400° F.
3. Remove from oven, cut dough into 3-inch squares.
4. Punch four rows of holes, four holes per row into the dough.
5. Turn dough over, return to the oven and bake another 30 minutes.
6. Turn oven off, leaving door closed.
7. Leave the hardtack in the oven until cool.
8. Crumble hardtack into fried pork, stir and serve.

Photo by Agostino von Hassell

(Opposite) Soup has always been a mainstay of naval food. Here, French sailors line up aboard a pre-World War I warship to draw soup rations for their comrades. Note the enormous size of the containers.

(Above) Wardrooms aboard naval ships are far more than a place to get nourishment. They are the unofficial social club where gossip is exchanged, games are played and "mid rats" are issued (peanut butter and jelly sandwiches and ice cream seem to be the most popular snacks on modern U.S. Navy ships).

Wardrooms served a grim purpose in the past: during battle, the large tables would be cleared and used as emergency operating theaters.

This is the officers' wardroom aboard the USS Nassau, one of the capital amphibious ships of the U.S. Navy and home for more than 4,000 U.S. Marines. The old tradition of a steak-and-egg breakfast before a landing, accompanied by the order "Land the landing force," is slowly fadin away. Food is typically simple and nourishing and often supplemented by treats from home. One Marine captain's family would regularly mail him boxes of his favorite cereal.

Some nights, special dinners would be prepared such as well-seasoned steak with grilled shrimp, fresh salad, and assorted pies for dessert.

LIQUID COURAGE

There are an untold number of beverages, alcoholic and otherwise, that have played important roles in aiding and abetting the sins of war, and in accompanying the fine dining that led to war, victories, and treaties. Wine, rum, sake, beer, and every form of spirits have been a mainstay of armies since the day they were formed.

Co-author Agostino von Hassell would routinely carry a small flask to the field with a most expensive and flavorful brandy to cut the edge from nervous nights in the field. "On long deployments, I would take a sip, hold it in my mouth for a few minutes, and then spit it back into the flask since a new supply was often thousands of miles away," complains Hassell.

During World War I, German, British, and French soldiers routinely "fortified" themselves before going over the top with a big drink of whatever was available, be it rum, scotch, brandy, or moonshine. Some reports from that terrible trench war suggest that many soldiers were actually quite drunk — understandable when you consider the stress of that war. Reports during the Napoleonic Wars indicate soldiers of all armies were heavily fortified with spirits in the heat of battle.

For 285 years, from 1685 through July 31, 1970, the British Royal Navy issued rum rations every day at noon. The rum, very much a result of the Royal Navy's conquests of key islands of the Caribbean, was Pusser's Rum. It was not sold on the commercial market until 1980 when the British Admiralty allowed public sale of this beverage with proceeds benefiting the Royal Navy Sailor's Fund. Pusser's is Royal Navy slang for "purser," the individual in charge of issuing rum rations aboard ship.

Alcoholic beverages can be found in almost all militaries with the rare exception of Muslim forces. The quality of the liquor differs dramatically from army to army: raw alcohol destined for tank maintenance

The History of Rum Making

yet "looted" for personal consumption by Soviet soldiers was a common health hazard in the 20th century. This is one extreme involving the lowest rank of the scale. On the opposite side of the spectrum, depending on the taste and budget of the regiment, one might find soldiers enjoying superb champagnes, vintage ports, and some of the finest Bordeaux vintages.

Beer and wine were the main alcoholic beverages of soldiers and officers of the ancient world. The processing and alcohol content killed many dangerous organisms. Diluted sour wine was usually imbibed by the ordinary Roman troops, with better wines being served on special occasions. Grain was fermented to make beer, which was most popular. A discharged Legionnaire is recorded as having set up one of Europe's first taverns with the small business serving beer to the military toward the end of the first century.

Settlers in the young United States had an amazing capacity for alcohol. They discovered early on that

(Opposite) Tsingtao Beer — China and Germany
In 1903, Germany's colonial government constructed the Germania (now Tsingtao) Brewery and imported German brew masters to oversee the work of supplying the German Imperial Navy with local beer. Tsingtao Brewery is now the largest brewery in China and Tsingtao beer is the No. 1 branded consumer product exported from China.

(Above) This stamp from the British Virgin Islands celebrates the custom of the Royal Navy to issue rum rations (or grog) to sailors. The custom continued for nearly 300 years until it was suspended in 1970. Rum was a product of the West Indies where Britain maintained numerous colonies. Rum was frequently referred to as "Nelson's Blood." The body of this preeminent hero of the Royal Navy was preserved in a barrel of rum after the battle of Trafalgar, and then brought back to London for burial.

those who drank coffee, tea, wine, or beer rather than plain water suffered fewer illnesses and lived longer. Coffee and tea were too expensive for most farmers, so homemade brew became the order of the day. Children as young as toddlers imbibed. Following the American Revolution, it became customary among families and regiments to toast their new country, sometimes as often as once for each state. Years of experience in drinking gave the colonials a tolerance for alcohol unheard of today. It is said that, in 1792, John Hancock gave a party for members of the Boston Fusiliers and at that single event eighty men drank 136 bowls of punch, 21 bottles of sherry, and a large but unspecified, quantity of cider and brandy. We are not sure if the punch used wine or hard liquor as a base, but either way it's still an enormous quantity of alcohol per person. Without a doubt, no one among the militiamen saw the whites of their eyes the next morning. But astoundingly, there were no reports of alcohol poisoning.

During the American Civil War, the Confederacy — perennially short on supplies — turned to all kinds of tricks to provide beer and wine to its Rebels. Beer was brewed using corn, potatoes, sassafras, persimmons, and spruce or pine needles. Wine was made from various berries and even dandelions.

Beer

Prince Otto von Bismarck gave his name to numerous dishes and products, some of which are still commonly available in German grocery stores. Bismarck had rather simple tastes that shocked Emperor Napoleon III after he surrendered to the Prussians at the Battle of Sedan on September 2, 1870. Bismarck was known to drink a bizarre mixture of brown beer and champagne.

While beer was a staple drink in ancient Egypt, it was not all that popular among the Roman armies, whose crusaders and many armed forces crisscrossed Europe for centuries. The lasting legacy of "military" beer came much later.

To put it simply, beer does not travel well. Beer rations loaded on Royal Navy ships that would see months, even years of duty in the Caribbean or in Asia would turn bad in only a few weeks. Beginning in 1655, rations of one pint of wine or a half-pint of spirit were substituted when the beer went bad. Wine and spirits would be diluted in a 3:1 ratio with water. Sugar and lemon or lime juice were added resulting in a mixture known as grog.

Co-author Agostino von Hassell has been served John Courage beer aboard Royal Navy ships. It is a Navy beer capable of withstanding the high heat of the tropics, arctic temperatures, and the constant movement of sailing ships. John Courage was brewed initially, and almost exclusively, for the Royal Navy. Some additions to the traditional brew allowed this ink-black ale with a strong kick to withstand the rigors of life at sea.

John Courage is just one example of the military

Drinking Songs
A soldier's life, oh, that means being merry.
Soldiers drink champagne, champagne
with their roast pork.
7th Hanoverian Infantry Regiment, 1864

So we live, so we live,
so we live every day
in the nicest of all drinking companies.
With brandy in the morning,
with beer at noon,
with the maiden at night
in the sleeping quarters.
Prussian Hussar Regiment No. 5, 1752

(Opposite) MOSCATEL DE SETÚBAL
"TORNA VIAGEM" (Return Trip)

During the nineteenth century, large sailing vessels majestically crossing the seas and trading goods at the ports of call conducted intercontinental commerce. Voyages were successful or not depending on favorable winds and the absence of storms and pirate attacks. They also depended on bartering the products in the holds for merchandise available at the ports of call.

In 1834, José Maria da Fonseca started to make contact with the captains of such vessels, to open up new markets for Portugal's Moscatel wines.

These wines experienced the effects of long journeys and different climatic conditions as they traveled around the world. They crossed the Equator and tropics, finding their way to Asia, South Africa, and South America, mainly to Brazil. Some of the wines were not sold and returned to Portugal crossing the Equator for a second time.

During these long voyages, the wines were improved by the temperature variations that refined their quality, while ageing them and giving them more complexity and style. Those that returned to Portugal even changed names. They became known as the "Torna-Viagem" (return trip) wines and were sought after as valuable rarities.

Some of these wines, ancient voyagers from the past century, still exist as shown in the picture. There are only sixty bottles, all registered in 1900. These bottles are part of the stock of Moscatel "Torna-Viagem" wine, a very special treasure kept at José Maria da Fonseca "frasqueira." The cellar where they are stored has maintained a steady balance of humidity, light, and temperature since 1775.

prompting a customized recipe. As Germans started to explore the world, and to seize their own colonies and trading ports, they brewed special "export" beers, the most famous of which is Beck's Beer.

But Germany, almost by accident, created what may be the world's largest beer brewery. After the German Imperial Navy seized the port of Tsingtao and the province of Kiauchow in China for the German Empire, it became quickly apparent they needed a local source of beer. In 1903, under the auspices of the Imperial Navy, the "Germania Brewery" was established in Qingdao, producing a typical German beer. Today, the same beer, put in green bottles virtually identical in shape to Beck's beer bottles, is still brewed in Qingdao by the Tsingtao

Brewery Group. It is one of the best selling beers in the world, courtesy of the German Imperial Navy.

Wine

Winemaking has been traced back to the early Sumerians and other ancient civilizations, but it was ancient Rome's imperial growth that created much of the wine culture that now dominates Europe's landscape and economic coffers.

Roman legions developed the skill, the know-how, and a thirst for winemaking that spread throughout the Roman empire and that envelopes Europe today. The Romans planted vineyards in locations as diverse as the Rhone Valley of France, the Mosel Valley in Germany and even in Southern Britain. Their motivation was based on the simple logistics of having local sources of wine and easing the load of the military supply system as they traversed Europe.

As Rome's legions moved north, land was set aside for retiring legionnaires as part of a complex policy to "Romanize" the empire. One result is the lower Rhone Valley near Orange, where many retirees of the V Legion settled and started the vineyards, which then became the foundation of this region's flourishing wine industry.

This tradition led to the practice of retired French Foreign Legionnaires producing wine. They often

(Opposite) It was customary in the elegant regiments of Czarist Russia to create miniature copies of the helmets worn by the officers. A distinctive miniature was placed in the mess at each officer's table setting. They served as small shot glasses for vodka. (From the collection of Christopher & Karin Ross, New York City).

(Below) Record book of the champagne house Veuve Clicquot indicating sales during World War II. The rather major "sales" to Germany were essentially confiscations by German military forces.

were, after all, heavy drinkers, although their history clearly shows that more Legionnaires died of thirst than of cirrhosis. Legionnaires enjoyed the natural medicinal qualities of wine, as well as its ability to properly reduce thirst.

Always true to its principle of never leaving its men behind, neither in combat nor in life, the Legion created a series of structures to support elderly Legionnaires. Among those structures is the "L'Institution des Invalides de Puyloubier," a place where retired legionnaires take great care in growing the grapevines that produce the widely acclaimed "Cotês de Provence." This vineyard, located at the base of Mount Sainte Victorie, receives an optimal amount of sun and rain for raising superb wine-making grapes. Varieties typical to the region include Grenache, Cinsault, Sirah and Mourvèdre. The wines produced reflect the qualities of this "terroir," with a typical Mediterranean climate and a somewhat clayish soil. The bottled wines are usually well-balanced, strong wines with heavy bodies and rich aromas, perfect for serving with meals.

In Portugal, most vineyards are referred to as Quintas; the word "Quinta" is derived from the Roman "quintilius" or one-fifth. Roman legionnaires typically claimed one-fifth of the land for the Empire and then often used that land to plant a vineyard and called it a "Quinta." Beyond just claiming the land, however, legionnaires developed novel wine-making procedures, some of which remain characteristic of Portuguese wines today. For instance, in the hot Alentejo region of Portugal, winemaking can be tricky. The extreme summer temperatures impact the aging of the wines, but Romans solved the problem by digging deep holes in the ground and inserting giant amphorae. Each day, a laborer would have to stir the contents of the large clay jugs, each containing as much as 5,000 liters of fermenting wine, allowing the cool fluid from the bottom to rise to the top.

The amphorae, called talha, are made of clay and are produced in a variety of dimensions. Approximately 2,000 years ago, clay was the best solution to overcome the problem of finding satisfactory wood appropriate for making barrels. Clay is quite porous and allows for fast oxygenation. The amphorae are lined with pine pitch so that the wine is not in direct contact with the clay. Wines produced this way typically have a harsh undertone from contact with the pine resin, a flavor many consumers do not enjoy. Several producers have even replaced pitch with a special paint in order to avoid its characteristic flavor. The Romans often used olive oil as a liner, but today's wine makers choose not to do it, claiming that it brings a rancid flavor to the wine.

In some vineyards, the technology has not changed, and one can still find vintners in the Southern Portuguese province of Alentejo using the same technique. One such wine is the famous Tinto da Talha, produced in the Redondo region, one of eight sub-divisions of the Alentejo. Tinto da Talha wines are produced at low temperatures maintained by pouring water over the amphorae. This wine is made without preservatives and, consequently, suffers a quick evolution. It is classified as a young, tasteful, and fruity wine that is best consumed within a year of being produced.

There are in the annals of history many references to wine, the role it played in conquering nations, and the

(Above) Canard-Duchêne is one of the best champagnes made in France. The label, decorated with a cavalry saber, carries the slogan: "Le Champagne que l'on saber." This indicates the old custom, still performed today, to use a saber and in one well-practiced swipe to remove the cork from the bottle.

(Right) This silver champagne bucket was made for a Prussian Hussar officer in the years before World War I — in the shape of a traditional fur shako. Note the Iron Cross engraved into the champagne bucket. The champagne bottle — empty now — is decorated with a miniature Royal Swedish military neck decoration. (From the collection of Christopher & Karin Ross, New York City).

(Opposite) Here is one of many advertisements for America's most famous soft drink. Other ads, which ran during World War II, featured Marines and other services.

results that developed from cultural interaction. Some outstanding examples include Britain's Admiral Horatio Nelson who was quite fond of fine cookery and a connoisseur of wine. Large quantities of Marsala are reported to have been served to the Admiral aboard ships he commandeered, especially during his many years of fighting the French.

Admiral Nelson's prime adversary was Napoleon, another leader who most certainly reveled in fine food and wine. Napoleon's favorite wine was a burgundy named Champertin and he had quite a reputation of consuming copious amounts of this wine while he ate with great haste, as was his custom.

Another important reference to wine in military history is "Jarhead Red," a cabernet developed by Adam Firestone, a former Marine captain and chief executive officer of California's Firestone Vineyard along with vineyard foreman Ruben Dominguez, a former Marine sergeant. Since 2001 the pair have been combining cabernet and merlot grapes into a palatable wine. A portion of the proceeds from each bottle goes to the Marine Corps Scholarship Foundation to benefit the children of killed or wounded leathernecks.

Like the Roman legionnaires of years' past, retired U.S. Navy Captain Richard Alexander, took to winemaking as well. He owned Hopelands Vineyards, a Rhode Island winery that produced a variety of delightful premium table wines. A portion of the proceeds from each bottle supported the Marine Corps Law Enforcement Foundation that awards scholarships to the children of fallen Marines and law enforcement officials who were Marines. Anyone who imbibed these fine wines did so with the knowledge that each sip supported the children of fallen comrades.

Returning to Italy, the heart of the Roman Empire, retired Colonel Giuseppe Coria has applied his rigid military discipline to the production of several fine wines in the Cerasuolo region of Sicily. Colonel Coria has turned his family estate into a model farm for cultivating grapes and producing his renowned Cerasuolo Stravecchio Siciliano, a wine that the colonel ages for as long as 40 years, after which it strongly resembles a fine sherry.

The colonel also produces a wine he calls Perpetuo, which is made using an ancient Sicilian custom that results in a perpetual wine. Aged in wooden barrels, the colonel draws a small quantity from each barrel every year and replaces the drawn amount with an equal amount of new wine. While the practice sounds simple, it is only successful with the right kind of wine under very stringent conditions.

Colonel Coria uses Stravecchio Siciliano for the Perpetuo as well, and the few bottles that become

That *Extra* Something!

...You can spot it every time

1863 "Stonewall Jackson taught us what *the pause that refreshes* really means."

A new idea joined the army in "the sixties". It was the rest pause . . . with refreshment. Here's what a Coca-Cola advertisement said about it in 1931:—

"Stonewall Jackson always got there first. On the march he gave his men rations of sugar and at intervals required them to lie down for a short rest. Thus he marched troops farther and faster than any other general in the field. Since his day all marching troops have been given a short rest period out of every hour."

To our fighting men and war workers everywhere that fact has new importance. A short pause helps you in any task. A pause for the energy-giving refreshment of ice-cold Coca-Cola helps you even more.

1943 Today *the pause that refreshes* with ice-cold Coca-Cola is a standby of men in the Army, Navy and Marine Corps—and a standby of the great army of men and women war workers. Every time you enjoy a Coke it tells you all over again what it means to morale.

Even with war and so many Coca-Cola bottling plants in enemy-occupied countries, our fighting men are delighted to find Coca-Cola being bottled in so many places all over the globe.

The best is always the better buy!

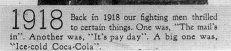

1918 Back in 1918 our fighting men thrilled to certain things. One was, "The mail's in". Another was, "It's pay day". A big one was, "Ice-cold Coca-Cola".

Coca-Cola 5¢

available each year are nearly impossible to acquire because of their popularity.

In the United Kingdom, many regiments have attempted to maintain high-quality wine cellars. Many British regiments still control stocks of superb old ports and decent clarets. Details on these stocks are hard to come by since the wine supply of the better regiments, such as the Irish Guards, is guarded nearly as closely as a state secret. Yet, a cursory review of existing menu cards from British regiments, some of which are reproduced here, show that the selection of wines would impress even the snootiest sommelier in Paris or New York.

Some military organizations have their own special wines bottled just for them. Even very small units have their own wines in Europe. For instance, the Papal Swiss Guards, now numbering just 100 active duty members, drink "Lugana doc" grown in the Lago di Garda region close to the Swiss border. It is an almost sweet white wine with a honey color. The Sovereign Military Order of Malta, often referred to as the Order of Malta or Knights of Malta, holds on to an impressive castle at Magione in Umbria, north of Rome, where they make red and white wines for exclusive use by the Order.

Champagne is yet another important story, especially in France. Most famous here is the delicate Canard-Duchêne, which is the "house" champagne of key French regiments such as the Republican Guards or the Military School at St. Cyr. The crossed swords decorating the labels come from the custom of "Sabre le Champagne," or using a sword to open the bottle. With a sharp cavalry saber, a soldier will, with some amazing skill, slice upwards with a movement similar to what a cavalryman would use to decapitate an enemy and "remove" the champagne cork.

Wines and war have been, and probably will always be, strongly linked. Wine is often war booty. For instance, record books from the famed French champagne house Veuve Clicquot Ponsardin show the quantity of bottles "sold" ("sold" equals looted here) to the German army in the Second World War:

1940: 463,962
1941: 910,914
1942: 802,740
1943: 1,060,708
1944: 686,732
1945: 0
Quantity of bottles "sold" to Allied forces:
1946: 153,536
1947: 13,290

Coca-Cola®

In modern history, Coca-Cola® has been a surprisingly significant drink.

Coke® or Coca-Cola® was largely a national drink in the nineteenth century, but by the outbreak of World War II "the drink that refreshes" was being sold in 78 countries. Some called it "soda" or "pop" or "soda pop."

Coca-Cola® opened its first plant in Germany in 1929, but initial sales were sluggish. Coca-Cola® entered an aggressive marketing campaign. During the 1936 Olympics in Berlin, Adolph Hitler, along with many international athletes and visitors, was photographed drinking the cola. Despite concerns by the Nazi health ministry over the caffeine content, the beverage was a huge success. Local soft-drink manufacturers were threatened by the popularity of the American soda and an executive of a German company producing Afri-cola went so far in 1936 as to steal Coca-Cola® bottle caps indicating the drink was kosher and using them to blast the beverage as "Jewish-American." In an effort to counter the marketing attack, Coca-Cola® GmbH executive Max Keith had his branch pass out "sodas" for free at Hitler youth rallies and displayed huge swastikas at bottling conventions. The gambit was a rousing success for Coca-Cola's® German branch; in 1939, Coca-Cola® GmbH sold 4.5 million cases of soda.

Coca-Cola's® marketing efforts back home in the United States were making headway as well. Coca-Cola® president Robert Woodruff was so moved by the loss of American lives at Pearl Harbor, that he gave a company order promising to "See every man in uniform get a bottle of Coca-Cola® for five cents wherever he is and whatever the cost to the company."

It was a brilliant maneuver. When Woodruff gave the order he had no idea that troops being forced to drink nasty-tasting, heavily chlorinated water would be so anxious to drink Coke® instead. And he did not realize how accommodating the military would be. General George C. Marshall signed a circular permitting theater commanders to order Coca-Cola® bottle plants to be built at the front line. Coca-Cola® employees, dressed in military drab flew to Europe as technical observers where they oversaw the construction of bottling plants behind enemy lines.

Coca-Cola® was a huge hit among American GIs and, in June 1943, General Dwight D. Eisenhower, seeing the need to improve the morale of troops fighting in the desert environment of North Africa, ordered eight Coca-Cola® bottling plants be sent to supply allied troops fighting there. By the end of World War II, Coca-Cola® had distributed more than 5 billion bottles of Coke®. In gratitude, sixty-four Coca-Cola® bottling plants built by the U.S. military were turned over to the corporation free of charge.

Then there was Marshal Georgi Zhukov, the Russian war hero. When General Eisenhower introduced Coke® to Zhukov at the Potsdam Conference in 1945, the Russian liked it. But he also knew how Stalin would react if one of his generals was seen drinking an American imperialist symbol. Allied General Mark Clark made a special request to Coke® executive Jim Farley and the folks at Coke® were as accommodating as could be. A chemist removed the soda's caramel color, and they put the drink in a clear bottle with a white cap and red star and sent it to Zhukov as "White Coke."

In World War II, Coke® was an American imperialist symbol, a kosher food, a fake communist beverage and the drink of Hitler Youth. Most people thought the war was about good, evil, competing ideologies and so on, but for Coca-Cola® the issue was simpler: more Coke® or less Coke®.

Naval Coffee

In modern times, coffee became the single most important drink aboard men-of-war and in naval services such as the United States or Royal Marines. Coffee is common in the senior or naval service, and all western land forces consume incredible quantities of coffee, typically black — no milk, no sugar, and occasionally a pinch of salt among submariners. Some Marines call this "lifer juice."

Co-author Herm Dillon can attest to this. While serving in Phu Bai, Vietnam, he was promoted to corporal and taken out of the field where he fixed Jeeps and other vehicles, often lying in mud and working in the monsoon rains. He was given a job as an office pogue, a Jarhead term for a non-fighting Marine. "Being a pogue was great," recalls Dillon. "I was dry, no longer covered in mud, grease and oil, and it was relatively safe. The only downside was that I had to share an office with a group of lifers, both NCOs and commissioned officers. They drank coffee constantly." In the office there was an electric coffee maker, placed in the charge of Cpl. Dillon.

Unfortunately, or fortunately, depending on how you look at it, the corporal didn't drink coffee nor did he know how to make it. "A strange thing happened

(Below) The Mystery of Naval Coffee – 1914
Coffee, more than rum, is lifeblood of naval forces. This set shows a Prussian coffee cup filled with black coffee. Admiral von Tirpitz acquired the teaspoon in Albany, New York's capitol, during a tour of the United States. Other Admiral von Tirpitz mementos include one of his Naval daggers, his model of a torpedo, his map for official writing papers, a book on battle ships built by the famous Schichau Yard, a handbook on naval combat fleets, a letter to his wife Marie, and a business card from Count von Zeppelin, who invented the dirigible while serving under Tirpitz.

(Above) Friendly rivalry among the branches of the U.S. armed forces doesn't stop at football. The Army and the Marine Corps both claim to have the recipe for the world's best mint julep. Whether you prefer your julep with spring water or branch, with rum or without, one thing is certain; the julep is ingrained in U.S. military socializing. Props in the photo include a set of 1914 U.S. Army Field Regulations, a 1991 model of the 45 pistol, and a medal from the United States Civil War.

almost immediately after I was promoted. The officers and staff began to receive daily compliments on my coffee. I just poured a bunch of grounds in and filled the coffeemaker with water, never bothering to measure anything. Moreover, and I think this was the key to my favored coffee, I never washed the coffee maker. There was no convenient place to wash it. I reckoned that taking it to a water buffalo and washing it with cold water without soap wouldn't help. The mess hall was the only place with hot water and soap and I avoided the pot washer like the plague. In time, the inside of the pot was brown, resembling the coffee itself. And the browner it got, the more my fellow Marines liked the coffee. On my last day in country before returning back to the U.S., Gunny Taylor told me that I would be sorely missed in the office because of the fine coffee I made. Yes, Marines, especially lifers, like their coffee."

Coffee is an essential ingredient in military rations and at formal military dinners. It is the fuel for long nights next to a radio, on watch, or on the bridge of a man-of-war. In many ways, the quality matters a lot, but that has not yet impacted on the suppliers to the U.S. military who insist on calling their instant coffees either "Type II" or "Type III." Your authors have never, ever seen "Type I."

During a war, access to coffee becomes a major quest. In World War II, German forces, cut off from most imports, resorted to "Erzatzkaffee" made of roots and chicory.

Throughout the Napoleonic wars, when shortages of imported coffee beans arose, Napoleon offered a major monetary prize for a substitute. The winner created a questionable concoction where one harvested the berries of a grown asparagus plant, dried them, and then roasted them in a coffee roaster or in a hot oven. The "beans" were then ground and used just like coffee with, reportedly, a nice caramel flavor.

The Mint Julep

Mint has been used to flavor foods and beverages for many centuries. Researchers have found references in recipes of Arabs, who referred to it as "julab," and the Portuguese called it "julepe." The Romans called it "julapium," and the French, well, the term "julep" is of French derivation. Using mint to flavor a drink with bourbon certainly comes from the Southern United States, but exactly where in the South, no one is really sure, both Virginia and Georgia lay claim to the recipe.

What is not debated is the popularity the drink has enjoyed among U.S. Army, Naval, and Marine Corps officers. The U.S. Army prides itself on a recipe published in a letter from Lieutenant General Simon Bolivar Buckner Jr. to Major General William D. Connor, who at the time was serving as the Superintendent of the United States Military Academy at West Point. General Conner had written to General Buckner in March 1937 requesting his "formula" for mixing mint juleps.

TYPES MILITAIRES

FRANCE 1865 ___ OFF.R DE DRAGONS

(Above) A French officer of Dragoons lifts a well-filled glass of champagne in a dramatic toast, probably to Bacchus. The other officers in attendance look quite horrified on this nineteenth Century French cartoon, at the presumably "boorish" behavior of a fellow officer.

General Buckner described it as a simple process consisting of whittling off the part of the mint that didn't look like an elephant. He went on to describe the process as a ceremony, so much for simplicity, and one that "must be performed by a gentleman possessing a true sense of the artistic, a deep reverence for the ingredients, and a proper appreciation of the occasion. It is a rite that must not be entrusted to a novice, statistician, nor a Yankee. It is a heritage of the Old South, an emblem of hospitality, and a vehicle in which the noble minds can travel together upon the flower-strewn paths of a happy and congenial thought."

General Buckner suggests you go to a spring where cool, crystal clear water bubbles from under a bank of dew-washed ferns. In a "consecrated" vessel, dip up a little water at the source.

Then find and gather the sweetest and most tender spearmint shoots and gently carry them home.

Select a decanter of Kentucky bourbon distilled by a master hand, mellowed with age, yet still vigorous

and inspiring. Prepare an ancestral sugar bowl, a row of silver goblets, some spoons, and some ice, and you are ready to start.

Into a canvas bag, pound twice as much ice as you think you will need. Make it as fine as snow, keep it dry and do not allow it to degenerate into slush.

Into each goblet, put a slightly heaping teaspoon of granulated sugar, barely cover this with spring water and slightly bruise one mint leaf into this, leaving the spoon in the goblet.

Then pour the elixir from the decanter until the goblets are about one-fourth full. Fill the goblets with snowy ice, sprinkling in a small amount of sugar as you fill. Wipe the outside of the goblets dry, and embellish copiously with mint.

Then comes the delicate and important operation of frosting. By proper manipulation of the spoon, the ingredients are circulated and blended until nature, wishing to take a further hand, and add another of its beautiful phenomena, encrusts the whole goblet in a glistening coat of white frost.

Thus, harmoniously blended by the deft touches of a skilled hand, you have a beverage eminently appropriate for honorable men and beautiful women.

It's not known whether United States Marine Corps Colonel Ben Finney ever saw General Buckner's "formula" for a mint julep but his ability to make one gained him some great fame and an interesting few days on R & R, while serving in France between wars. Needing some time away from the field — Paris that is — Colonel Finney asked a friend if he knew of a place where he could get away for a few days and rest up. His friend, Cole Porter, the jazz musician, suggested a cozy hostelry called the Bas Breu in a small town called Barbizon about 60 kilometers south of Paris. The colonel tells the story in this way in his book *Once a Marine - Always a Marine*.

"Egon (his German attaché) and I didn't arrive at the Bas Breu until the next afternoon. We were escorted through an open courtyard to our room. There was only one person in the courtyard, a fairly large, athletic-looking man sitting at one of the tables. After stowing my gear, I returned to the courtyard. As I did, the man at the table asked me in a loud voice if I knew how to make a mint julep. 'Certainly, I do. I'm from Virginia!' I answered. 'I don't give a damn if you're from the Ides of March,' he came back, 'if you know how to make a julep. There's a big bed of mint over there, and I've got a case of damned

good bourbon (hard to get in France), but these Frog bastards don't know what a julep is, let alone how to concoct one.' 'Break out the bourbon while I cut some mint. Your problem is solved,' I told him. I made so many juleps, the Frogs learned the knack, and from then on it was simply a case of Ernest Hemmingway and I sitting still and sticking our noses in mint."

The Colonel wrote that "at the end of four days there was an elegant sufficiency of mint left, but a case of good bourbon lasts only so long."

Colonel Finney acknowledges that most people have heard of a mint julep but few "mixologists" know how to properly make one. Here is his recipe:

Break and drop into a dry, 10-ounce silver or pewter tankard, with handle, 15 or 20 (depending on the size of the leaves) fresh, I repeat, fresh mint leaves.

Add a scant half-teaspoon of granulated sugar and two tablespoons of water.

Then muddle the leaves until they are well crushed and the sugar is dissolved.

Pack the tankard with finely crushed ice.

Pour, not measure, enough bourbon into the tankard to come to about an inch below the rim. After thoroughly stirring, add crushed ice up to the rim and float thereon a teaspoon of Barbados rum.

Insert two large or three small, sprigs of mint to the right of the handle, allowing mint to protrude two inches above the rim.

When imbibing, allow your nose into the protruding mint and sniff and quaff at the same time.

Recipe author's note: Oh boy! My mouth is watering.

After reading the two recipes, which have some admitted similarities, it's easy to understand why Marines are known as "First to Fight," in that Finney's preparation of an exquisite mint julep takes a shorter course.

Apart from bourbon and mint, sugar is a key ingredient. And this is another fruit of military prowess. Sugar, which would become a major ingredient in the lavish banquets of the Stuart and Tudor societies and the courts of kings and princes all over Europe, made its first true entry into Europe as a result of the Crusades. While the ancient Egyptians, Persians, and even the troops of Alexander the Great knew sugar, it remained virtually unknown in Europe until the thirteenth century. And even then, sugar remained a rare commodity, available only to the richest families. The Crusaders encountered sugar all over the Middle East and even in Sicily. Arabs had large plantations of sugar cane and taught the Crusaders how to refine the precious substance from the cane. Slowly and over time, sugar replaced honey, the main sweetener of ancient Rome and subsequent years. Note that sugar was often prized loot when English privateers seized Spanish or Portuguese galleons, ranking in importance and value just below gold and silver. ✄

SPRUCE BEER

Spruce Beer is made all over Europe. The German black beer is made from spruce, and the Russian Army used to have a special brew enlivened with horseradish, ginger, mustard, and an assortment of spices. Spruce beer is also a good source of vitamins and is proven to help prevent scurvy. This recipe has the laconic New England touch:

Ingredients
1 pint good spruce extract
12 pounds treacle
7 gallons water
1 pint yeast

Instructions
1. Bring spruce extract, treacle and 3 gallons of water to a boil, then let stand 1 hour.
2. Add 3 or 4 gallons of hand warm water and the yeast.
3. Pour into a 10-gallon cask.
4. Bung her up.
5. Bottle her off.

Civil War soldiers in the United States were just as ingenious, and just as thirsty, as any other soldiers, and whenever they were in camp long enough, they set about constructing their own personal (and discreet) brewing and distilling operations. Both armies had mountaineers with long experience in clandestine whiskey production, and they used their talents just as cleverly as they had at home. New England troops were reported to have been fond of a special homemade brew. No one knows exactly what was in it, but it was called "forty-rod," supposedly because the drinker could down a cupful and still stagger forty rods before he collapsed. Southern troops had a beverage, which they fondly called "pine tops," or "Spruce Beer." They made it from fresh young pine boughs, but the result was just the old-fashioned spruce beer similar to the preceding recipe with perhaps an extra dash of turpentine in it.

Ingredients
sprigs of spruce or pine
water
molasses

Instructions
1. To brew spruce beer, take the young tender sprigs of spruce or pine and boil them in water for three hours.
2. Strain the resulting liquor into a wooden cask and add one quart of molasses to every six gallons of liquor.
3. Contemporary accounts note that ". . . it will be a great advantage to the men not to drink it till it is two days old."
4. For thorough fermentation, a longer period would be desirable.

CHATHAM ARTILLERY PUNCH

One example of a regimental punch is the Chatham Artillery punch. The punch commemorates the famous unit organized in 1786 in Chatham County, Georgia, by veterans of the Revolutionary War. Chatham Artillery is still active today and its punch is one of the best, as well as one of the strongest. To make it, begin with a base of pink Catawba wine with a little brown sugar and a few lemons for flavoring. Then add equal quantities of rum, brandy, rye whiskey, and gin, and finally, when ready to serve, add a triple quantity of champagne. It tastes like fruit juice and kicks like a 32-pounder. This recipe will make twelve gallons, enough for 100 parched people with little to spare. The stock must be aged for one or two weeks prior to serving if the punch is to be smooth and mellow. Without this blending period, the taste will be somewhat harsh.

Ingredients
1 pound green tea in 2 gallons of cold water, allowed to stand overnight, then strained
3 gallons pink Catawba wine
1 gallon rum
1 gallon brandy
1 gallon rye whiskey
5 pounds brown sugar
2 quarts cherries
juice of 3 dozen lemons
1 gallon gin (to make it smooth)
12 quarts champagne

Instructions
1. Mix the tea and juice together first, preferably in a cedar tub, but any clean container will do.
2. Add the sugar, cherries, Catawba wine, and liquors.
3. Let this stock sit for a week or two covered, preferably in glass bottles.
4. When ready to serve, pour over a block of ice in a punch bowl and add the champagne.
5. The stock and finished juice should be stirred well. Once chilled, serve, and enjoy.

(Opposite) Serving superb wine in the mess has long been a hallmark of British regiments as these menus from the 1950s show. A dinner on June 20, 1958, held by the 264th (7th London) Field regiment in the Royal Artillery Mess in Woolwich, featured costly wines such as Chateau Perron 1953 and the famous Chateau Lynch Bage 1953 from Bordeux. A rare 1922 Warre's Vintage Port was also served at a dinner on January 30, 1959 held by the Essex Yeomanry. At that dinner, a Chateay Gruaud la Rose 1948 and a 1952 Chablis accompanied a roast capon and a turbot. A Royal Artillery dinner on June 3, 1955 again featured the elegant Warre's 1922 along with other wines.

PROGRAMME OF MUSIC

1.	March	Cockleshell Heroes	Dunn
2.	Selection	Dvorak Memories	Dvorak
3.	Suite	Three Light Pieces	Fletcher
4.	Waltz Potpouri	...Classical...	Arr Hildebranot
5.	Tango	The Golden Tango	Sylvester
6.	Selection	My Fair Lady	Loewe
7.	Waltz	Eton Boating Song	Kaps
8.	Galop	Leaps and Bounds	Brianne

REGIMENTAL MARCHES

Essex Yeomanry
Slow March Past   "The Duke of York"

Quick March Past   "The British Grenadiers"

Trot Past   "The Keel Row"

Canter and Gallop   "Bonnie Dundee"

The Royal Artillery Slow March
(Composed by H.R.H. The Duchess of Kent, 1843)

MENU

——

Turtle Soup

Fillet Sole Duglère

Roast Spring Chicken
Brussels Sprouts
Parisienne Potatoes

Omelette en Suprise

Coffee

WINES

Fileno

Sainte Elise

Beaujolais

Warre '22

WINES

Fileno

Sainte Elise

Beaujolais

Warre '22

... "...erations" ... Mozart.

...from "The Chocolate Soldier" ... J. Strauss.

5. Petite Suite de Concert ... O. Straus.

6. Intermezzo ..."Forgotten Dreams"... Coleridge Taylor.

7. Tunes from ... "My Fair Lady" ... Anderson.
Loewe.

Quick March Past   "The British Grenadiers"

Trot Past ...   "The Keel Row"

Canter and Gallop   "Bonnie Dundee"

The Royal Artillery Slow March
(Composed by H.R.H. The Duchess of Kent, 1843)

Melon

Fillet Sole Bonne Fe...

Roast Aylesbury D...
Green Pea...
New Potat...

Strawberries and...

Croute Tamis...

Coffee

WINES

Fileno
Chateau Perron '53
Chateau Lynch Bages '53
Archilles Freres
Warre's '22
Cognac
Liqueurs

WINES

——

Fileno
Chateau Perron '53
Chateau Lynch Bages '53
Archilles Freres
Warre's '22
Cognac
Liqueurs

MENU

Grape Fruit Cocktail

Supreme de Turbot Bonne Femme

Roast Capon

Garden Peas
New Potatoes
Fruit Salad and Cream
Barquette de Jambon

Coffee

WINES

Fileno
Chablis '52
Chateau Gruaud la Rose '48
Vinay Pere et Fils '45
Warre '22
Cognac

1.	March	"Sea Songs"	Vaughan Williams.
2.	Overture ...	"The Bohemian Girl" ...	Balfe.
3.	A Selection from the Ballet	"Les Sylphides"	Chopin.
4.	Waltz	"Gold and Silver"	Lehar.
5.	Descriptive Piece	"The Grasshopper Dance"	Bucalo...
6.	Some of the Borodin Melodies from	"Kismet..."	arr...

Quick March Past   "The British Grenadi..."

Trot Past ...   "The Keel Row"

Canter and Gallop   "Bonnie Dundee"

The Royal Artillery Slow March
(Composed by H.R.H. The Duchess of Kent, 1843)

WINES

Fileno
Chablis '52
Chateau Gruaud la Rose '48
Vinay Pere et Fils '45
Warre '22
Cognac

Tuba

On the Pacific front during the Second World War, Allied enlisted men were denied the expensive opportunity to get good liquor, but once again American ingenuity prevailed. If they couldn't buy liquor, they simply made their own, and literally thousands of brewing and distilling operations sprang up throughout the entire South Pacific area. One of the favorite drinks the budding brew masters produced was tuva or tuba, named after a native palm beverage and produced on Guam, New Guinea, the Philippines, and numerous other islands. It had the advantage of being almost instant alcohol.

To make it, the thirsty Marine sliced the top of a young coconut and added sugar and raisins to the milk inside. Then he either put the top back on or plugged up the holes and propped the nut up in the sun for fermentation to take place. He didn't have long to wait. As a general rule, tuba was graded as 2-hour, 4-hour, or 6-hour. Six-hour tuba was the acme of the brew.

The Bottle of Death

Soldiers throughout the ages have been known to save a good bottle of their favorite libation for special occassions.

The pilots of Escadrille had no need to suffer for want of their favorite beverage, and they celebrated that happy situation by naming their two lion cub mascots "Whiskey" and "Soda." Of all the whiskey available, however, there was one extra-special source for a drink. This was a bottle of aged bourbon that ground soldier Paul Rockwell gave his flying brother Kiffin. Rockwell and his fellow flyers promptly declared the bottle sacrosanct. Dubbed "The Bottle of Death," it could only be tapped by a pilot returning from a kill. Each drink from its precious contents celebrated the downing of an enemy plane.

Jungle Juice

A first cousin of raisin-jack, jungle juice was made from fruit of any kind, sugar, water, and when possible, raisins. These ingredients were put in a container and set out to ferment. Five-gallon water cans were the favorite containers, but washtubs and old barrels or drums of every sort were pressed into use. The soldiers preferred closed containers, because the number of fruit flies that clustered around the open ones attracted the attention of officers who might confiscate the brew just as it reached the drinking stage. When they did use a closed can, however, they had to be sure to vent it. Otherwise it would explode, and explosions around the perimeter of a camp always attracted unwanted attention. As popular as it was during the island campaigns of the Pacific in WWII, jungle juice is one beverage that few veterans have yearned to encounter ever again.

Ingredients
3 pounds sugar
1 quart canned peaches or other fruit in syrup
1 box yeast
5 gallons water

Instructions
1. Put sugar, fruit, and yeast in a five-gallon water can.
2. Fill the remainder of the can with water.
3. Close can but vent to release fermentation gases and place in the sun from four days to two weeks or until the bubbling ceases.
4. Clean off the scum or strain through cheesecloth.

The brewers on Sir Graham Moore Island created their own potato-based version:

Ingredients
10 pounds dehydrated potatoes
20 pounds sugar
6 ounces 91 proof grain alcohol
10 gallons of water

Instructions
1. Pour potatoes, sugar, and alcohol into a ten-gallon drum.
2. Add enough water to fill the drum almost to the top.
3. Cover mixture and allow to stand for five weeks.
4. Remove scum.
5. Fill canteens.

B₂C₂

Many a veteran can still reminisce happily over the memories of the time his outfit found a real cache of contraband liquor and liberated it — sometimes by the truckload. One of these occasions led to the invention of a memorable drink with a name like a chemical formula: B_2C_2. The time was the spring of 1945, and the U.S. 21st Corps had just crossed the Rhine when word flashed into the Corps G-2 office that a Wehrmacht liquor storage cavern had been located. Acting with their usual dispatch and acumen, the men of G-2 promptly sent a jeep and trailer, and a 2 1/2 ton truck to the discovery site. Both returned with fine liqueurs, which were generously distributed throughout the corps. Here was a challenge, and G-2 set out to lick it. They determined to invent a combination of these beverages that would be both palatable and suitable for serious drinking. After considerable patient and selfless experimentation, they produced a concoction that was exactly right. It was made of equal parts of brandy and Benedictine (B_2), a like amount of cointreau, and enough champagne (C_2) to fill the remaining portion of a tall glass. Here is how this smooth and delightful beverage was made in western Germany in the spring of 1945:

Ingredients
1 jigger Benedictine
1 jigger Brandy
1 jigger Cointreau
champagne - enough to fill a tall glass
Optional: Ice, sliced fruit

When drunk by its originators, the liquors of the B_2C_2 were at cool room temperature, for no ice was available. In the summer of 1945, however, veterans of U.S. 21st Corps G-2 met in New York on their way to take part in the expected attack on Japan, and they decided to reminisce over a pitcher of B_2C_2 at the café Trouville. Money was no object to men with such a short time in the States and such a future, so they duly initiated the bartender into the mysteries of their invention. They found his version of the beverage much improved by the addition of ice and various fruits, which he cut up and stuffed into the pitcher. Ice and sliced fruit have been accepted as optional ever since.

(Above) The Papal Swiss Guards have their very own wine, Lugana (doc). It is produced in Italy south of Lake Garda in a small area between Peschiera and Desenzano. The wine has roots in Roman times and was mentioned as excellent by Pliny. Bacci, in his De Naturali historia vinorum, described Lugana as a "regal wine." It has been described as a "straw-yellow wine with a brilliant taste, featuring the best characteristics of the wines from the Lugana area."

(Right) Two neck-labels of special bottling of Canard-Duchêne: One for the French military academy — the West

Point of France — at St. Cyr, and one for the famous Ècole Polytechnique, which was founded in 1794 and is one of the premier universities of France.

The famous and rather costly Bordeaux wine in the Medoc "Château Palmer" has strong military roots. The estate was acquired by one of the generals who served under the Duke of Wellington. Major General Charles Palmer purchased the vineyard in 1814 after the Napoleonic Wars. Originally, the property was called Château d'Gascq.

An den
Halbardier
Andreas Wicky, GSP
Citta del Vaticano

FRONT LINE FAVORITES: ANECDOTES OF MILITARY DINING

In the year 640, a Welsh army was fighting Saxons in Great Britain. The Roman Catholic Church had lost power and anarchy reigned. Identifying the enemy posed a difficult problem since they dressed and looked alike. Welsh military leaders ordered that each Welsh soldier wear a leek fixed to his helmet so they did not accidentally kill each other. The novel identification worked, and the Welsh soldiers went on to victory against their Saxon enemy.

The leek would go on to become the national emblem of Wales.

Sorbet a British Tradition, Not French

In 1191, England's King Richard I (commonly known as Richard the Lion Hearted) embarked on a Third Crusade and gained a brilliant victory over the Saracen leader Saladin at Arsuf, leading the Christians to within a few miles of Jerusalem.

Legend says it was a particularly hot day, and the English foot soldiers battled well into the afternoon. The knights were held back, sweltering in their armor, their shielding acting like ovens, but they obeyed their king and never broke rank. When Saladin's men were exhausted, Richard's knights charged forward, dispatched the Saracen forces, and captured Saladin. It is said that Saladin was so impressed with Richard that he offered the Crusaders a refreshing dish made from fruit and snow. The English loved the "charbet" and brought the recipe back across Europe where it became known as sorbetto in Italy, sorbet in France, and sherbet in England.

Bread, Not What It Used to Be

King Arthur and the Knights of the Round Table enjoyed some of the finest feasts any soldier could ever imagine. But one of the main parts of those feasts, bread, was "banal." Aye, the bread in Britain's famous castles was baked in large communal ovens that were called "Four Banal," which refers to a community oven for which there were standards for construction and use. Everyone in the castle, from the lowest ranking person to the lord of the castle ate the same bread, which led to the origin of the word "banal," or commonplace.

It was there, however, that banality in the banquets of knights and squires ended. Their feasts were grand

(Opposite) This dessert is served by the nuns of the Order of Baldegg to the Swiss Guards who protect the Pope. The sweet is typically served with Vin Santo.

affairs that included an abundance of wild game, including every type of bird imaginable, in particular unusual birds such as peacocks and swans. Fish and shellfish were also delicacies and were typically prepared in complex sauces and served in an elaborate fashion.

Unfortunately, few written recipes from English castles remain today, but there are general descriptions that give us some idea of what knights ate. Professional cooks prepared food using peasant suppliers for everything from pans and utensils to grains, meat, poultry, pork, fish, and fresh fruit.

Among the most famous kitchens of Europe was that of the Dukes of Burgundy, which served the Knights of the Golden Fleece. One of the most common dishes served to these grand knights consisted of a peacock stuffed with a swan, which in turn was stuffed with a duck and the duck stuffed with a chicken that was stuffed with a quail or pheasant. After roasting, the outer skin of the peacock was re-dressed so it appeared as if a live bird was being served.

The repast was served on five-day-old bread sliced thick so that it was stiff enough to hold the dinner and soak up the various juices and sauces that were served with the meal. This slice of bread was called a trencher. Guests were required to bring their own knives to cut their portions from prepared food, and then they mostly ate with their knives and their fingers, as forks were not invented yet. Nevertheless, using one's knife and fingers was no small matter as there were rules of etiquette on how to cut meat, to sip (not slurp) soup, and to drink and toast.

When the meal was finished, the trencher, now soaked with the juices of the meal, was thrown to the dogs.

Pistolets

When co-author Agostino von Hassell was a child in the Rhineland (Near Cologne and Bonn), certain long thin rolls were called Pistolets, or little pistols. The name dates back to the seventeenth century when French occupation troops put such rolls, rather than weapons, into their pistol holsters.

Alexis Bénoit Soyer

Alexis Bénoit Soyer grew to become known as the greatest chef of the nineteenth century. Born on February 4, 1810, to a family of French grocers, Soyer ignored the wishes of his parents to become a minister and instead followed the career of brother Philippe, who had moved to Paris and established himself as a celebrated chef. In Paris, Soyer attended the Grignon, today known as the Institut National Agronomique

Paris-Grignon, and took a job working at the Douix, Boulevard des Italiens in Paris. Here, at the age of 17, he was a success with 12 chefs working under him, but once again he followed his brother. On the eve of the July Revolution, Alexis sailed to England where Philippe was chef for Adolphus Guelph, the duke of Cambridge.

In 1831, Soyer took employment in the duke of Cambridge's kitchen but soon moved on to become the chef for the duke of Sutherland. He later cooked for the marquis of Waterford and other celebrated London nobles. On June 28, 1838, he prepared a breakfast for 2,000 guests attending Queen Victoria's coronation at London's Reform Club.

Despite all of this success in designing and developing cookery for Europe's richest families, Soyer became concerned about starving people in Ireland and began to write about the famine in Ireland. In April of 1847, Soyer was sent to Dublin by the British government where he built and opened kitchens from which he sold soup and meat at half the price of what other establishments charged. While there, he wrote a book titled *Soyer's Charitable Cookery*, and gave the proceeds, which were most likely limited in that not too many people cared about the plight of the starving Irish, to charities.

Soyer's charities did not, however, go unrecognized. In September 1848, Colonel Dunne investigated efforts to aide the famine victims. The gallant colonel wished to know why Soyer, of the Reform Club, had not been rewarded for his commissariat services. The hint was not lost upon the Irish Ministers. Soyer went on to be known as the "Gastronomic Regenerator of Ireland" and nicknamed by the Irish as "the broth of a boy."

Soyer eventually left the employ of the Reform Club and opened his own restaurant named Gore House in Kensington. The restaurant failed, but he did not. In February 1855, he offered to go to Crimea at his own expense to advise on cookery for soldiers fighting there, and he began revising dietary standards for hospitals. During a visit to Baklava, he worked with Florence Nightingale and the medical staff of hospitals in establishing new provisioning standards. He also spent time as a cook for Britain's fourth division army fighting in Crimea. On returning to London, Soyer lectured at the United Service Institution on cooking for the army and navy, and he designed and built a model kitchen at London's Wellington Barracks.

Soyer was to gain one final nickname after his death in 1858. Historians often refer to him as the man who time forgot. It's said that following his death, all of his belongings were seized by a creditor, possibly the same man that helped him build the Soyer Field Stoves that Soyer had donated to the army. All of Soyer's notes were lost, including all of the humanitarian work he performed on behalf of the British armed forces and the Irish. Beyond being considered to be the greatest chef in the world during his time,

some say he likely saved more lives in his work with the kitchens in military hospitals than did Florence Nightingale. His three books, *A Shilling Cookery Book for the People*, *Soyer's Culinary Campaign*, and *Instructions for Military Hospitals*, changed the basis of nutrition for generations to come.

Historic Recipes

British infantry Captain Henry Rudyerd, who commanded the 15th Regiment during a war of rebellion in Canada (1837-1838), is a wonderful example of how military officers were concerned about food quality. He maintained a detailed book of recipes, called *Memoranda*, that listed wonderful dishes such as a Bengal Curry, various recipes for making curry powder, and Ginger Cordial. Rudyerd grew up in India, where his father served in the British Army, and many of his recipes are based on Indian food. The recipe book is now kept at the Toronto Reference Library.

Ice Cream: Military Food or Not?

It's reported that during the 1940s ice cream became so thoroughly associated with Americans that Japanese military leaders discouraged their soldiers from eating it. Ice cream would never be served to the soldiers in a mess because they viewed it as a food of the meek and one that could never support a hardened soldier.

The Japanese weren't alone in their view. Marine Corps General Lewis B. "Chesty" Puller shared their sentiments. Chesty boasted that the appropriate nourishment for Marines was beer and whisky, not ice cream. The Pentagon did not support the alcohol diet, however, and instituted a regulation that all soldiers fighting in the hot Pacific climate should be served ice cream at least three times a week.

Wiener Schnitzel

Many sources attribute certain Viennese specialties to military exploits. The famous breaded veal cutlet — typically known as Cotoletta Milanese or also as Wiener Schnitzel — may have been brought to Vienna first by Field Marshal Radetzky and later by Emperor Franz Joseph. This often-repeated story is somewhat unproven, but this dish of breaded veal certainly did not originate in Milan. It probably originated with the Spanish soldiers serving under Emperor Charles V. When these troops moved south toward the famous sack of Rome, they reportedly breaded their veal and then fried it.

Tabasco® Sauce

Gourmets throughout the world know Tabasco® sauce, which originated at Avery Island, Louisiana, as the essential hot pepper sauce. It was invented on this

(Opposite) Well-cooked grits, also known as "mealy-pop," and collards are typical field food for Zulu warriors. The short fighting spear, battle stick, and water bottle made from a squash gourd are also typical among Zulu warriors.

hot and humid island in 1868 by the McIlhenny Company, which immediately sent cases to President Ulysses S. Grant.

It was used by Roosevelt's Rough Riders and others on many military campaigns. Since World War II, it has been the single most important culinary ingredient used by American soldiers. Some soldiers have strange beliefs and claim that Tabasco® will kill bacteria and viruses in food (unlike other hot sauces from Louisiana) and improve any dish.

Search the packs of any U.S. military unit and you are likely to find Tabasco®. Aboard ship and in mess halls, gallon-sized Tabasco® bottles are standard. Small camouflaged holsters for sauce bottles are common. And to this day Tabasco® sauce remains one of the few brand-name items in MREs. While all other food is packed in drab envelopes marked with incompre-

hensible language such as "Coffee Type II," some MRE pouches contain miniature 1/8-ounce glass bottles with the familiar bright Tabasco® label.

Much of the success of Tabasco® with the military must be credited to Brigadier General Walter S. McIlhenny, USMC (Retired) whose family owns the brand and the pepper plantations. This general was truly effective in marketing the sauce.

Sicily

Maria Carolina, the wife of Ferdinand I and the sister of Marie Antoinette, imported French chefs to the royal court in Palermo in 1805. Specifically, the very first was Monsieur Robert who was the chef to French Marshall Joaquin Murat.

These chefs became known as "Monzu," a corruption of the word *monsieur*. Gradually the Sicilians and

(Above) Prussia, World War I
Sauerkraut with smoked sausages and capers, served in a standard-issue World War I canteen along with buttered bread. The dish is served on a "Kriegskarte" of the Middle East and shown here with a German Mauser infantry rifle and standard issue bayonet.

(Opposite) Imperial Russia, August 1914
This typical field lunch for a senior Czarist officer includes a special borscht with sausages and assorted meats, black Siberian bread, a spicy cucumber salad, pink Champagne from Russia's Georgia, tea, and jam for the tea. Also pictured are a "Broom-Handle Mauser," a set of eyeglasses manufactured before World War I, Gagarin family silver, a small field icon, a nineteenth century Samovar, and a Fabergecopper cooking pot.

Neapolitans who had apprenticed under the French Monzu took over the kitchens and continued to bear the prestigious title.

Today some chefs in Sicily still proudly carry the title Monzu.

Arab Pasta

At least one historian of pasta secca believes that macaroni was invented by nomadic Bedouin utilizing the newly found properties of hard wheat: it could be dried, made small, and transported for long periods of time, up to many years.

Others suspect that future historians may discover that it was some Arab general in charge of logistics. He would have had to feed the armies of Islam as they exploded out of the Arabian Peninsula in the seventh century, sweeping across North Africa, south-western Europe, and the Middle East over the next two centuries.

Their food needs were enormous, the aridity of these regions meant they couldn't rely on local agriculture — they needed food that was transportable and could be stored for years. What better food than dried macaroni and dried legumes?

Hardtack from Spain

Hardtack, also called ships' biscuit, first appeared in thirteenth century Spain, where it was called *bizcocho*. This twice-baked, unleavened wheat biscuit could easily be carried in the haversacks of troops and would not spoil easily. Thirteenth century notary records of naval affairs of Marseilles and Genoa indicate it was a favorite among mariners.

Ironically, bizcocho also became a misnomer for sponge cake — a light cake made with lots of eggs and cornstarch or potato starch. Even today, bizcocho can mean either sponge cake or biscuit in Spain.

(Above) This shows a menu and music program for the annual dinner of the Order of St. George in Moscow on November 26, 1885. One of the dishes featured on this menu, Chaud-Froid de Foie-Gras a la Carême, is shown on page 119. The medal between the two cards represents the Order of St. George (Imperial Russian Knight's Cross). Directly above the Knight's Cross is a silver brooch by Faberge and above that is a miniature vodka cup handed down from a Life Guard Grenadier serving in the Pavlovski Regiment. (From the collection of Christopher & Karin Ross, New York City)

Sauerbraten

French occupation forces in the seventeenth century in the Rhineland left a lasting impact on that region's cuisine, now commonly seen as "German food." It is said that the French troops invented sauerbraten to help the local populace eat less than savory meat. The preparation's "sour" flavor helps camouflage the taste of old and almost spoiled beef.

Military Leaders and Good Food

Numerous dishes in France, Spain, and Portugal are called "The Admiral's Sauce," or the "Admiral's Sole." We were unable to find any connection to a specific admiral and believe it was just the fancy of the chef who created a specific dish. Similarly "Sole Biron" is apparently named after Armand de Gontaut, Baron de Biron, a famous French Marshal who died at the siege of the noted Champagne town of Epernay on July 26, 1592. While Marshal Biron certainly may have eaten well, it is uncertain whether he personally inspired Sole Biron, a rich

dish of folded sole fillets poached in white wine sauce and garnished with truffles.

Folklore connects the creation of mayonnaise to the chef to the Duc de Richelieu, who allegedly created this condiment after the victory of Mahon (hence "Mahonaise"). While this tale is frequently recounted, historical basis seems lacking.

Prince Otto von Bismarck gave his name to numerous dishes and products, some of which are still commonly available in German grocery stores. The reason why "Bismarck Herring" is a popular product cannot be explained with any certainty.

It is different with French General George Louis Humbert who, in the nineteenth century, had his chef create "Eggs Humbert," a sophisticated concoction of eggs, chopped ox tongue, eggplant, tomato sauce, and green peppers.

Salisbury Steak

This standard dinner item is named after James H. Salisbury, a medical doctor who was born in 1823 in Scott, New York. During the War between the States he somehow figured out that he was able to cure diarrhea —a common problem in the field — of soldiers by a bizarre diet of coffee and broiled beefsteak. He invented this "cure" while stationed at Camp Dennison near Cincinnati, a Yankee army post selected by General George McClellan.

After the war, using his wartime experience, he refined this diet, promoting a thrice-daily intake of chopped lean beef, heavily seasoned with Worcestershire sauce (based in part on Rome's "garum"), or mustard, horseradish, or lemon juice. In later years, he probably would have recommended Tabasco®. ✂

APRICOT SHIPS OF THE HOLY FATHER'S SWISS GUARDS (APRIKOSENSCHIFFLI BALDEGGER ART)

This unusual recipe was developed by the nuns that cook for the Swiss Guards in the Vatican. They belong to a Swiss-based order known as "Orden der Göettlichen Vorsehung von Baldegg." Baldegg is close to the home of many of the Swiss Guards, most of whom come from the German-speaking section of Switzerland. It is worth noting that the Swiss Guards eat quite well, being served typical Swiss food.

Ingredients

1 dozen 4 x 4 inch squares of puff pastry sheets
24 apricots (fresh or use dried apricots reconstituted in warm water for 30 minutes)
½ cup hazelnuts, ground
1 tablespoon granulated sugar
2 egg yolks, well beaten
1 cup powdered sugar
1 teaspoon lemon juice

Instructions

1. On each square of puff pastry add two apricots, cut into halves.
2. Sprinkle with ground hazelnuts and a very light sprinkling of granulated sugar.
3. Fold the sheet from the corners so that the filling shows.
4. Brush with egg yolk.
5. Bake at 350° F for 15 minutes.
6. Combine powdered sugar and lemon juice to make glaze.
7. When pastries are completely cool, cover tops with glaze.

QRITFA

This recipe from Gafsa in Tunisia is quite common with Arab troops and nomads and Bedouins. Gafsa is an oasis town in southwestern Tunisia.

Ingredients

1 tablespoon tomato paste
2 quarts plus 1 cup water
½ cup dried fava beans, picked over, soaked overnight in enough water to cover, and drained
½ cup plus 1 tablespoon extra virgin olive oil
2 medium-size onions, chopped
1 bunch Swiss chard (about 1¼ pounds), stems removed and leaves ripped into pieces
1 qarnit (small dried octopus; if using fresh octopus, see note to the right)
1 cup waztaf (small dried fish)
½ cup drained, cooked chickpeas
2 tablespoons dried brown lentils, picked over and rinsed
¼ pound dried apricots, quartered
1 teaspoon garlic powder
2 cups canned or fresh tomato puree
salt to taste
1 pound nawasar (or substitute quadratini pasta)
2 tablespoons samna (clarified butter)

Instructions

1. Dissolve the tomato paste in 1 cup of water.
2. Cover the drained fava beans in a medium-size saucepan with plenty of fresh water; bring to a boil, and boil until their skins can be peeled off, 5 to 15 minutes.
3. Drain the beans, allow them to cool, then peel off skins.
4. In the bottom portion of a couscousiere or a pot that can fit a colander on top, heat ½ cup of olive oil over medium-high heat, then cook the onions until soft and golden, about 7 minutes, stirring.
5. Pour the diluted tomato paste in with the onions, add the Swiss chard leaves, and cook until wilted, about 1 minute. Add the qarnit, wazaf, chickpeas, fava beans, lentils, apricots, garlic powder, 2 quarts of water, and tomato puree. Stir well. Reduce heat to medium and season with salt.
6. In a large bowl, mix the nawasar with the remaining tablespoon of olive oil, tossing well so every square is oiled (this way they won't stick together as they steam).
7. Put the nawasar in the top portion of the couscousiere or the colander, and place the top portion or colander over the broth in the bottom portion or pot. Cover and steam until tender, about 2 ½ hours. Mix the nawasar as well as the broth occasionally with a wooden spoon to distribute the flavors.
8. Remove the nawasar from the heat and stir to separate any pasta pieces from each other. Mix in 1 tablespoon of the samna and return to steam for another 30 minutes. Remove the pasta and transfer to a platter.
9. Mix in the remaining tablespoon of samna and toss. Cover with the sauce and serve.

Note: If substituting fresh octopus, use 1 ½ pounds of octopus, washed and cleaned. Put the octopus in a pot and cover with water and 1 cup white vinegar. Bring to a boil, reduce the heat to medium, and simmer, covered, for half an hour. Drain and wash well in cold water, peeling off the skin. Add as directed in step 5.

Many of the ingredients for this dish can be found in Middle Eastern grocery stores; for dried fish and octopus, Chinese grocery stores are another possible source.

Indonesian Flank Steak with Hot Peppers

This dish, adapted by Agostino von Hassell, was served in the field by a unit of Indonesia's army. It is easy to make, yet spicy and best served with solid quantities of refreshing beer.

Ingredients

1 pound flank steak, thinly sliced
½ pound hot peppers, sliced (any type of peppers will do)
soy sauce to taste (if available, use sweet Indonesia soy known as Kecap Manis)
salt
palm oil
3 cups cooked rice

Instructions

1. Combine the flank steak and peppers in a large bowl and season with soy sauce and salt. Let it sit for about 30 minutes.
2. In a large sauté pan, heat palm oil until very hot and almost smoking.
3. Add the steak and peppers to the pan and quickly stir fry. Depending on the thickness of the steak, frying should take no more than 10 minutes.
4. Serve with rice.

You can vary this dish by substituting the steak with thinly sliced tenderloin of pork or chicken.

Lombardy Egg-Drop Soup from Pavia (Zuppa Pavese)

The story surrounding this dish is that when Charles V of Spain (1500-1558) defeated King Francis I of France (1494-1547) at the battle of Pavia in 1525, Francis tried to take refuge in a nearby farmhouse. The badly wounded ruler was captured immediately by Spanish harquebusiers, and he was taken to Madrid as a prisoner. Historian Ferand Braudel suggested that the Battle of Pavia, besides being a triumph of the harquebusiers, was also the triumph of empty stomachs because Francis's army was too well fed, while the Spanish and Lombards he fought made do with a simple broth like this zuppa.

Ingredients

2 tablespoons unsalted butter
4 slices French or Italian bread with crust
¼ cup freshly grated Parmigiano-Reggiano cheese
1 ½ quarts veal broth
4 small eggs
1 tablespoon fresh finely chopped parsley leaves
ground white pepper to taste

Instructions

1. Preheat oven to 200° F. Warm four ovenproof soup bowls.
2. In a large skillet, melt butter over medium heat and lightly sauté the bread on both sides until golden, making sure you do not blacken the edges.
3. Place a slice of bread in each bowl. Sprinkle 1 tablespoon of Parmigiano-Reggiano on each slice of bread.
4. Bring the broth to a rolling boil. Without breaking the yolk, crack 1 egg onto each slice of bread and carefully ladle or pour the boiling broth over the egg until the bowl is filled.
5. Sprinkle with parsley and a pinch of white pepper and serve immediately.

Add more cheese at the table if desired.

Tough Beef

Tough beef, typically from old cows or oxen, is one of the pitfalls of living in the field. It is believed that British troops serving in the Boer Wars (South Africa) created this dish to deal with tough cuts.

Ingredients

8 pounds tough beef
2 large onions, chopped
1 pinch pickling spices
1 cup chopped mixed herbs (whatever is available)
1 cup wine vinegar
2 bottles dark beer

Instructions

1. Tie the beef up with string, making a roll.
2. Take a large ovenproof casserole and place the beef in it.
3. Cover it with onions, pickling spices, herbs, vinegar, and the dark beer.
4. Bring to a simmer.
5. Simmer for 2 to 3 hours or until the meat is tender.
6. Remove from the casserole and slice the beef.

Note: British troops would serve this with plain, boiled potatoes or red cabbage.

(Opposite) Indonesian military forces commonly partake of this dish of strips of flank steak, garlic, and hot peppers sautéed with coconut oil.

ANZAC Biscuits

ANZAC (Australia New Zealand Army Corps) is best known for their losses at Gallipoli during World War I. Thirty-three thousand Australian and New Zealander lives were lost to the Turks between 1914 and 1918. To put this in perspective in terms of the population at the time, 1 in 65 Australians and 1 in 17 New Zealanders were killed. When New Zealander and Australian soldiers joined forces in this war, becoming the ANZAC, a biscuit was made to celebrate. In addition to being cheap and easy to make, the biscuits kept well and were nourishing. This enabled families in New Zealand and Australia to send the biscuits to ANZAC troops overseas in food parcels. They were usually eaten with hot tea, a standard ration, which also made them quite tasty. The recipe has strong links to Scottish Oatcakes, which settlers brought to New Zealand.

Ingredients
1 cup rolled oats
¾ cup desiccated coconut
1 cup plain flour
1 cup sugar
¼ pound butter, melted
1 ½ tablespoons bicarbonate of soda
2 tablespoons boiling water
1 tablespoon golden syrup

Instructions
1. In a large bowl, combine all dry ingredients except soda.
2. Add melted butter and syrup.
3. Add soda to the boiling water.
4. Add water soda mixture to the bowl.
5. Place spoonfuls on a greased cookie sheet.
6. Bake at 300° F for about 20 minutes.
7. Allow to cool.
8. Store in an airtight container.

Zulu Warrior Grits

This is a common dish among African tribes, including the elite Zulu warriors. One of the many names for this nourishing dish is "mealy-pop." While it seemingly lacks elegance, versions of the very same are served now in elegant American southern restaurants in Savannah, Georgia; and Charleston, South Carolina.

Ingredients
water
2 teaspoons salt
2 pounds collard greens, well rinsed and roughly chopped
1 pound coarse grits, polenta, or corn meal
palm or peanut oil
pepper to taste

Instructions
1. Bring two large saucepans, each filled with about 2 quarts of water, to a rapid boil.
2. Add one teaspoon of salt to each saucepan.
3. Into one saucepan, add the chopped collards and boil for about 45 minutes or until tender.
4. In the second saucepan, slowly pour in the grits while stirring constantly.
5. Keep stirring the grits for about 15-20 minutes until creamy.
6. Drain the collards and place on a warmed serving platter.
7. Add the grits to the platter.
8. Liberally dribble palm or peanut oil over both the grits and collards and add pepper to taste.

To "spice" up the dish, you can add some pepper vinegar to the collards and some thinly sliced spicy sausage to the grits.

(Opposite) Order of St. George, Moscow: This dish is a recreation from a military dinner held in Moscow on November 26, 1885. This was an annual dinner held in St. George's Hall in the Kremlin amid paintings and statues of earlier awardees. The Order of St. George was established on November 26, 1769, by Empress Catherine II. The order has four classes. During World War I, the Order of Saint George was bestowed upon officers for exceptional bravery.

The food shown is Chaud-Froid de Foie-Gras a la Carême. This classic preparation of poached and then chilled foie-gras is covered in a thick sauce and glazed in aspic. The dish was refined by Antonin (Anton) Carême, one of the most famous chefs of all time. He worked for Czar Alexander of Russia for several years around 1820.

On the right, a dramatic silver candelabra of British design celebrates the sacrifices of the wars against Napoleon. (From the collection of Christopher & Karin Ross, New York City)

(Right) Moscow's 1, Red Square restaurant recreates fancy military dishes from Czarist times.

PORTUGAL:
WHAT ONE COUNTRY CAN OFFER

João Luís Santos sat on the gunwale of his Portuguese caravel. The ship, the *Espírito Santo,* weighed anchor on June 13, 1553. She carried square sails on her fore and main masts and a lateen sail on the mizzen. The square sails filled like parachutes and propelled the ship at speeds faster than most other ships of 16th-century design, while the lateen gave the ship precise maneuverability. Speed and maneuverability were important, in fact, essential for a fishing vessel.

João watched the green swells of the north Atlantic flow by as his ship eased through each one, speeding to Portugal's new-found treasure, the New Foundland coast. Portugal by 1502 had already claimed and named the coast "land of the King of Portugal." To this day there are Portuguese maps that identify New Foundland as a Portuguese discovery, and many early maps show towns with Portuguese names. New Foundlanders would not agree.

It was from here that ships were returning to ports throughout Europe with reports of a fish, a large fish sometimes as big as a man, with the whitest meat and soft bones. Swimming in the water it was graceful, looking more like a bird than a fish, with five fins unfurled and a white stripe running up its side. Unlike most fish, it had a squared-off tail and a strange appendage hanging from its chin, the appendage many believe is used for feeling the ocean floor.

(Opposite) Alcobaça Monastery — Codfish Dish: The Cister monks built the monastery of Saint Maria of Alcobaça from 1178 to 1254. The kitchen depicted here was built on orders from King Dom Afonso VI (1656–1667). The "new kitchen's" dimensions are impressive: 32 yards long by 7 yards wide and 20 yards high. The main chimney is located in the center of the room and supported by eight floor-to-ceiling columns. A heavy stone table sits between the chimney, and the water tank (perfect for washing vegetables) is filled by a tributary of the Alcoa River. Tiles dated from 1752 cover the walls. French, British, and Portuguese troops used this monastery during the Peninsular War.

In 1762, there were 139 monks in the monastery plus a large number of servants and guests. There could be more than 500 people to be fed at a single meal, and consequently, the kitchen was of central importance.

The codfish dish pictured is still commonly served to the Portuguese army and navy. Codfish sautéed with onions and layered with mashed potatoes and spinach leaves, then covered with white sauce and breadcrumbs, makes an easy and balanced dish with both a strong taste (from the codfish) and a velvety taste (from the white sauce).

Fish was not new to the Portuguese diet and was already a staple of the populations of many countries along with meat and grains. But the cod was different in texture and flavor, and most importantly, it could be salted and stored for long periods of time, just as meat was stored.

Portugal was fortunate in having a plentiful supply of salt to complement the cod. Salt was an extremely important commodity, not only because it is necessary to the human diet, but also because it preserves and flavors the food.

For the Portuguese, who were already heavily involved in trade around the world, salted cod not only became a staple at the dinner table, but one more product that could be traded for valuable spices and other merchandise.

Cod meat has virtually no fat and eaten fresh is more than 18 percent protein. When properly dried and salted, it becomes concentrated 80 percent protein. For this reason, cod became important for sailors out at sea for many months and even European armies that often spent long periods in the field. The other benefit to cod is that there is virtually no waste to the fish. Most say that the head tastes better than the body of the fish, and the throat, referred to as a tongue, and small disks on either side of the fish called cheeks, are also considered delicacies. The roe is eaten fresh or smoked, and New Foundland fishermen are said to be especially fond of the female gonads, a two-pronged organ nicknamed "the britches" because they resemble a pair of trousers. Years ago in Iceland they used to eat milt, the sperm in whey, and the Japanese are still especially fond of the milt today.

This was João Luís Santos's first trip across the Atlantic. He had read the reports of Portuguese Captain Estêvão Gomes who had originally sailed with Magellan and in 1525 was charged by Emperor Charles V to discover the Northwest Passage. Gomes charted a course similar to that of John Cabot who had failed in his attempt to find a route through North America, but as Gomes explored the North American coast from New Foundland to the Chesapeake Bay, his reports included details of the shallow banks that stretch from New Foundland to Southern New England, describing huge shoals off the continent where there was sufficient food to support impressive numbers of codfish.

This led to many trips that João would make across the Atlantic, at times crossing in rough seas through wicked storms, usually leaving from his home town of Cascais, Portugal, in the spring. He would fish all

summer and return home in the fall. For João it was an exciting life. That is, until the war started.

Who would have thought that great nations would fight over fish, much less one specific fish, the cod?

It is ironic that it wasn't the codfish itself that brought France and England to the brink of war, but the salt used to preserve the codfish. England, of course, was a nearer sail to New Foundland than was France, Spain, or Portugal. It was also closer to Icelandic cod fishing, where England came into dispute with the Germans of the Hanseatic League, a group of German merchants that controlled trade along the Kiel "salt road."

England, of course, had an impressive fleet of ships. What it lacked was salt. Salt, or "wich," which is the Anglo–Saxon word for "a place that has salt," was so important in Great Britain that British towns with names ending in "wich" were towns where salt could be found.

Salt taxes imposed by governments made them wealthy, but also led to their downfall. The French, with little salt of their own except that which was made from brine and tasted inferior, were forced to buy salt from the British for many years. Without a sufficient supply of salt, Great Britain turned to Portugal, which had a massive saltworks at Aveiro. The town became and remains today the salt center of not just Portugal but of all of Europe because of its abundance and fine taste. In exchange for salt, the British gave the Portuguese protection on the high seas from the French who were reputed to have taken more than 300 Portuguese ships within a decade.

The Portuguese alliance with Britain lasted until 1581, when Filipe II, king of Spain, became also Filipe I, king of Portugal. A few years later, the British destroyed the entire Spanish fishing fleet primarily to protect their cod interests and then sank Spain's military fleet when the Spaniards attempted to invade England (1588). Many Portuguese ships sank with the Spanish fleet. Sailors like João Luís Santos continued to sail the North Atlantic for many years after that, and his descendants continued fishing the Grand Banks until 1986 when the Portuguese were expelled by the Canadians. The Portuguese salt cod industry ceased, never growing into the dominant international industry it once appeared it would become.

Cod wars continue today, although there are less and less for fisherman to fight over. The cod population off New Foundland and New England has diminished

(Right) Cover of the menu of a reception given by the chairman of the Joint Chiefs of Staff to the Military Committee composed of the Chiefs of Staff of NATO member countries, held in the S. Julião da Barra Fortress on September 29, 1977. Many military functions include elegant menus among the finer details, especially when entertaining international guests. The cover depicts an officer of a high rank in a "Great Uniform" (ceremonial uniform) from 1834, in accordance with the "Plan of Uniforms to the Army," published by the Military Order no. 9, from 22/11/1834, pages 1 to 12. This watercolor pictured on the menu is part of a collection of watercolors by Colonel Ribeiro Artur (1851–1910) in the Historical Military Archive of Lisbon.

(Opposite) Lunch at the Officers' Mess in Lisbon — Papaya stuffed with shrimp.

Located in Barbacena Palace, a building that survived Lisbon's powerful earthquake of 1755, the Officers' Mess in Lisbon enjoys a magnificent view of the National Pantheon (previously called Saint Engrácia church) and the Tagus River. In the heart of Alfama, the "cradle" of the city, the building is a good example of Portuguese baroque, with its impressive seigniorial façade and roomy parlors overlaid with ornamental tiles of great historic and artistic value. The 18th–century tiles depict hunting scenes, banquets, and other social occasions.

The table is laid with the mess china, crystal glassware, and fine cutlery. At each place, a papaya stuffed with shrimp and cocktail sauce lies on a lettuce leaf, a beautiful presentation for the eye and the palate.

S. JULIÃO DA BARRA, 29 SETEMBRO 77

to a small fraction of the fish that João Luís Santos went seeking. Those that were "nearly as big as a man" no longer exist, and what few fish can be found are diminutive in size. Most of the cod fishing fleet has been converted for other sea purposes.

Some hope that the cod disappeared due to a rise in the water temperature, which forced them off to cooler waters. As yet no one has found cod in those cooler waters, and the fish that fed armies and navies around the world for centuries sees its stocks diminishing at an amazing rate. That is a reason why the cod is now considered a "protected species" under several countries legislations.

Cod, however, was not the only important dish to go to sea with Portuguese explorers. There is a dish, still renowned today, known as Porto Style Tripe in the northern city of Oporto. There are many legends surrounding Porto Style Tripe, but a visit there several years ago established the one with the most historical significance. It surrounds the Oporto-born Prince Henry who needed meat to supply his caravels that were preparing to depart Portugal to conquer Ceuta. Concerned that he would not have sufficient supplies for the voyage, Prince Henry asked his fellow townspeople to help him with the victuals.

The people of Oporto immediately set to filling wooden barrels with salted meat, keeping the tripe, which they cooked into a thick stew with sausages and fatty meat, and served the feast accompanied by dark rye bread.

(Above) Codfish "patanisca" with beans and rice is a typical dish in Portuguese homes, as well as in the navy Officers' Mess in Lisbon, and is normally served with a green salad.

The "patanisca" itself is a spoonful of fried dough prepared with codfish, eggs, parsley, milk, and flour. The rice is prepared with red beans that have been sprinkled with parsley, acquiring a special taste and consistency to match the strong flavor of the "pataniscas."

(Opposite) Escola Prática de Infantaria de Mafra —Infantry School of Mafra, Portugal (built ca. 1717)

Lunch is about to be over at the Infantry School of Mafra, and around 300 young recruits, almost all in their late teens, are getting ready to clear their tables and leave the dining hall.

In the background there is a painting that was used by Napoleon's army to improve their marksmanship during the Peninsular War, when Napoleon tried to conquer Portugal (1807–1814).

The school is located in the old monastery devoted to Saint Anthony of Lisbon, a part of the Mafra monument complex. The impressive baroque monument was started in 1717 and finished in 1730. King D. João V (1689–1750) and his wife, Queen D. Maria Ana of Austria, had it built to thank God that they were granted an heir. The entire monument is composed of a palace, a basilica, a library, and the monastery. It includes 880 rooms, 300 convent alcoves, 5,400 windows and doors, 154 staircases, and 29 courtyards.

(Below) Odivelas Institute Military Kitchen – "Tripas à moda do Porto": This dish has a special place in military history. It was served during a seige of the city of Porto to the soldiers defending the city.

The dish is shown in a building that has stood for more than 700 years. Legend says that King D. Dinis survived an attack by a bear and honored his patron saint, Saint Dines, by erecting a monastery for the Cister nuns. Begun in 1295 and completed in 1302, the building served as a convent until 1834, when Portugal abolished religious orders.

In 1900, the "Infante D. Afonso Institute" was founded as a school to properly raise and educate the daughters of army officers, and it continues to operate as such. After several designations, it was named "Odivelas Institute" in 1942, after the name of the convent.

The kitchen of the institute is famous for 18th–century tiles that completely cover the walls and chimney, as well as its collection of copper pots, where the famous quince marmalade of the convent used to be prepared.

The photo depicts "Tripas à moda do Porto," the most popular dish of Oporto. Its ingredients are tripe, pig trotter, veal trotter, a piece of fat dry–cured ham, a "salpicão" (sausage of pickled loin of pork or smoked ham), a "chouriço," (dry Portuguese sausage), carrots, butter beans, lemon, pepper, salt, and paprika.

(Opposite) Carrot and turnip leaves soup: Officers' Mess in Évora, Portugal.

A simple carrot puree is improved by using turnip leaves, water crest, or spinach. The greens create a more powerful visual element and a more complex flavor.

Here the soup is being served on a plate of the "Manutenção Militar – MM," the Military Logistics, together with wine from the same source. The clay pitcher keeps water cool in the region's hot, dry weather.

Marble and basalt, both native to the Lisbon area, were used to make the washbasin in the dining hall.

The man who concocted the send-off provisions for the caravels also sailed with them. He discovered new foods and ingredients, the most important of which was the butter bean. The dish today is an important part of the culinary history of the city, usually flavored with cumin and black pepper with homemade sausage and chicken fat.

These early explorations were only the beginning for Portugal. Portuguese sailors are credited with developing one of the most important trade routes in the history of the world. During the 15th and early 16th centuries, Portuguese sailors were lured to the Orient where they discovered precious spices, most of which were in great demand in Europe. They settled Portuguese colonies like Goa, a small region of India; Malacca, a region of Malaysia; and Macao. The grand Portuguese traders made fortunes from introducing new foods and seasonings, including saffron, garlic, yellow onions, vinegar, olive oil, red and green peppers, and even cayenne peppers or a derivative known today as the piri piri pepper, ever popular in modern-day Portuguese cuisine.

The Portuguese used these spices in their own foods, not just in Europe, but in their territories, as well. Just as importantly there was a blending of foods and spices that came from the territories back to Portugal and Europe. The integration of new flavors also went from Europe and the territories to Asia. An example of this was the introduction of roasted suckling pig to the east. ✄

(Below) Details are important. For instance, even the sugar packets of the Portuguese military carry the coat of arms of the logistics unit of Portugal's Armed Forces.

CODFISH WITH SPINACH AND WHITE SAUCE (BACALHAU COM ESPINAFRES E MOLHO BRANCO)

Ingredients — Main Dish
4 slices of thick salted codfish
pinch of nutmeg
2 tablespoons olive oil
2 onions, finely sliced
3 cloves garlic, minced
2 pounds of potatoes, peeled and diced
2 cups of milk, warmed
4 tablespoons butter
½ teaspoon nutmeg
salt to taste
pepper to taste
1 egg yolk
1 pound fresh spinach
¼ cup grated Parmesan cheese

Ingredients — White Sauce
2 tablespoons of butter
3 teaspoons of flour
2 ½ cups of milk, warmed
salt to taste
pepper to taste
nutmeg to taste
2 egg yolks, lightly beaten

Instructions — Main Dish
1. Soak codfish in water for 24 hours, changing the water 3 or 4 times. Remove the skin and the bones. Place cod, enough milk to cover the cod, and a pinch of nutmeg in a medium saucepan. Bring to a boil and cook just long enough to get the pieces of codfish softer.
2. Prepare a "refogado" (onions fried until a bit more than transparent in olive oil) with the olive oil, finely sliced onions, and minced garlic. Add the codfish and fry on medium heat until golden.
3. Prepare a generous amount of mashed potatoes by placing potatoes in a medium pan, covering with water, and boiling until they are soft. Mash or grind the potatoes in a food mill until achieving a puree. Add the warmed milk and mix until smooth. Add butter, nutmeg, salt and pepper and egg yolk. Mix and heat again until the yolk is cooked.
4. Parboil the spinach for five minutes. Drain thoroughly and fry in butter until limp and tender.
5. Spread the mashed potatoes in a greased oven dish of clay, ceramic, or glass, pretty enough to be taken to the table. The dish can be rectangular (13" x 9") or round (11" diameter). On top of the potatoes, add a layer of codfish and then the spinach. Cover with the white sauce and top with grated cheese. Broil on low just long enough to melt the cheese "au gratin" and let some brownish bubbles appear on the top of it.

Instructions — White Sauce
1. Melt the butter at a low temperature and mix in the flour, stirring or whisking until it makes a smooth paste.
2. Slowly add the warm milk, and keep stirring to avoid lumps.
3. Season with salt, pepper, and nutmeg.
4. Raise the burner to medium heat and stir constantly until the mixture begins to thicken.
5. Remove from the heat and allow to cool.
6. Add the egg yolks, stirring quickly or whisking so that the sauce does not curdle.
7. Bring pot to a gentle boil, and let quietly simmer for another 2 or 3 minutes.

(Below) Military forces have always been known for precise record keeping, including such details as provisions purchased and disbursed. During excavations at Hadrian's Wall in Scotland, detailed Roman army records were found regarding shipments of cheese and animals purchased for slaughter. This Portuguese book, "Auxiliary Book of the Supervision and Treasury of the Royal Domains, in reference with the Crown Materials, War Ammunitions and Provisions," 1776–1792, provides similar documentation. [Paper, manuscript, leather binding and cold engraving, 201 pages. Reference 2265, "Biblioteca Central da Marinha – Arquivo Central" – Portuguese Navy Central Library – Central Archive]

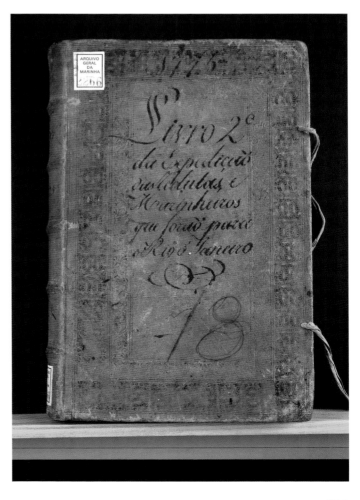

GAME PIE
(EMPADÃO DE AVES)

Ingredients
2 ¼ pounds of pheasant, partridge, turkey and hare
10 ounces, slab bacon or fat back
10 ounces, sausage
1 or 2 cloves garlic
8 to 10 grains of black pepper
2 tablespoons vinegar
1 onion
bunch of parsley
water
salt and pepper to taste
30 ounces flour
lard (to grease pan)
2 eggs, beaten

Instructions
1. Preheat oven to 450° F. Put ingredients from pheasant through parsley in a large pot. Cover with water and bring to a smooth boil.
2. Reduce heat to low and simmer until meats come away from the bones, without going into pieces.
3. Remove meats from the broth. Strain broth and set aside to cool.
4. In the meantime, remove meat from bones and cut into little chunks. Cut the sausage and the bacon or fat back into little chunks also.
5. Mix all the meat together and add a bit of the strained broth, just enough to keep the meat moist.
6. Season the cooled broth with salt and pepper to taste. Skim the fat from the top with a spoon, saving it in a clean container for the next step.
7. Sift the flour into a large bowl and add the fat from the broth. Knead together, adding small amounts of broth as needed to form dough. The dough has to be very well "worked" so that it can be rolled out flat and very thin.
8. Divide dough in half.
9. Roll out one piece of dough on a floured surface until it is large enough to line the baking pan.
10. Grease and flour a 9-inch deep-dish round baking pan, pretty enough to serve in, or spring-form pie pan and line with dough.
11. Place meat mixture into pie, adding more broth if needed to keep mixture moist.
12. Roll out dough for a top crust and place over pie pan. Use your fingers to gently pinch the edges of the two crusts to seal together.
13. Make a central hole, to work as a chimney for the steam to escape. You can support the hole by using a piece of cardboard rolled as a little cylinder.
14. Brush the top part of the pie with the beaten eggs. The top crust can be decorated with pieces of dough making letters, flowers, leaves, or small crowns.
15. Bake the pie until crust is slightly golden or brownish.

Remove cardboard and serve hot.

NOTE: A spring–form pie plate can be used. It should allow the top part to be removed to allow the bottom part to support the pie.

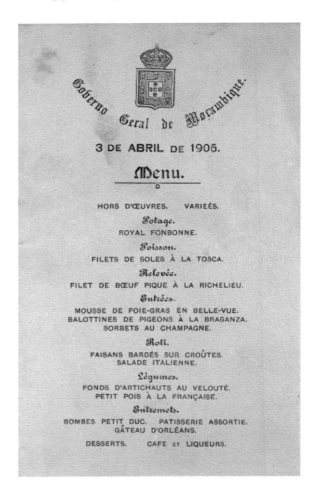

(Above) This menu is from a reception held on July 8, 1897, to celebrate the 400th anniversary of the "Departure of Vasco da Gama from Lisbon to India," or, in other words, the discovery of the sea route from Portugal to India.

The dinner was held aboard the Portuguese navy vessel *África* while it was anchored in Livorno. The menu is a testament to Portugal's reputation as discoverers with several of the dishes cooked "the French way," "the Italian way," or "the English way."

The ship's logs describes the day as follows: "Service of July 8 to 9, 1897, Thursday to Friday. Anchored in Livorno — Good weather — Usual and regulated service — Banquet to be served — Gig lowered being ready to go to land and pick up the guests for the dinner celebrating the 4th centenary of India. Came aboard Mr. Ferreira do Amaral, and other guests — The mast was full of little flags. No news during the night. Washing up of the desk — Usual services — Nothing more — Delivery of the bread and meat to be later distributed among the crew."

(Above) A young Portuguese private holds a bottle of olive oil produced for and bottled by Portuguese Military Logistics. Two different types of olive oils (90% extra–virgin and 10% virgin) are bottled and distributed among all the military installations throughout the country.

This particular warehouse has the capacity to store 2 million liters of olive oil (approximately 530,000 gallons). Today about 14,000 men compose the Portuguese army. The warehouse was built to store the olive oil needed during the colonial wars, when around 130,000 men were enlisted in the army. The amount of olive oil consumed by the Portuguese in general and by the Portuguese army is an impressive figure, especially compared to countries where other types of vegetable oils are more frequently used.

ANDALUSIAN-STYLE CHICKPEAS (GARBANZOS A LA ANDALUZA)

In the 16th century, chickpeas were the staple diet for the adventurers and soldiers manning the Spanish presidios along the Barbary Coast. In the Spanish province Andalusia, cooks make this dish in a variety of ways, sometimes adding sweet potatoes or rice.

Ingredients
1 ½ quarts water
2 cups dried chickpeas (about 1 pound), picked over, soaked in cold water to cover overnight, and drained
1 medium-size onion, quartered and layers separated
½ pound Canadian or Irish bacon, cut into large squares
1 cup dry white wine
1 bay leaf
salt to taste
1 tablespoon extra virgin olive oil
1 green bell pepper, seeded and sliced into rings

Instructions
1. Bring water to a boil in a large saucepan, add drained chickpeas, reduce the heat to low, cover partially, and cook for 1 hour. The water should always just cover the chickpeas.
2. Add the onion, bacon, wine, and bay leaf, and season with salt. Cover partially and simmer until the chickpeas are soft, another 2 to 3 hours, replenishing with boiling water so the chickpeas are always covered. The older the chickpeas, the longer you will need to cook them.
3. In a medium-size skillet, heat olive oil over medum-high heat, and cook the green pepper until soft, stirring frequently, about 20 minutes.
4. When the chickpeas are done, transfer to individual serving bowls or a serving platter, cover with the sautéed green pepper, and serve hot.

(Right) This is yet another example of elegant dining offered by Portugal's military. Featured are consommé Regina, sea trout "mousseline" sauce, veal "bouquetiére," an elegant traditional preparation of partridge (a game bird hunted in the vast open fields of Portugal's Alentejo region), and green beans with cream. Sicilian ice cream was served for dessert and the wine list included Monroy, Barolo Mirafiore, Heidsieck Monopole Brut, and Porto.

(Opposite) Officers' Mess in Lisbon — Detail of a tile panel depicting a banquet

CATALAN SPONGE CAKE (PA DE PESSIC)

Ingredients
1 cup granulated sugar
8 large egg yolks
¼ teaspoon pure vanilla extract
zest of 1 lemon
½ cup unbleached all-purpose flour
½ cup cornstarch
¼ cup unsalted butter, melted
confectioners' sugar for garnish
ground cinnamon for garnish

Instructions
1. Preheat the oven to 350° F. Beat the granulated sugar, egg yolks, vanilla, and lemon zest together in a large bowl. Work in the flour and cornstarch a spoonful at a time. Stir in the melted butter. The batter will be thick and very stiff.
2. Butter a 9-inch round cake pan on the bottom and sides. Spread the batter evenly in the pan. Bake for 35 minutes. Remove the cake from the pan to cool on a wire rack.
3. Once the cake is completely cooled, dust the top with confectioners' sugar. Decorate the top by making a diamond or heart, for instance. To make a heart stencil, fold a piece of stiff paper in half. Cut half a heart out along the edges.
4. Open the paper, smoothing crinkled edges and gently place over the cake. Dust the heart cut-out with ground cinnamon. Carefully remove the paper and serve.

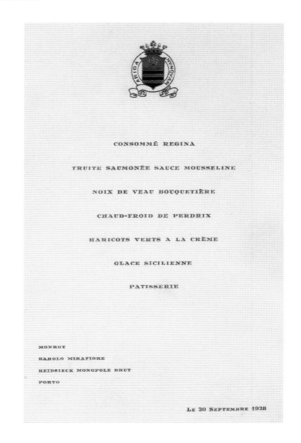

CONSOMMÉ REGINA

TRUITE SAUMONÉE SAUCE MOUSSELINE

NOIX DE VEAU BOUQUETIÈRE

CHAUD-FROID DE PERDRIX

HARICOTS VERTS A LA CRÈME

GLACE SICILIENNE

PATISSERIE

MONROY
BAROLO MIRAFIORE
HEIDSIECK MONOPOLE BRUT
PORTO

LE 20 SEPTEMBRE 1928

COMMANDO-STYLE BRAISED RABBIT WITH TOMATO AND CHOCOLATE SAUCE (CONEJO ALMOGAVAR)

The Almogavar were commandos trained to carry out raids into enemy territory on the Iberian Peninsula. These soldiers were an important part of armies in the Middle Ages. It is doubtful a mess cook of the Middle Ages ever made this recipe. First of all, chocolate and tomatoes were yet to be imported from the New World and, even in later centuries, both are unlikely to have been available to a field cook. In any case, this seemingly unusual recipe is quite good.

Ingredients
1 rabbit (about 4 pounds), cut into 4 pieces
salt and freshly ground black pepper to taste
3 cloves garlic, peeled
6 blanched whole almonds, toasted
¼ cup finely chopped fresh parsley
½ teaspoon freshly ground white pepper
1 ounce semisweet chocolate
1 small hard roll (preferably a dried hard wheat biscuit)
1 cup dry white wine
½ cup rabbit or chicken broth
2 tablespoons pork lard
1 medium-size onion, chopped
1 cup crushed tomatoes, canned or fresh

Instructions
1. Remove and save the rabbit liver. Season the rabbit with salt and pepper.
2. Put the garlic, almonds, parsley, white pepper, chocolate, hard roll, and rabbit liver in a food processor. Run it in short bursts for about 1 minute and then run continuously while slowly pouring in the wine and broth.
3. In a large non-reactive casserole, melt the lard over medium-high heat, then brown the onion and rabbit pieces on all sides until the rabbit is golden, about 10 minutes.
4. Reduce the heat to medium-low, add the tomatoes, and cook until the tomato sauce is thick, about 45 minutes. Keep the sauce covered.
5. Pour the contents of the food processor over the rabbit and continue cooking until the rabbit is fork-tender, about another two hours.
6. Check the rabbit to see if it is cooked and add up to 1 cup of water if the sauce is drying out.
7. Season with salt and black pepper to taste and serve.

Braised Partridge (Perdiz à Conde von Alten)

This dish was served to Major General Sir Charles Count von Alten, who was also lieutenant general in the Royal Hanoverian Army, in late 1812, just north of Lisbon. At that time (the middle of the Peninsular War), General von Alten commanded the Light Division, which included key British regiments such as the 43rd, 52nd, 95th, and the (Portuguese) 1st Caçadores. Partridge is one of the premier game birds of Portugal and to this day makes a delicious fall dinner. It is likely that the superb marksmen of the Portuguese Caçadores (hunters) shot the bird for the general's table.

Ingredients
1 large Savoy cabbage, cored and cut into wedges
salt and pepper to taste
4 partridges, cleaned and trussed
¼ cup olive oil
6 thick slices of bacon
1 tablespoon crushed juniper berries
1 cup of dry white wine (preferably Tapada de Coelheiros, but any decent dry white can be used)
2 cups chicken broth
4 carrots, thinly sliced
cloves
3 bay leaves
4 sprigs dried or fresh thyme
1 yellow onion
1 teaspoon flour

Instructions
1. Preheat oven to 350° F.
2. Boil water, add salt and cabbage, and boil for about 8 minutes. Drain and rinse with cold water.
3. Generously season with salt and pepper the inside and outside of the partridges.
4. Heat the olive oil in a casserole and brown the partridges for about 12 minutes on all sides. Remove the birds.
5. Line the base of the casserole with bacon. Add half the cooked cabbage, the crushed juniper berries, and more salt and pepper.
6. Place the partridges on top of the bacon with the remaining cabbage, the wine, chicken stock, carrots, celery, herbs, and onion. Cover the casserole and bake for 90 minutes.
7. Remove the partridges.
8. Remove the cabbage, carrots, celery, and bacon, and place on a serving dish.
9. Boil the remaining stock and juices from the birds and vegetables until reduced by half; add the flour and stir.
10. Place the partridges on top of the vegetables, cover with the sauce and serve.

Note: Mashed or French-fried potatoes make a good side dish. Serve with a strong, intense, red wine such as Mouchão.

Pork Cubes (Rojões)

Served by Major General Ferreira dos Santos of Portugal in 2002, then commander of the Rapid Operational Euroforce (EUROFOR) located in Florence, Italy, at a formal dinner for his staff.

Ingredients
3 pounds lean pork
7 ounces Vinho Verde (a light green wine typical from Minho region)
2 ounces olive oil
2 cloves garlic
1 bay leaf
1 teaspoon cumin seeds
salt

Instructions
1. Cut the pork into 2–inch cubes.
2. Place in a pan with the wine, olive oil, garlic, bay leaf, cumin, and salt. Allow to boil until there is no more wine. Add more salt to taste.

This dish is often served with boiled potatoes that have been browned in the fat used to cook the pork. Shelled, roasted chestnuts can also be added. Serve the meat, potatoes, and chestnuts garnished with slices of lemon.

(Above) "Messe dos Oficiais do Exército" – The Officers' Mess in Lisbon (ca. 1750) — This brass plaque is at the entrance of this club, which is located in Barbacena Palace, with a reflection of the National Pantheon (previously called Saint Engrácia church).

Pork with Peas (Porco com Ervilhas)

This dish was served to Agostino von Hassell by elements of the Portuguese marines corps (Corpo de Fuzileiros) at Alfeite, in the area of the Naval Base of Lisbon, in 1989. It was served with a light green and almost sparkling wine known as Vinho Verde. This refreshing wine is a perfect complement to a dish that emphasizes fresh peas.

Ingredients

3 tablespoons of good olive oil (see page 131 for Portuguese military olive oil)
1 large yellow onion, diced
2 pounds pork tenderloin, cut into 1–inch cubes
2 cups of white wine
3 cups fresh, shelled peas (may substitute frozen peas, but fresh are better)
2 large eggs
fresh flat–leaf or Italian parsley, chopped
salt and pepper

Instructions

1. Preheat the oven to 350° F. Heat the olive oil in an ovenproof casserole.
2. Add the onion and stir until the onion turns soft and translucent.
3. Add the pork cubes and quickly brown on all sides.
4. Add the wine and bring to a boil.
5. Cover the casserole and bake for 30 minutes.
6. Remove from the oven, stir in the peas, and cover the casserole again. Return to the oven for an additional 20 minutes.
7. While the peas cook, combine the eggs and chopped parsley.
8. Remove the casserole from the oven and stir in the egg and parsley mixture. Season with salt and pepper. The heat from the pork will cook the eggs and thicken the dish.

Grilled Swordfish (Espadarte Grelhado)

This simple dish was served to Agostino von Hassell aboard the Portuguese frigate *Comandante Hermenegildo Capelo*. The ship is named after Hermenegildo Carlos de Brito Capelo, a former Portuguese naval official who gained fame for his explorations of the interior of Angola and Mozambique, in the late 19th century.

Ingredients

5 swordfish steaks, cut into 1–inch cubes
1 large lemon
½ cup olive oil
1 clove garlic, peeled and minced

Italian parsley, finely chopped
salt and pepper
wooden skewers soaked in water for at least 30 minutes

Instructions

1. In a large bowl, sprinkle the swordfish cubes with lemon juice, olive oil, garlic, parsley, salt, and pepper, and marinate in a refrigerator for about two hours.
2. Meanwhile, heat a gas grill or build a hot fire in a charcoal grill.
3. Remove the fish from the marinade and place about five cubes on each skewer.
4. Place on grill for about six minutes on each side.

Note: Serve with fresh lemons, rice, and chopped kale, steamed, and then fried in olive oil.

(Above) The menu depicts a reception given by the Spanish army for the Portuguese army in Alcazarquivir on August 4, 1942, with the peculiar detail of presenting a meal prepared in the Moorish style. The dishes served were Pinchitos (little cubes of meat on a spit), Moruno Lamb, couscous, and fruits, followed by tea and pastries. The Moorish occupation of Spain and Portugal strongly influenced the culinary traditions of both countries. It is unusual that this dinner took place in the middle of World War II, even though both Portugal and Spain remained neutral.

THE NEW EMPIRE: MILITARY FOOD IN THE UNITED STATES THE PAST, PRESENT AND FUTURE

"I Am Uncle Sam"

Sam Wilson was born on September 13, 1766, a decade before the American Revolution, in a place known as Menotemy, which is now called Arlington. His parents were colonists, so fully committed to the fight against British tyranny that they sent their two eldest sons to fight in General Washington's army.

When Sam was fourteen years old, his family moved to Mason, New Hampshire, where he later met the daughter of Captain Benjamin Mann. The two fell in love. Before he could marry, however, Sam knew he would have to provide for Betsey Mann in the fine manner to which she was accustomed as the daughter of a senior army officer. With little enterprise available in Mason, Sam and his elder brother Ebenezer devised a scheme to move where they could find work and save some money. Sam was 22 years old when he left Mason. The brothers reported walking 150 miles through deep snow to the town known then as Vanderheyden, now Troy, New York, near the state's capital of Albany.

Initially, Sam and Ebenezer became brick makers and later meatpackers. They both worked tirelessly, and after having saved some money and establishing himself, Sam returned to Mason to fetch Betsey and marry her. The two were married in January 1797 and returned to Troy. They had four children, although only two survived to adulthood.

In Troy, Sam's meatpacking business began to thrive. He made his own barrels for packaging meat, and had his own docks and ships that distributed his products along the Hudson River and down to New York City.

At the outset of the War of 1812, Sam was asked to supply meat for the American forces serving in the northern states. His reputation garnered such a high level of respect, he was subsequently asked to become the inspector for beef and pork for the United States Army.

One day, in a patriotic move, Sam began painting the initials U.S. for United States on his barrels of meat. At the time, the initials were rarely used to identify the country, which was more popularly known as the United States or America. On a shipment south one day, someone asked what the U.S. stood for on the barrels of meat, and jokingly one of Sam's workers replied that it stood for Uncle Sam. From that day on the story spread to everywhere Sam's meat was

Much More than Spam®
I love my Canned Bill, I never knew
How good that stuff could taste in stew.
I love it hot, I love it cold
Corn Willie never will grow old.

If you walked into the kitchen
When through your morning drill,
You could bet your old "Tin Derby"
There you'd meet your friend "Corn Bill."

It's the thing that licked the Kaiser
In that land across the sea –
And it drove away our troubles,
As we fought for Liberty.

"Bill" was our iron–rations
And we packed the stuff for miles.
It was always worth the effort,
As it filled our face with smiles.

He fought through all the battles,
Just the same as you and me –
And I don't see what ever keeps them,
From giving "Bill" a D.S.C.

From Rhymes of a Lost Battalion Doughboy
by Buck Private McCollum

(Opposite) Lamb stuffed with oysters, a dish served to General Washington at a victory in New York, and spoon bread. Photographed at the Old Mill in Millwood, Virginia. The mill supplied grain to revolutionary soldiers and soldiers from the North and South during the Civil War. The cooking instruments belonged to General Daniel Morgan who won the battle at Saratoga, New York.

shipped, and the initials U.S. were understood to be the identity of Uncle Sam Wilson. Ironically, as the Army began identifying everything from blankets to rifles with the initials U.S., they came to be known as Uncle Sam.

Samuel Wilson died in 1854 at the age of 88. Little did he know at the time of his death that he would become associated with the nation's namesake, Uncle Sam. He is buried in Oakwood Cemetery in Troy, New York.

Uncle Sam isn't alone in his culinary tribute to the United States. On February 20, 1991, *The New York Times* wrote of Tom Miner's determination to honor "the General." Miner was the executive chef at Fraunces Tavern® Restaurant at 54 Pearl Street in Lower Manhattan, and he was interested in recreating the dinner that General Washington and his officers enjoyed at the tavern in celebration of the ousting of the British in 1783.

Fraunces Tavern® was originally the Queens Head Tavern when it began serving in 1763. The proprietor and superb chef was Samuel Francis, who later changed his name to Fraunces. Born in the French West Indies, Fraunces is reputed to have been an avid anti–Royalist and arranged for clandestine meetings of groups like the Sons of the American Revolution and The Vigilance Committee, who in 1774 used the tavern to protest the tea tax and the landing of British tea. It was New York's response to the Boston Tea Party. The *Times* reports that a verse written by Philip Freneau documents how Fraunces was unduly punished.

> Scarce a broadside was ended
> Till another began—
> By Jove! It was nothing but
> Fire away Flanagan!
> At first we supposed it
> Was only a sham,
> 'Til he drove a round–shot
> through the roof of Black Sam.

Fraunces was rewarded after the war when General Washington chose his tavern for a meal following a victory march down Broadway on British Evacuation Day in 1783. According to reports, the 100 or so officers accompanying General Washington consumed an exorbitant amount of alcoholic punch and spruce beer along with 133 bottles of Madeira, port, and claret. Miner went to great lengths to recreate the famed feast.

A New Nation and New Culinary Skills

New culinary skills may be a stretch because early immigrants to America brought their own culinary skills with them. But it didn't take long for Yankee ingenuity to develop new and efficient ways to supply the fledgling nation with food. And it came from military leaders. There are too many stories to tell,

but this one is often told at the Millwood Mill in Clarke County, Virginia — in an area where being called a Yankee is somewhat of an insult.

Brigadier General Daniel Morgan is credited for doing more to turn the tides of battle for the colonies than any other war hero, aside from General Washington. Credited as the innovator of precision shooting for the infantry, which typically shot haphazardly in the direction of the enemy, General Morgan began using new tactics of war in 1777 by having his riflemen concentrate their fire on British officers, leaving the enemy troops leaderless. The British were furious, but his tactics led to the new country's victory at Saratoga, which prevented the Red Coats from splitting the colonies and gaining control of the Hudson Valley.

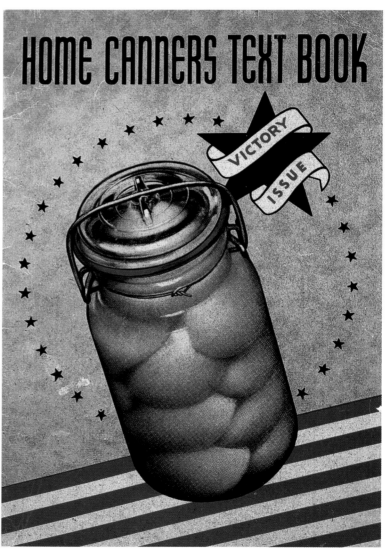

(Above) World War II brought some rationing to the United States even though the deprivations were miniscule compared to countries such as Britain or Germany. Yet home canning — as in this 1945 "Victory Issue" — was encouraged as an essential contribution to the war effort.

Contemporary records from the Revolutionary War strongly suggest that General Morgan loved his food and also made a major effort to maintain decent rations for his men. General Morgan, whose personal cooking pots and pans are now on display in Millwood, Virginia, built a farm called Saratoga (named after one of his victories) close to Millwood, right after the war. The photograph showing spoon bread and lamb stuffed with oysters was prepared using General Morgan's personal cooking utensils.

Thomas Jefferson considered Colonel Nathaniel Burwell to be the ablest businessman in Virginia. Burwell was charged with developing the Village of Millwood from 1785 to 1800 in what has been characterized as the one of America's most illuminating and absorbing post–Revolutionary histories of the nation.

Under orders from President Thomas Jefferson, Colonel Burwell visited Millwood and reckoned that Virginia could not develop an economy solely on tobacco but needed crops that could be turned over more quickly. Burwell foresaw that establishing a gristmill to process corn and wheat could create opportunities for an agrarian economy in the region. General Morgan was interested in pursuing the endeavor with Burwell, and he agreed to provide 500 Hessians to work at the mill. The German Hessians, now free, constructed the Millwood Mill in 1782 (completed in 1785) on Colonel Burwell's property. The mill became a hub for numerous other commercial endeavors including a general store, tannery, blacksmith, a wagoner, two distilleries, a tavern, and a post office. Millwood would become a model for many post–Revolutionary War villages in America initiated by military leaders and founded on the economic opportunities afforded by a mill.

The Millwood Mill, by the way, has been restored and remains one of the finest examples of Revolutionary War–era food manufacturing in America today. The mill was state of the art when it was built and is a true piece of industrial art, in addition to representing what we might call one of the first "food factories" in the United States.

Legend has it that a well–known Pennsylvania specialty, Pepper Pot, originated with George Washington at Valley Forge.

During that brutal winter of 1777–1778, the troops were cold, ragged, and half–starved. To boost morale, General Washington is supposed to have ordered a good meal one night, only to learn all that was available was tripe, a few scraps, and peppercorns.

The cook did much with little and created a soup he named, after his hometown, Philadelphia Pepper Pot. At least that is the story told in the Delaware Valley where the dish remains a cold weather favorite. It is a historical fact that troops in snow–swept Valley Forge were served this dish, but it may have originated in Africa, making its way to the United States through the West Indies. In the African recipe, fish, not tripe, was the focus of the soup.

General Ulysses S. Grant, fond of both food and spirits, was served an ultra fancy dinner in New York, in 1880, at the Hotel Brunswick. Prepared for just ten guests, Grant was served:

Oysters:
Soup, Consommé Royal.
Fish:
Fried smelts, sauce Tartare.
Releves:
Boned capon.
Entrees:
Sweetbreads, braised Quails, a la Perigord.
Sorbet au kirsch.
Game:
Broiled woodcock, Canvas–back duck.
Terrapin.
Vegetables:
Cauliflower, Spinach, Artichokes, French peas
Dessert:
Biscuits Diplomatiques, Frozen pudding,
Meringue Chantilly, Assorted cakes.
Fruit. Coffee. Cigars.
Liquors.

Another menu from a dinner that honored Grant, this one held in Cincinnati, is reproduced on p. 11.

During the War between the States, Grant didn't go hungry. The Yankees, unlike the Rebels, had ample food supplies. It appears Grant ate well. "I will not move my army without onions!" General Ulysses S. Grant declared in an 1864 advisory to the federal government. It is a stark contrast to General Robert E. Lee's comment, "I have been up to see the Congress and they do not seem to be able to do anything except eat peanuts and chew tobacco, while my army is starving. ..." One of Lee's colonels stated in 1863, "I cannot fight more until I get something to cook in!" The onions that Grant demanded (he was immediately sent three train cars full of the tasty bulbs) were appreciated by soldiers for both their flavor and antiseptic properties when used to treat powder burns.

That terrible war created a revolution in food, with dehydrated milk being just one of the accomplishments. Very much like the Roman's, the Quartermaster Corps of the United States Army emerged as a major force, providing superb logistics and a steady supply of food. Not necessarily tasty food, but food nonetheless.

The United States has probably done more than any other nation to develop food that can be packaged safely and eaten years later. Co–author Agostino von Hassell, recalls eating C–rations in 1973 that dated from the Korean War. The canned ham and eggs had turned a bit green, but a liberal dose of Tabasco ® covered up this questionable look.

America developed food that is both hated and loved. No section on American military cuisine would be complete without mentioning Spam®, the mainstay of World War II. Spam®, developed by World War I Army veteran Jay Hormel, is a contraction of the words spice and ham. It is still made, with considerable success, by Hormel Food Corporation in Austin, Minnesota. While no longer official issue in the military, check the packs of soldiers and you are likely to find a can or two of Spam®.

Complex K–Rations and C–Rations were served to fighting forces until the late 1970s when MREs made their appearance (based in part on technology developed by NASA for the space program). Processed cheese, powdered milk and freeze–dried coffee that were first invented for the government are now sold in supermarkets throughout the United States.

The general thinking has always been that the less said about U.S. combat rations the better. No matter which ones – the hardtack of Civil War days, the K–Rations, the C–Rations, and now the MREs — their reputation has never been great. Many combat soldiers will claim that the desire to consume rations increases with the distance from the front lines. Early MREs had a horrible reputation. One Marine called smoky frankfurters "the four fingers of death." Other descriptions are unprintable.

The value of U.S. rations as "trading goods" is low. In uncountable peace–keeping missions and joint operations with allies, U.S. soldiers try, often in vain, to trade their rations with the rations of their allies, perceived as superior.

A U.S. Army installation in Natick, Connecticut, houses the lab of future military food. It is there that scientists (we can't exactly call them chefs) create unusual MRE items for the future, such as oriental chicken with Thai sauce, seafood jambalaya and decent pasta. During the preparations of this book, the food stylist Harry McMann, a most accomplished chef himself, pronounced the MRE rations as tasty and well prepared. Actually, once removed

Photo by Agostino von Hassell

Photo by Agostino von Hassell

(Above) Technically this miniature can opener — once worn by most GIs on their dog tags — is known as the "P–38." At least that is the term used in the U.S. Army. The U.S. Marine Corps, with its flair for distinction, used to call it a "John Wayne." This can opener used to be essential field gear to open canned food issued in World War II, Korea, and Vietnam. These K– and C–Rations have since been replaced by MREs, packaged in plastics bags that do not require can openers. This can opener is a marvelous design since it is self–sharpening and ultra easy to use.

(Right) On top is a United States Marine heating his canned C–Ration meal on a small fire. Many soldiers used to use C–4, a flammable plastic explosive, to rapidly heat cans of ham, scrambled eggs, or meat-balls. The C–4 has been replaced by technology: today's "high–tech" rations are self–heating.

Below shows Marine recruits at the famous Marine Corps Recruit Depot, Parris Island, South Carolina, in the late 1970s. Today on Parris Island, such chow lines have been replaced by salad bars and almost elegant dining facilities. Yet the old standby — chipped beef on toast known as S.O.S. — is still served and remembered with fondness by many Marine veterans.

(Opposite) During warfare exercises in Northern Germany these Marines spent hours waiting, hanging out on their tank. With a helmet as a har-vest basket, a nearby potato field provided the raw material for a nourishing meal. The potatoes were quickly sliced and pan–fried until done. We used the C–Ration processed cheese as grease and spiced this wonderful plate of "home fries" with additional cheese, Tabasco® sauce, salt, and pepper. It was delicious.

Photo by Agostino von Hassell

(Below) U.S. Marines host allies for an elegant dinner served in a tent on the beaches of Gallipoli in Turkey in 1989. Solid red wine, steaks with a wine sauce, green beans drizzled with olive oil, spiced rice, and a fine pie, along with U.S. Navy coffee, was served in the field by U.S. Marine Corps cooks on U.S. Navy china.

(Right) The ever–efficient U.S. military must have produced hundreds of cooking manuals during World War II, giving guidance for harried cooks that had to supply meals for almost 12 million men and women in U.S. uniform. Every conceivable aspect of food preparation was covered — including how to use dehydrated food, and how to butcher and properly cook lamb aboard ship.

(Opposite) In 1983, during the civil war in Beirut, these United States Marines — then stuck in a hot combat zone and subject to frequent shelling and sniper fire — were served a treat from home. Perfectly fried chicken was prepared aboard ship and flown ashore, then served on top of barbed wire.

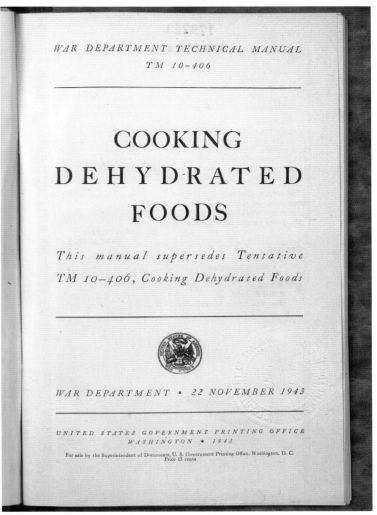

WAR DEPARTMENT TECHNICAL MANUAL
TM 10–406

COOKING
DEHYDRATED
FOODS

This manual supersedes Tentative TM 10–406, Cooking Dehydrated Foods

WAR DEPARTMENT • 22 NOVEMBER 1943

UNITED STATES GOVERNMENT PRINTING OFFICE
WASHINGTON • 1943

For sale by the Superintendent of Documents, U. S. Government Printing Office, Washington, D. C.
Price 15 cents

from the olive–drab pouches and served on proper china, this food is superb.

Will superb food emerge from U.S. military kitchens? Yes, it does already. Senior generals and admirals can have their chefs assemble dinners equal to or better than the grandest restaurants around the nation. Hudson Valley Foie Gras was one featured item at one dinner of the superintendent of the United States Military Academy in West Point.

Annual culinary competitions in the armed forces show the array of talent within the military. It is impressive and it is no wonder that former military cooks end up with great careers in the competitive commercial restaurant scene. A prime modern example is former Marine John Besh who served with distinction in the first Gulf War. While in Marine Corps service, he kept a detailed diary of dishes he wanted to cook once back in civilian life. With that diary and a strong drive, as only the Marine Corps can supply, Besh ended up running award–winning restaurants in his native New Orleans.

But taste may not be able to defeat technology. About the worst "food" we encountered were plans for the "Transdermal Nutrient-Delivery System" in early stages of development at Natick. It is a patch, similar to patches used to quit smoking, that is equipped with a tiny computer that measures a soldier's food needs and then delivers nutrients through the skin. It's hard to put Tabasco® on that! ✂

(Above) Looted Lobster Salad. General Thomas Jonathan "Stonewall" Jackson, CSA, had raided a Yankee supply depot near Manassas Junction on August 29, 1862. His troops then made off with fresh lobster and other victuals, such as ham and superb cigars. Simply prepared in the field with fresh lettuce, this became a famous dish from the War between the States. Props include an 1863 McCullen cavalry saddle, a Civil War period sword, a Civil War canteen, a glass bottle dating back to 1711, and a knife and fork from the Civil War. The dish was served with captured Rhine wine, even though Jackson objected to alcohol and had his men destroy most the liquor supplies during this "supply raid."

LOOTED LOBSTER SALAD

Ingredients
4 cups cooked lobster, chopped
2 cups celery, chopped
¼ cup green or red peppers, chopped
¾ cup mayonnaise
2 tablespoons sour cream
1 tablespoon Dijon or regular mustard
2 tablespoons lemon juice
½ teaspoon salt
⅛ teaspoon pepper
lettuce

Instructions
1. Combine all ingredients.
2. Serve chilled.

(Above) The food served in trenches during the various wars of the 20th century created the lasting bad reputation of U.S. military food.

JOHNNY CAKES

Johnny Cakes were a staple of Confederate Forces. But they were also a staple of colonial times, taking advantage of the growing bounty of corn. Some early colonial records suggest that the name comes from "Journey Cakes," indicating that the finished cakes could be easily packed and taken along. Many Confederate soldiers did carry Johnny Cakes in their haversacks. This recipe is adapted from *Virginia Housewife*, a cookbook published in 1824 by Mary Randolph, a member of an influential aristocratic Virginia family whose descendants still live in the Commonwealth.

Ingredients
1 cup course yellow cornmeal
½ teaspoon of salt
1 cup boiling water
½ cup of whole milk
vegetable oil or butter
maple syrup
butter for serving

Instructions
1. Combine the cornmeal and salt in a saucepan.
2. Add boiling water, and stir constantly until the mixture is smooth and without lumps.
3. Add milk and continue to stir.
4. With butter or oil, grease a heavy, 12–inch frying pan (ideally cast iron).
5. Heat to medium heat.
6. With a tablespoon, drop three or four dollops of the batter onto the surface of the pan.
7. Cook until golden. This takes 5–6 minutes.
8. Turn the cakes with a spatula and cook for another 5–6 minutes.
9. Serve.

You can serve the hot cakes — very much like pancakes — with maple syrup and melted butter. For use on a "journey," wrap the cakes in parchment paper. They can be reheated over a campfire.

Martha Washington's Famous Great Cake

December 26, 1776, was a great day for General George Washington. His troops won the Battle of Trenton, and one of his wife's fruitcakes arrived safely at his camp. One look at the ingredients will explain why it was known as a great cake; it was meant to feed a crowd.

At the time, fruitcakes were popular for special occasions and celebrations and were topped with very stiff, egg–white–based icing and flavored with rosewater or orange–flower water.

The Mount Vernon Ladies' Association, the private, nonprofit organization that maintains historic Mount Vernon in trust for the people of the United States, graciously provided this recipe.

Ingredients
40 eggs
4 pounds butter
4 pounds sugar
5 pounds flour
5 pounds fruit
½ ounce mace
½ ounce nutmeg
½ pint wine
brandy

Instructions
1. Take 40 eggs, divide the whites from the yolks, and beat them to a froth.
2. Then work 4 pounds of butter to a cream and put the egg whites to it a spoon full at a time till it is well worked.
3. Then put 4 pounds of sugar finely powdered to it in the same manner.
4. Then put in the egg yolks and 5 pounds of flour and 5 pounds of fruit.
5. 2 hours will bake it.
6. Add to it half an ounce of mace and nutmeg, half a pint of wine, and some fresh brandy.

S.O.S. (U.S. Air Force Recipe)

S.O.S. is a standard military breakfast item with every mess hall, every ship, every unit having different recipes. The basics are the same … sautéed ground beef on toast. Far from basic, S.O.S. increasingly is featured on the breakfast menus of the finest hotels around the United States.

Ingredients
1 pound ground beef
¼ cup flour
2 cups milk
3–4 drops Tabasco®
salt and pepper to taste
white bread, toasted

Instructions
1. Brown and chop ground beef. Remove ground beef with slotted spoon and drain on a paper towel.
2. Sprinkle flour into the fat remaining in the pan to make a roux.
3. Cook for a few minutes over low heat.
4. Add milk a little at a time while stirring.
5. Add Tabasco®.
6. Cook until thick and bubbling.
7. Add ground beef, and salt and pepper to taste.
8. Serve over toasted white bread "shingles."

(Opposite) Wherever there are United States Marines, they will celebrate the birthday of their famous Corps, which was founded by the Continental Congress on November 10, 1775. The first recruiting office was — appropriately so for thirsty Marines — at Tun's Tavern in Philadelphia.

Birthday celebrations will take place in a combat zone, aboard a ship, or at a Marine Corps base, but no matter where, it is a solemn occasion always concluded with a cake (sometimes in battle zones with canned fruitcake — either made from C–Rations or shipped from home). The cake will be cut, with great ceremony, with a Marine Corps sword. The first piece goes to the guest of honor, the second piece to the oldest Marine present, and the third to the youngest Marine. Eating a piece of cake is believed by some to provide strength and commitment for another year of service to Corps and Country.

THE COMMANDANT'S ANTIPASTO

This recipe is served at elegant cocktail parties hosted by the commandant of the United States Marine Corps at his official residence. The mansion is one of the few structures in the neighborhood to survive the fires set by the British during the War of 1812. It is often the site of elaborate dinners, garden parties, and cocktail parties, attended by senior military officers, foreign military dignitaries, Medal of Honor recipients, members of Congress, members of the administration, and occasionally the president of the United States. The house is located at the famous original Marine Barracks at 8th and I Streets in Washington, D.C. The recipe was provided by Gunnery Sergeant D. E. Blakeman, USMC.

Ingredients
1 8–ounce block cheddar cheese
1 8–ounce block Monterrey Jack cheese
1 roll Italian salami
1 roll pepperoni
2 jars pickled baby corn on the cob
2 jars marinated artichoke hearts
1 12–ounce can ripe olives
1 jar stuffed green olives
1 jar marinated mushrooms
1 jar cocktail onions
1 12–ounce jar Italian dressing

Instructions
1. Cut cheese and meats into bite–sized cubes.
2. In a large bowl add all ingredients together and mix thoroughly.
3. Refrigerate for several hours.
4. Place on a serving tray or plate. Serve with toothpicks.

This dish may be made a day in advance.

Makes 10 to 12 servings.

FRIED APPLES AND BACON

Used with permission from Mr. William Lee Harmison, Berkley Springs, West Virginia.

Ingredients
½ pound bacon
1 pound tart apples, pealed, cored, and cubed
3 teaspoons sugar

Instructions
1. Fry the bacon in a skillet until crisp.
2. Place bacon on paper towels to drain. Keep warm.
3. Pour out all but ¼ cup of bacon fat from the skillet.
4. Add apple cubes to the skillet and sprinkle with sugar.
5. Cover and cook on low heat for about 10 minutes, turning midway.
6. When apples are lightly browned, remove.
7. Place apple cubes on a serving dish, surround with bacon, and serve.

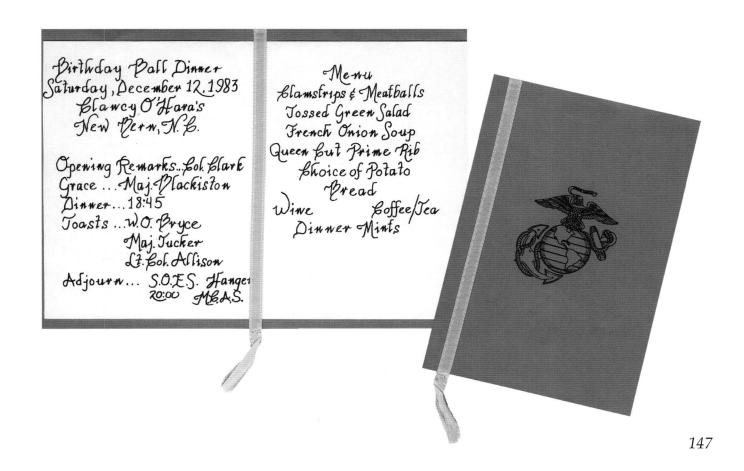

Birthday Ball Dinner
Saturday, December 12, 1983
Clawcy O'Hara's
New Bern, N.C.

Opening Remarks... Col. Clark
Grace ... Maj. Blackiston
Dinner...18:45
Toasts ...W.O. Bryce
      Maj. Tucker
      Lt. Col. Allison
Adjourn... S.O.E.S. Hanger
      20:00   M.C.A.S.

Menu
Clamstrips & Meatballs
Tossed Green Salad
French Onion Soup
Queen Cut Prime Rib
Choice of Potato
Bread
Wine   Coffee/Tea
Dinner Mints

GENERAL SHERMAN'S BAKED VENISON

General William Tecumseh Sherman, who served in the United States Army during the Civil War, loved fine wines and good food. It is said that he would have his troops hunt deer for one of his favorite dishes, baked venison. The following recipe is adapted from the *Manual for Army Cooks* published in 1896 by the Government Printing Office in Washington, D.C.

Ingredients

4 pounds fresh venison loin
1 stick butter (unsalted)
4 cups flour
2 cups beef stock, boiling hot
pepper
salt
ground nutmeg
ground cloves
2 sprigs rosemary

Instructions

1. Trim and wash the venison and pat dry.
2. Rub it all over with butter.
3. Mix the flour with a bit of water to make a thick paste and cover the meat with about half an inch of the paste.
4. Place the venison in a baking pan and add the beef stock.
5. Bake at 375° F, about 15 minutes per pound.
6. Baste every 10 minutes with the beef stock.
7. Ten minutes before the meat is fully baked (for a 4–pound piece of venison about 50 minutes after start of baking), remove the meat from the pan and remove the flour crust.
8. Return the venison to the baking pan and bake 10 more minutes.
9. Remove venison from the pan and let it rest for 15 minutes. Then slice it and serve on a warmed platter.
10. While the meat is resting, take some additional flour and quickly brown it in butter.
11. In a stockpot, combine the stock in which the venison baked with the browned flour. Add pepper to taste, one cup of hot water, salt, ground nutmeg, ground cloves, and rosemary and bring to a boil until reduced by about half. Stir frequently.
12. Serve this gravy on the side.

Note: General Sherman enjoyed this meal with green beans cooked for several hours with ham hocks and country ham. He also enjoyed a sweet Rhine wine or Riesling with this meal.

HANNAH DAVIS' BAKED APPLE CRUNCH

This recipe, associated with George Washington, is courtesy of Robert C.D. Norden. Mr. Norden is a direct descendant of Hannah Davis, known as "the first widow of the American Revolution." She was the wife of Captain Isaac Davis who was killed at Concord on April 19, 1775.

Ingredients

For the filling:
2 pounds tart apples, peeled, cored, and sliced ¼ inch thick
½ cup sugar
1 teaspoon cinnamon
½ teaspoon nutmeg
½ teaspoon ground cloves

For the topping:
½ cup flour
4 tablespoons sugar
3 tablespoons butter
1 teaspoon vanilla extract
confectioners' sugar for garnish

Instructions

1. To make the filling, combine the apples, sugar, cinnamon, nutmeg, and cloves in a large bowl.
2. Stir to coat the apples.
3. Spoon the mixture into an 8– or 9–inch pie plate and set aside.
4. Preheat oven to 350° F.
5. To make the topping, combine flour, sugar, butter, and vanilla in a medium–size bowl.
6. Work mixture between fingers until crumbling, then drop crumbs on top of apple filling.
7. Bake for one hour, or until topping is golden.
8. Allow it to cool slightly, sprinkle with confectioners' sugar, and serve.

(Opposite) The rivalry among the various U.S. military services remains legendary. Thus imagine the sense of isolation felt by the wives of Army officers attending a course at the Naval War College in Rhode Island. But isolation was quickly replaced by pride; once settled in, these ladies would go out of their way to demonstrate to the United States Navy that the Army too could serve superb food. Recipes included a strange drink called Idiot's Delight — a seemingly lethal concoction with corn whiskey, sugar, oranges, bananas, milk, and chocolate syrup. Other dishes of this circa 1965 booklet include a Pumpkin Chiffon Pie and detailed instructions for Sherry–Glazed Spareribs.

GENERAL PICKETT'S SHAD

This recipe is attributed to Major General George Edward Pickett, CSA, who would gain lasting fame for his daring yet futile attack during the Battle of Gettysburg known as "Pickett's Charge." General Lee fired General Pickett, because Pickett was absent from his command, attending a "Shad Bake" with some other generals, while his division was getting cut up in battle. This happened during the April 1, 1865, Battle of Five Forks at Dinwiddie, Virginia. To this day, the Virginia Democratic Party hosts an April 1st shad bake or "shad–planking."

Ingredients
8 to 10 fresh shad fish (whole)
long, flat oak boards or shingles that have been soaked in water for several hours
salt
pepper
cornmeal
bacon fat

Instructions
1. Split the shad length–wise.
2. Remove the roe from the female shad and reserve.
3. Nail the fish, skin side down, to the oak boards.
4. Stand the board close to a blazing and very hot fire (a brick or large rock will help secure the board in a vertical position).
5. Cook the fish for about 8 minutes.
6. Pull board away from the fire, remove the fish from the board, and nail it back on with the skin on the surface.
7. Return to the fire for another 8 minutes.
8. Serve on a platter, accompanied by fresh spring onions.
9. While the fish is cooking, dredge the roe in cornmeal and quickly fry in bacon fat in a heavy, cast–iron skillet over the fire.
10. Salt and pepper both fish and roe to taste.

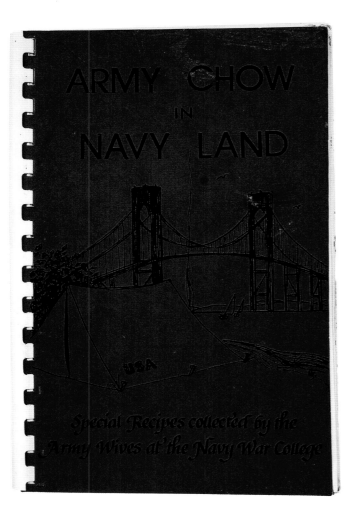

CANNON BALLS

The following recipe is adapted from the *Manual for Army Cooks,* published in 1896 by the Government Printing Office in Washington, D.C. This dessert has been associated with the Indian wars. A very different and more sophisticated version of this dessert is served at the U.S. Naval Academy in Annapolis Maryland (see www.usna63.org/news/FactBalls.html). The recipe here is suitable for a large gathering or as the manual states it is "sufficient for 22 men."

Ingredients
1 ½ pounds suet
6 pounds flour
3 pints molasses
1 pint water
old linen towels or kitchen towels cut into 8–x–8–inch squares
twine
powdered sugar to dust Cannon Balls

Instructions
1. Chop the suet and mix with flour.
2. Mix the molasses with water.
3. Place the flour into a large bowl and slowly pour the molasses into the flour while stirring (slowly!).
4. Mix, if necessary, by hand.
5. Form small cannon balls by hand (bigger than a golf ball but smaller than a baseball).
6. Tie each ball into a towel square, not too tightly.
7. Boil for about 90 minutes.
8. Remove from the cloth, dust with powdered sugar and serve.

Note: The Army manual also states, "These, with lime–juice sauce, are an excellent anti–scorbutic, and will keep good for twelve months, and longer. They should be made before going on any long voyage, and given out as rations. In the tropics, where fruit is cheap, the fruit is mixed with the molasses, but less fat is used."

Minced Pie of Beef

Ingredients
4 pounds boiled beef, chopped fine and salted
6 pounds raw apples, chopped
1 pound beef suet
1 quart of wine or rich sweet cider
1 ounce mace
1 ounce cinnamon
2 pounds sugar
1 whole nutmeg, ground
2 pounds raisins
butter
flour
egg whites

Instructions
1. Combine beef, apples, suet, wine, mace, cinnamon, sugar, nutmeg, and raisins.
2. Bake in a paste made as follows: to any quantity of flour, rub in three fourths of its weight of butter, (whites of eggs to a peck) rub in one–third or–half, and roll in the rest.
3. Bake 45 minutes.

Lamb Stuffed with Oysters

The Norden family operated the Fraunces Tavern® for more than 100 years and served this dish at the British Evacuation Day dinner reenactment in 1991. This recipe is courtesy of Robert C. D. Norden, proprietor, The Old '76 House. Located in Tappen, New York, '76 House is the oldest restaurant in the Hudson Valley.

Ingredients
1 cup bread crumbs
2 hard–boiled egg yolks, mashed
3 anchovies filets, soaked in water for at least 4 hours
¼ cup yellow onions chopped
½ teaspoon salt
⅛ teaspoon black pepper, freshly ground
1 teaspoon dry thyme or 1 tablespoon of fresh thyme, minced
⅛ teaspoon dry savory or 1 tablespoon of fresh summer savory, minced
⅛ teaspoon ground nutmeg
12 oysters, shucked
2 eggs
1 leg of lamb, about 4 ½ pounds, boned and butterflied

Instructions
1. Preheat oven to 325° F.
2. In a large bowl, mix the bread crumbs, egg yolks, anchovies, onions, salt, pepper, thyme, savory, nutmeg, and oysters.
3. In a food processor, mince the ingredients and slowly add the eggs to make a paste.
4. Spread oyster paste over the inside of the leg of lamb.
5. Roll and tie the lamb with butcher's twine.
6. Bake 2 hours and 15 minutes, or until internal temperature is 150° F on a meat thermometer.
7. Let it rest for 15 minutes, and then slice and serve.

General Basil Duke's Kentucky Cavalry Burgoo

Brigadier General Basil W. Duke, CSA, fought in the Civil War with General Braxton Bragg, CSA, then commander of the army of Tennessee. The famous U.S. Army base Fort Bragg in North Carolina is named after him. Duke's memoirs, *The Civil War Reminiscences of General Basil W. Duke, C.S.A*, first published in 1911, contains many references to food and camp life. "Kentucky Burgoo" is the stew that is served in Kentucky on Derby Day. General Duke wrote, "As for the 'burgoo,' no description can give one who has never tasted it an idea of its luscious excellence."

Ingredients
1 pound mixed meats (beef, lamb, pork, chicken) cut into quarter–inch cubes
½ gallon chicken stock
¼ gallon beef stock
1 cup fresh tomatoes, skinned, seeded, and diced
1 large yellow onion, diced
2 stalks celery, diced
2 red bell peppers, diced
3 large Idaho potatoes, peeled and diced
2 large carrots, diced
1 cup fresh or frozen okra
1 cup cooked or canned lima beans
kernels cut from two ears of corn or 1 cup frozen white corn
1 tablespoon garlic, minced
salt
pepper
Tabasco® sauce to taste

Instructions
In a large saucepan, combine all the ingredients and bring to a slow simmer. Allow to cook for at least two hours, until the meat starts falling apart. The mixture will have the consistency of a heavy, thick soup. Serve with fresh corn bread.

PHILADELPHIA PEPPER POT

Legend has it that this famous Pennsylvania specialty originated with General Washington at Valley Forge. During that brutal winter of 1777–1778 the troops were cold, ragged, and half-starved. To boost morale, General Washington is supposed to have ordered a good meal one night, only to be informed by his cook that the only food available was tripe, a few scraps, and peppercorns — not very promising. But the cook, and ingenious fellow, used his imagination and came up with a soup he called Philadelphia (after his home) Pepper Pot. Some Philadelphians like to credit this improvised dinner with the success of the Revolution. Other Philadelphians are spoilsports and claim the dish existed long before Valley Forge. It is quite possible that it had its origins in Africa by way of the West Indies. There fish, not tripe, was the basic ingredient. Transplanted to Philadelphia with West Indian cooks, it took on a local flavor.

Ingredients
1 ½ pounds tripe, well washed
1 veal knuckle, washed
4 tablespoons butter
¾ cup finely chopped onion,
½ cup finely chopped celery
2 tablespoons finely chopped leek
½ cup diced green pepper
1 garlic clove, diced
⅛ teaspoon cayenne pepper (may add more to taste)
1 teaspoon cracked black peppercorns
1 bay leaf
3 sprigs of parsley
1 teaspoon marjoram
1 teaspoon basil
½ teaspoon thyme
1 teaspoon salt
4 cups chicken broth
4 cups beef broth
2 large potatoes, diced
2 tablespoons flour
1 cup milk or heavy cream

Dumpling Ingredients
¼ pound butter, softened
1 cup flour
⅛ teaspoon salt
ice water

Instructions
1. Place tripe in a stockpot and add enough water to cover by 2 inches. Bring to a gentle boil and cook for 2 hours.
2. Discard liquid. Allow tripe to cool then cut into ½-inch cubes.
3. Return tripe to stockpot, add knuckle and enough water to cover and simmer for two hours.
4. Melt 2 tablespoons butter in a skillet and add onion, celery, leek, and green pepper. Sauté until tender, taking care not to brown.
5. Transfer onion, celery, leek, and green pepper to the stockpot. Add all seasonings, chicken broth, and beef broth and simmer for 1 hour.
6. Remove knuckle, and cuts bits of veal from the bone. Discard bone.
7. Return veal meat to the stockpot, and add potatoes and enough water to cover. Simmer one hour.
8. Remove bay leaf and parsley and discard.
9. In a large measuring cup, mix 2 tablespoons butter with 2 tablespoons flour to form a paste. Add broth one teaspoon at a time to paste until paste dissolves. Transfer to the stockpot and simmer until soup begins to thicken.
10. Make dumplings by working butter, flour, and salt together to make dough, adding ice water drop by drop as needed until mixture reaches a pasty consistency.
11. Shape this mixture with floured fingers to make marble-size dumplings.
12. Drop dumplings into soup, a few at a time.
13. Cover pot and allow to cook for 10 more minutes.
14. Add more black or red pepper to taste.
15. Add milk or cream and serve.

BRAISED SPANISH ONIONS

A note in Martha Washington's *Rules for Cooking* says that this dish was served at Washington's farewell dinner to his officers, held in New York in 1783 at Fraunces Tavern®.

Choose a large-sized onion with a flat top. Just cover it with equal parts of milk and water and let it boil about 10 minutes. Take off the outer skin and drain the onion.

Line the bottom of a pan with bacon fat, put in the onion, and pour second stock almost half-way up it. If it suits better, use water with 2 tablespoons of glaze instead of stock. Let it simmer, but never boil, for 2 or 3 hours until tender. When you have taken out the onion, skim the half-glaze and serve as a sauce with it. Another version says, "Give just a glaze in the oven when fully done with a bit of fresh butter on top."

BIBLIOGRAPHY

Aide-Memoire Militaire a L'usage des Officiers D'Infantrie et de Cavalerie. Paris: Ch. De Fouan, J. Dumaine, 1844.

Allen, Frederick. *Secret Formula.* New York: Harper Collins, 1994.

Anthimus. *De obseruatione ciborum (On the observance of foods).* Translated and edited by Mark Grant. England: Prospect Books, 1996.

Ashkenazi, Michael and Jeanne Jacob. *The Essence of Japanese Cuisine.* Richmond, Surrey, Britain: Curzon Press, 2000.

Baer, Winifred and Isle. *The Prussian Service. The Duke of Wellington's Berlin Dinner Service 1817-1819.* Berlin: Verwaltung der Staatlichen Schlösser und Gärten, 1989.

Baker, Alan. *The Knight.* Hoboken, N.J.: John Wiley & Sons, Inc., 2003.

'Banquetting Stuffe.' ed. Wilson, C. Anne, The fare and social background of the Tudor and Stuart Banquet. Edinburgh: Edinburgh University Press, 1991.

Barboza José N. *Formulário de Alimentação para o Exército ou Guia do Director do Rancho.* Lisbon, Portugal: Typographia Portugueza, 1865.

Beveridge, N.E.. *Cups of Valor.* Harrisburg, Pa.: Stackpole Books, 1968.

Black, Maggie. *The Medieval Cookbook.* New York: Thames and Hudson, 1992.

Braudel, Fernand. *Capitalism and Material Life 1400–1800.* London: George Weidenfeld and Nicolson Ltd., 1973.

Breasted, J.H. *Ancient Records of Egypt - Volume II.* Chicago: The University of Chicago Press, 1906.

Bremzen, Anya von and John Welchman. *Please to the Table. The Russian Cookbook.* New York: Workman Publishing, 1990.

Brennan, Jennifer. *Curries and Bugles: A Memoir and a Cookbook of the British Raj.* New York: Harper Collins, 1990.

Brosse, Jacques and Bernard Nantet, Michel-Claude Touchard, Nadine Beauthéac, Maguelonne Toussaint-Salnat. *A Rota das Especiarias.* Lisbon, Portugal: Edições Inapa, 1989.

(Below) "Royal Biscuit Plant of Vale de Zebro" describes how the biscuits used to feed the Portuguese navy were prepared. When it was written in the 18th century, the biscuit was a foundation of sailor nutrition and consequently of major importance.

The left side lists the amount of biscuits prepared during the month of March and the beginning of April in the year 1787. Featured on the right is the elaborately decorated, hand–tooled leather cover of the 1788 inventory book.

These two books belong to the Portuguese Navy Central Library–Central Archive.

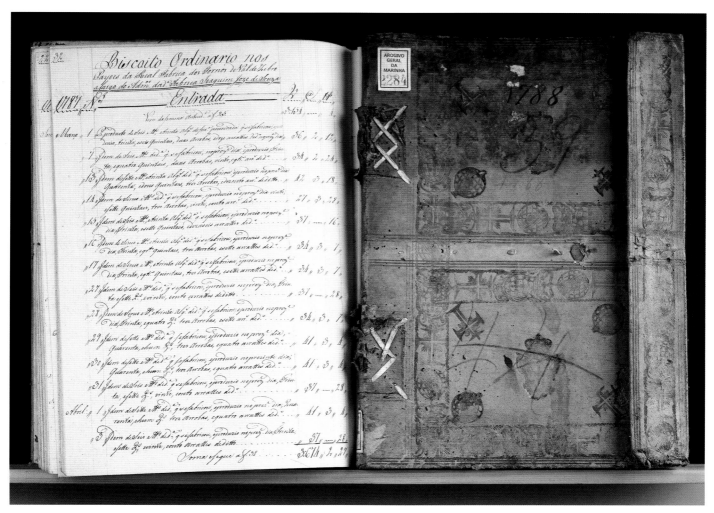

Caldicott, Chris and Carolyn. *The Spice Routes: Recipes and Lore*. San Franscisco, Calif.: Frances Lincoln Limited, 2001.

Cerwinske, Laura. *Russian Imperial Style*. New York: Prentice Hall Editions, 1990.

Ceserani, V., Ronald Kinton and David Foskett. *Practical Cookery*. London: Hodder & Stoughton Educational Division, 1987.

Childs, George Kohn. *Dictionary of War*. New York: Checkmark Books, 1999

Commissary General of Subsistence. *Manuel for Army Cooks*. Government Printing Office, Washington, D.C., 1896.

The Cookery Book of Lady Clark of Tillypronie edited by C.F. Frere. Constable & Company: London, 1909.

Dalby, Andrew and Sally Grainger. *The Classical Cookbook*. Malibu, Calif.: The J. Paul Getty Museum, 1996.

Davies, Roy W. *Service in the Roman Army*. New York: Columbia University Press, 1989.

Davis, Liz. *Army Chow in Navy Land: Special Recipes collected by the Army Wives at the Navy War College*. 1960.

Davis, William C. *The Civil War Cookbook*. Philadelphia: Courage Books, 1993.

Davis, William C. *A Taste for War: The Culinary History of the Blue and the Gray*. Mechanicsburg, Pa.: Stackpole Books, 2003.

Der Artillerist. Der Rekrut. Berlin: Verlag Offene Worte, 1924.

Department of the Army. *Army Mess Operations*. TM 10-405. Washington, D.C.: Government Printing Office, 1967.

Department of the Army. *The Army Food Service Program. Army Regulation 30-1*. Washington, D.C.: Government Printing Office, 1986.

Department of the Army. *Army Recipes (Meat, Poultry, Fish, Gravies, Sauces and Dressings)*. TM 10-412-1. Washington, D.C.: Government Printing Office, April 1957.

Department of the Army. *Army Recipes (Salads and Salad Dressings)*. TM 10-412-4. Washington, D.C.: Government Printing Office, May 1961.

Department of the Army. *Garrison Bakery Operations*. TM 10-417. Washington, D.C.: Government Printing Office, January 1948.

Department of the Army. *Quartermaster Service in Theater of Operations* FM10-10. Washington, D.C.: Government Printing Office, 1947.

Department of the Army. *Technical Manual TM 10-412*. Recipes. Washington, D.C.: Government Printing Office, 1950.

Department of the Army. *U.S. Army Support, Survival, Assault, Combat Rations and Supplements. Quarter Master Corps Manual*. QMC 17-3. Washington, D.C.: Government Printing Office, 1947.

Department of the Navy. *Manual for Supply Officers Afloat*. New York: Military Publishing Co., 1917.

Diner, Dan. *Verkehrte Welten: Antiamerikanismus in Deutschland. Ein historischer Essay.Frankfurt am Main: Eichborn Verlag*, 1993.

Driver, Christopher and Michelle Berriedale-Johnson. *Pepys at Table. Seventeenth century recipes for the modern cook*. London: Unwin Hyman, 1986.

A Epopeia das Especiarias. ed. Guerreiro, Inácio, Lisbon, Portugal: Edições Inapa e Instituto de Investigação Científica Tropical, 1999.

Escoffier, Auguste. *Souvenirs Inedits*. Marseille, France: Editions Jeanne Laffitte, 1985.

Feldienst-Ordnung (F.O.). Berlin: Ernst Siegfried Mittler und Sohn, Königliche Hofbuchhandlung, 1908.

Fernadez-Armesto, Felipe. *Near a Thousand Tables: A History of Food*. New York: The Free Press, 2002.

"Feuchte Stimme Amerikas," *Der Spiegel*, Hamburg, Germany: July 13, 1950, pp. 28-30.

Finney, Ben. *Once a Marine - Always a Marine*. New York: Crown Publishers, Inc., 1977.

Flandrin, Jean-Louis and Massimo Montanari. *Historia da Alimentação. Vol. 1: Dos primordios a Idade Media; Vol. 2: Da Idade Media aos Tempos Actuais*. Lisbon, Portugal: Terramar, 2001.

Fort Myer Officers' Open Mess, Arlington, Virginia. *Catering Department*. January 1962.

Fortescue, The Hon. Sir John. *A Short Account of Canteens in The British Army*. Cambridge, Britain: Cambridge University Press, 1928.

Gabbori, Mona. *Recipe Memories of Desert Storm*. Riyadh, Kingdom of Saudi Arabia: Support Industry Printing Center, 1992.

Garnsey, Peter. *Alimentação e Sociedade Na Antiguidade Classica. Aspectos Materiais e Simbolicos dos Alimentos*. Lisbon, Portugal: Editora Replicacao, 2002.

Giacosa, Ilaria Gizzini. *A Taste of Ancient Rome*. Chicago: The University of Chicago Press, 1992.

Grossman, Anne Chotzinoff and Lisa Grossman Thomas. *Lobscouse & Spotted Dog: Which it's a Gastronomic Companion to the Aubrey/Maturin Novels*. New York: W.W. Norton & Company, 1997.

Halici, Nevin. *The Historical Evolution of Turkish Cuisine*. Issues 42-43, 1991.

Hartley, Dorothy. *Food In England*. London: Macdonald & Co. (Publishers), Ltd., 1954.

Hassell, Ulrich von. *Erinnerungen aus meinem Leben 1848-1918*. Stuttgart: Chr. Belsersche Verlagsbuchhandlung, 1919.

Herodotus. *The Histories*. trans. by Aubrey de Selincourt with notes by John Marincola. New York: Penguin, 1996.

Hoffmann, Eleanor. *Feeding our Armed Forces*. New York: Thomas Nelson and Sons, 1943.

Hughes, Kristine. *The Writer's Guide to Everyday Life in Regency and Victorian England. From 1811-1901*. Cincinnati, Ohio: Writer's

Digest Books, 1998.

James, Kenneth. *Escoffier: The King of Chefs*. London: Hambledon and London, 2002.

Jeanneret, Michel. *A Feast of Words: Banquets and Table Talk in the Renaissance*. Chicago: University of Chicago Press, 1987.

Jourdin, Michel M. and Jehan Desanges. *As Rotas Milenares*. Lisbon, Portugal: Edições Inapa, 1989.

Kladstrup, Don and Petie. *Wine & War: The French, the Nazis & The Battle for France's Greatest Treasure*. New York: Broadway Books, 2001.

Kurlansky, Mark. *Choice Cuts: A Savory Selection of Food Writing from Around the World and Throughout History*. New York: Ballantine Books, 2002.

Laribe, J. *Manuel du Cuisinier Militaire en Campagne*. Paris: Edition Chiron, 1940.

Le Livre du Grade D'Infantrie. Paris: Berger-Levrault, Editeurs, 1913.

Le Repas du Guerrier. Catalogue to an exhibition of military food, November 3, 1990 - March 31, 1991, at the Musee de L'Alimentation, Vevey, Switzerland.

Louis, J. C. and Harvey Z. Yazijian. *The Cola Wars*. New York, Everest House Publishers, 1980.

Major L. *The Pytchley Book of Refined Cookery and Bills of Fare*. London: Chapman and Hall, 1887.

Mintz, Sidney. *Tasting Food, Tasting Freedom: Excursions into Eating, Power, and the Past*. London: Beacon Press, 1997.

Mitchell, Patricia B. *Cooking for the Cause. Confederate Recipes* Chatham, Va.: Self-published, 1988.

Mitchell, Patricia B. *Union Army Camp Cooking*. Chatham, Va.: Self-published, 1991.

Moh'd, Amir A. *Zanzibar Traditional Cookery*. Magomeni, Zanzibar: Good Luck Publishers, 2000.

Murphy, Margot. *Wartime Meals*. New York: Greenberg, 1942.

Nantet, Bernard and Patrick Rance, Françoise Botkine, Ninette Lyon, Jean-Claude Ribaut. *Cheeses of the World*. New York: Rizzoli

International Publications, Inc., 1993.

Neeb, Karen Jensen. *Brigade, Seats! The Naval Academy Cookbook*. Washington, D.C.: Glasgow Company Ltd., 1984.

Neumann, Gerhard. *Bayerischer Märchenkönig und Pommerscher Junker. Essen und Trinken in der Zweiten Halfte des 19. Jahrhunderts*. Akzente, June 1992.

A New System for Domestic Cookery; formed upon Principles of Economy by "A Lady", John Murray: Albemarle-Street, London, 1819

Nicholas & Alexandra: The Last Imperial Family of Tsarist Russia. From the State Hermitage Museum and the State Archive of the Russian Federation, New York: Harry N. Abrams, Inc., 1998.

Oliver, Thomas. *The Real Coke, The Real Story*. New York: Random House, 1986.

Pack, James. *Nelson's Blood: The Story of Naval Rum*. Annapolis, Md.: Naval Institute Press, 1983.

Palmer, Paul. *The Conspirators' Cookbook*. New York: Alfred A. Knopf, 1967.

Paston-Williams, Sara. *The National Trust: The Art of Dining. A History of Cooking and Eating*. London: National Trust Enterprises Limited, 1993.

Pendergrast, Mark. *For God, Country and Coca-Cola: The Unauthorized History of the Great American Softdrink and the Company that Makes It*. New York: Charles Scribner's Sons, 1993.

Pereira, Ana M. *Mesa Real - Dinastia de Bragança*. Lisbon, Portugal: Edições Inapa, 2000.

Peukert, Detlev J.K. *Inside Nazi Germany: Conformity, Opposition, and Racism in Everyday Life*. New Haven, Conn.: Yale University Press, 1982.

Pitte, Jean-Robert. *Gastronomie Française: Histoire et geographique d'une passion*. Paris: Fayard, 1991.

The Quartermaster School. *Conference Notes: Q.M. Corps - Rations*. Washington, D.C.: Government Printing Office, January 1949.

Ray, Elizabeth. *Alexis Soyer: Cook Extraordinary*. Lewes, East Sussex, Britain: Southover Press, 1991.

Rebora, Giovanni. *Culture of the Fork*. New York: Columbia University Press, 1998.

Rocha, Rui. *A Viagem dos Sabores*. Lisbon: Edicoes Inapa, 1998.

Root, Waverly. *The Food of Italy*. New York: Vintage Books, a Division of Random House, 1992.

Root, Waverly and Richard de Rochemont, . *Eating in America: A History*. New York: The Ecco Press, 1981.

Schivelbusch, Wolfgang. *Tastes of Paradise: A Social History*

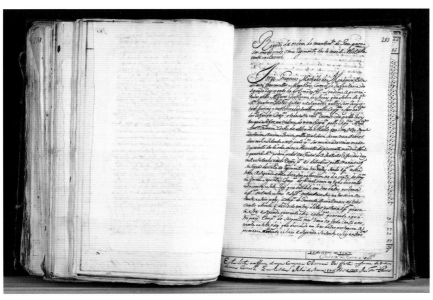

(Left) The 2nd Regiment of the Royal Navy kept detailed records of their time at the Fortress of São Julião da Barra. This 441-page book records rules, maps and food supplies from 1763-1764 and provides insight into 18th century life at the Fortress. This book belongs to the Portuguese Navy Central Library-Central Archive.

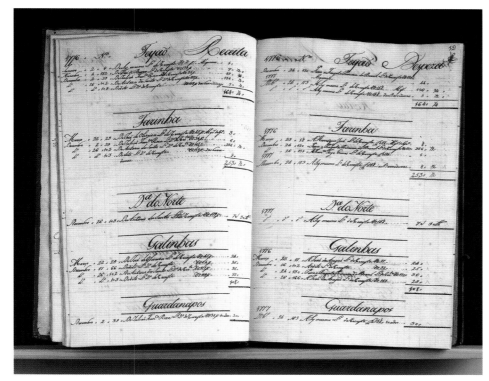

(Left) Effective movement of men and materials is vital to maintaining a top-notch military. Logistics depends upon knowing the location and quantity of each item a soldier might need. The leather-bound volume pictured above contains auxiliary listings of war ammunitions and provisions (i.e., food). This book belongs to the Portuguese Navy Central Library-Central Archive.

Uwe, George. *We true gedient hat…Die Regiments- und Erinnerungsteller der Meissner Porzellanmanufaktur 1900-1945.* Osnabruck: Biblio Verlag, 1985.

Verdon, Jean. *Boire au Moyen Age*. Paris: Perrin, 2002.

Vie, Gerard. *A La Table des Rois*. Paris: Art Lys, 1993.

of Spices, Stimulants, and Intoxicants. New York: Pantheon Books, 1992.

Schraemli, Harry. *Von Lukullus zu Escoffier*. Germany: Ceres-Verlag, Bielefeld, 1991.

Sekunda, Nick. *Food and Drink - Greek Military Cuisine*. Internet Article. http://www.hoplites.co.uk/pdf/hoplite_food_and_drink.pdf

Shaw, Timothy. *The World of Escoffier*. New York: The Vendome Press, 1995.

Simmons, Amelia. *American Cookery: or, The Art of Dressing Viands, Fish, Poultry and Vegetables*. Albany, New York: C.R. Webster, 1796.

Skillman, Commander J.H. (S.C.), USN. "Eating Through the Years," *Proceedings*. Vol. No. 67, No. 3 , Whole No. 457 (March 1941): pp 361 - 367.

Smith, Henry. *Classical Recipes of the World with occasions for their use and master culinary guide*. London: Practical Press Ltd., 1954.

Soyer, Alexis. *A Culinary Campaign*. Lewes, East Sussex, Britain: Southover Press, 1991.

Soyer, Alexis, compiled by Andrew Langley. *The Selected Soyer: The writings of the legendary Victorian Chef*. London: Absolute Press, 1987.

Soyer, Nicolas. *Soyer's Paper-Bag Cookery*. New York: Sturgis & Walton Company, 1911.

Stanhope, Henry and Tank Nash. *The Colonel's Table*. Washington and London: Brassey's, 1994.

Stern, Philip Van Doren. *Soldier Life in the Union and Confederate Armies*. New York: Gramercy Books, 2001.

Strong, Roy. *Feast: A History of Grand Eating*. London: Jonathan Cape, 2002.

Stukenbacher, Robert. *Das Diner: Praktische Anleitung zu dessen Service und Arrangement*. Berlin: Rudolf Mosse Verlag, 1896.

Tannahill, Reay. *Food in History*. New York: Crown Publishers, Inc., 1988.

Visser, Margaret. *The Rituals of Dinner*. New York: Grove Weidenfeld, 1991.

Walker, Mort. *The Unofficial MRE Recipe Booklet*. Avery Island, La: McIlhenny Company, undated.

War Department. *Cooking Dehydrated Food*. TM 10-406. Washington, D.C.: Government Printing Office, 1943.

War Department. *Cutting and Preparing Lamb*. TM 10-408. Washington, D.C.: Government Printing Office, 1943.

War Department. *Extracts from Manual for Army Cooks*. Washington, D.C.: Government Printing Office, 1917.

War Department. *Technical Manual: Emergency Food Plants and Poisonous Plants of the Islands of the Pacific*. TM 10-420. Washington, D.C.: Government Printing Office, 1943.

War Shipping Administration - Food Control Division. *Cooking and Baking on Shipboard*. United States Government, 1945.

Wer will unter die Soldaten. Deutsche Soldatenlieder. Leipzig: Insel-Verlag, 1934.

Willet, Ralph. *The Americanization of Germany, 1945-1949*. London: Routledge, 1989.

Woodward, Sarah. *The Ottoman Kitchen*. Modern recipies from Turkey, Greece, the Balkans, Lebanon, Syria and beyond. New York: Interlink Books, 2002.

Wyvern (Colonel Arthur Robert Kenney-Herbert). *Culinary Jotttings for Madras: A Treatise in Thirty Chapters on Reformed Cookery for Anglo-Indian Exiles*. Madras: Higginbotham, 1885.

Yin-Fei Lo, Eileen. *Chinese Kitchen*. New York: William Morrow and Company, Inc., 1999.

Young, Carolin C. *Apples of Gold in Settings of Silver: Stories of Dinner as a Work of Art*. New York: Simon & Schuster, 2002.

Zagalho, Bernardo A. *Projecto de Regulamento para a Organização e Administração do Exército - Apresentado no Senado, em Sessão de 29 de Janeiro de 1840*. Lisbon, Portugal: Imprensa Nacional, 1840.

Conversion Chart

Volume

Standard American (pint)	Metric (ml)
1	473
2	946
3	1419
4	1892
5	2365

Standard American (oz)	Metric (ml)
1	30
2	60
3	90
4	120
5	150
6	180
7	210
8	240
9	270

Standard American (lb)	Metric (gram)
1	450
2	900
3	1350

Oven Temperatures

Fahrenheit	Celsius	Gas Mark
275 degrees	140 degrees	1
300 degrees	150 degrees	2
325 degrees	160 degrees	3
350 degrees	180 degrees	4
375 degrees	190 degrees	5
400 degrees	200 degrees	6
425 degrees	220 degrees	7
450 degrees	230 degrees	8
475 degrees	240 degrees	9

WEIGHT

Standard American (oz)	Metric (gram)
1	28
2	57
3	85
4	113
5	142
6	170
7	198
8	226
9	255
10	283
15	425
18	509

Standard American (lb)	Metric (gram)
1	450
2	900
3	1350

Research for this book took our team all over the world. Pictured on a photo shoot in Portugal are (clockwise from upper left): Keith Crossley, Agostino von Hassell, Herm Dillon, Leslie Jean-Bart, Teresa Caiado Ramirez, Harry McMann with Maria Dog, Kristin Leigh Hoelen with George Dog

ACKNOWLEDGMENTS

This book would not have been possible without the assistance of many individuals and institutions around the world. We thank them with all our hearts.

Mr. Christopher Ross of New York City kindly allowed us to use his sterling collection of pre-World War I militaria for sets and detail shots. His collection on Manhattan's East Side is unique. He has brought together the very finest collection of dress uniforms, military art, swords, table decorations and helmets of the five major monarchies of pre-World War I Europe: The German Empire, the Austro-Hungarian Empire, the British Empire, the Russia of the Czars and France. His cooperation was as exemplary as his selfless dedication to preserving the images of a by-gone world.

We thank Abby Daniels who worked for an entire summer in performing some of the initial research that helped set the direction, tone, and content of this book.

We thank Susan Babson who helped collect details on the Royal Navy and specifically the food served on the HMS *Manchester*. We also thank the captain and the crew of this British ship.

In Portugal we received extensive help. We want to express our gratitude to Portuguese Navy Commander Rodrigues Pereira, who introduced us to the appropriate naval officers; to Commander João Carlos Filipe, Director of the Navy Central Archive; Ms. Isabel Beato, the main archivist, who was industrious in researching appropriate books and related information; and to Commander António Moita Gorreana, from the Navy Officers Club in Lisbon who was always helpful and ready to receive our team.

We thank the following members of Portugal's Army: Lieutenant Colonel Palma Ferro, from CEME, who in the name of the Chief of the General Staff, authorized the team to visit several military facilities and granted full support to the project; Colonel Manuel Ribeiro de Faria, Director of the "Military Museum in Lisbon," who was valuable both in terms of military history, and in providing props for some of the pictures; Lieutenant Colonel Carlos de Aguiar Santos, of the "Infantry School" in Mafra; Lieutenant Colonel Manuel Lopes Calado and Lieutenant Pinheiro, from the Officers' Mess in Évora; Colonel António Pereira Cardoso, Director of the "Military Logistics;" Ms. Margarida de Raimond, Director of "Instituto de Odivelas;" and Captain Nuno Reis, Director of the "Officers Mess in Lisbon."

Also in Portugal, we would like to thank Mr. António Soares Franco from "José Maria da Fonseca Vinhos Lda," who gave us permission to take pictures of the company's special cellar, the Public Relations team, Ms. Maria João Aguiar and Ms. Carla Ribeiro, as well as the always present and kind Mr. João Araújo; Ms. Gabriela César from the "Commerce and Trade Delegation

(Above) Cielo Peralta from Murray's Cheese, Bleeker Street, New York City, is a master of cheeses. His secret is to match a cheese to his customer, not just to their favorite wine. Peralta carries 400 kinds of cheese yet can narrow the selection down to four choices based on customer preferences, such as strength of flavor, texture, and saltiness.

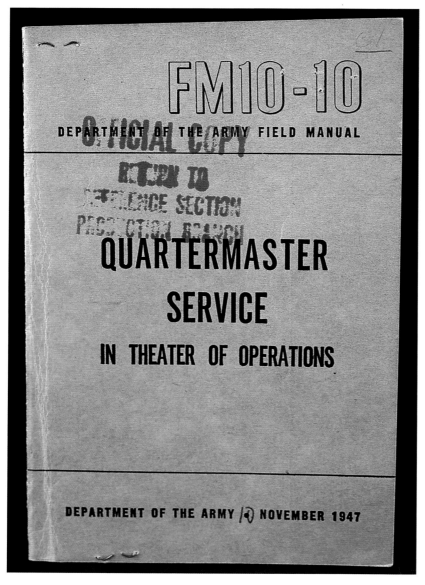

(Above) The United States Army Field Manual pictured above is just one of hundreds of documents, anecdotes and pieces of memorabilia the authors have collected over the years. Their passion for good food, their love for the military and the interesting discoveries they made while researching around the world led to the creation of this history of military cuisine.

We would like to extend our gratitude to Mr. Roland Schaefer, who provided all the wines from the "Légion Étrangère" used in this book.

We also would like to thank Reverand Michael C. Osborn of the Holy Roman Catholic Church who assisted us with obtaining the recipe from the Pontifical Swiss Guards.

In the United States, we want to express our thanks to Colonel Roy S. Batterton, USMC (Ret.) who lent us his dress sword as well as the cooks at the Washington Marine Barracks at "8th & I." Thanks go to the Mount Vernon Ladies Association and Robert C. D. Norden of The '76 House for providing revolutionary-era recipes. We appreciate the kind assistance of Amy Northrop Adamo, Director, Fraunces Tavern® Museum, and the Whitney Collection of the New York City Public Library during our colonial research.

Heartfelt thanks go to Phil Egginton, Secretary, the Historical Maritime Society, for verifying information on Britain's Royal Navy.

Carl Tribble, Jr. is a superb baker located at Carl's Breads!, Red Gate Farm, Summit Point, West Virginia. He — with our thanks — baked a special dark bread for the Russian photo on page 116 and a crusty white bread for the World War I photo on page 117. Thanks also go to Mr. Robby Ambrose of Berkley Springs, West Virginia for lending us original Civil War implements used in the photo on page 148. Thanks are also due to Colonel Bob Moberly, U.S. Army (Ret.) who helped with authentic period weapons.

Mr. Cielo Peralta of Murray's Cheese in New York City helped with patient advice and counsel on cheeses that originated with the Roman Empire. Professor Patrick Kelly of Adelphi University in New York assisted with the research on the Germania Brewery (now Tsingtao Beer) in China. Dr. Giorgio Migliavacca, the President of the BVI Philatelic Society, Tortola, British Virgin Islands, assisted with a stamp showing rum issue aboard a British man-of-war.

Priscilla Mary Isin in Turkey provided us with art and information related to the famous Ottoman officer and chef Mahmud Nedim bin Tosun (see www.ottoman-cuisine.com).

But most of all, we want to thank countless United States Marines, members of Italy's Marine Corps, the San Marco Battalion, and the Royal Marines who gave help and support, and often shared sparse meals in locales as diverse as the snowy mountains of northern Norway, the dusty landing beaches at Gallipoli in Turkey, or the war-torn streets and villages of Lebanon. ✂

of Macao in Lisbon;" Ms. Isabel Costeira, Director of the Alcobaça Monastery, as well as Ms. Celeste Gil and Ms. Júlia Machado, who took the time to accompany the team and accommodate us as well as possible; Ms. Maria Ilda Gonzaga Ribeiro, owner of the restaurant "Frei Bernardo" in Alcobaça, who allowed a group of "strangers" to use her kitchen and her tools; Mr. Eduardo Ambar, Director of "Pousadas de Portugal" and especially Ms. Maria Gabriel, Vice Director of the "Pousada dos Lóios" in Évora; Mr. Paulo Garcia, Director of the restaurant "Casa Leão" in Lisbon; and Ms. Filomena Barata from IPPAR ("Portuguese Institute of Architectural Heritage"), in Évora and especially Mr. Rafael Alfenim.

RECIPE INDEX

INDEX

The Grace before Dinner will be sung by the Men,
at the sound of the bugle.

"Be present at our table, Lord,
Be here and everywhere adored;
These creatures bless, and grant that we
May feast in Paradise with Thee."

RATIONS

Over the top and the best of luck - 6.30 p.m.

JOINTS.

ROAST BEEF.   BOILED BEEF.
ROAST LAMB.   YORK HAM.
CHICKEN.   TONGUE.
(Bully and Biscuits, IF PREFERRED.)

VEGETABLES.

HOT POTATOES.
(March carefully over the Allotments.)

PICKLES.   SALAD.

SWEETS.
(Plum and Apple, napoo !)

TRIFLE.   PASTRIES.   JELLIES.
BLANC-MANGE.   FRUIT and CREAM.
HOT PLUM-PUDDING and SAUCE.

CHEE

BEER (Gravity—Umpteen)

Smoke clouds will be liber

TOAST LIST.

"His Majesty the King."
Proposed by The LORD BISHOP OF HEREFORD.

"Our Guests."
Proposed by The LORD BISHOP OF HEREFORD.
Responded to by Major the Rev. E. H. BEATTIE, M.C., S.C.F.
and Sergt. J. DAVIES, V.C.

"The Committee and Helpers."
Proposed by Sergt. DAVIES, V.C.
Responded to by Mr. J. C. MACKAY (Chairman) and
Mr. GEORGE WHITTAKER, O.B.E. (Hon. Sec.).

BISHOP for presiding.
on. and Very Rev. The DEAN OF

1914. — 1919.

The Great European War.

HEREFORD'S

Welcome Home

TO RETURNED

Sailors, Soldiers and Airmen.

Saturday, 6th September, 1919.

THE HEREFORD TIMES LTD.

Complimentary Mess
BY THE
Newcastle & Durham
Engineer Volunteers
ON THE OCCASION OF
Presentation of Sword of Honour
TO
General Graham, K.C.B. &c.
Assembly Rooms, Newcastle-on-Tyne,
19th July, 1884.

Lieut.-Col. C.M. Palmer, M.P., Chairman.

Menu.

Vins.

Potages.   Printanier à la Royale.
                Fausse Tortue à la Londres.

Poissons.   Saumon, Sauce Piquante.
                 Filets de Merlans aux Champignons.
                 Concombres et Salade Mayonnaise.

Entrées.   Escalopes de Veau aux Olives.
                Salmis de Canetons à la Bigarade.

Relevés.   Quartier d'Agneau.
                Aloyau Rôti.
                Poulets Chipolata aux Jambon.
                Legumes Variés.

Entremets.   Soufflé aux Abricots.   Chartreuse aux Fraises.
                  Bavarois au Chocolat.
                  Gelée Brillanté.
                  Anchois à la Wolfrannen.
                  Croûtes de Caviare à la Russe.
                  Fromages Variés.

Glaces.   Plombiere à la Nesselrode.

Dessert.

Café Gloria.

Toasts.

"The Queen,"

"H.R.H. the Prince and Prin
and other Members of the R

"Navy, Army, and Reserve Forc

"General Graham, K.C.B., &c

MENU

HUITRES DE ZELANDE

CONSOMMÉ À LA GOSSELIE

SOLE DORÉE
SAUCE BLANCHE

NOIX DE VEAU
À LA PARISIENNE

CHOUX DE BRUXELLES

PURÈE DE

GATEAU E

BOUCHE

DE

C

JAN 14 '19.

MENÙ

COPA DE PEROLA
SALADA À PORTUGUESA
CHOU-FLOR
COSTELLETAS DE GAZELLA
POMO CON ARROLAS
CARNES FRIAS
PATO RECHEADO
LOMBO ASSADO
ESPARGOS

SOBREMEZA

VINHOS
BUCELLAS COLLARES PORTO CHAMPAGNE
CAFÉ E LICORES

1 This menu from September 6, 1919, celebrates the homecoming of British servicemen. The soldiers, sailors, and airmen were served a complex dinner evoking war, the food proper was listed as "rations."

2 A sword of honor was presented to British General Sir Gerald Graham at Newcastle-on-Tyne at a dinner held by the Newcastle & Durban Engineer Volunteers on July 19, 1884. Graham earned his Victoria Cross during the Crimean War, and later served in China and in the Egyptian War of 1882. This feast included an apricot soufflé, and a large variety of wines and champagnes.

3 This was the menu of an elegant dinner held by the headquarters staff of the 37th U.S. Division right after World War I in Eastern France and close to the German border. Dishes featured included oysters and fresh sole.

4 This menu comes from Mozambique and details a dinner for Portuguese army officers held on December 10, 1900. Included on the menu were cutlets of gazelle.